# Congress and the Crisis of the 1850s

**Perspectives on the History of Congress, 1801–1877**
Donald R. Kennon, Series Editor

*Congress and the Emergence of Sectionalism:*
*From the Missouri Compromise to the Age of Jackson,*
edited by Paul Finkelman and Donald R. Kennon

*In the Shadow of Freedom: The Politics of Slavery in the National Capital,*
edited by Paul Finkelman and Donald R. Kennon

*Congress and the Crisis of the 1850s,* edited by Paul Finkelman and Donald R. Kennon

# Congress and the Crisis of the 1850s

Edited by Paul Finkelman and Donald R. Kennon

Published for the
United States Capitol Historical Society

by Ohio University Press • Athens

Ohio University Press, Athens, Ohio 45701
www.ohioswallow.com
© 2012 by Ohio University Press

Printed in the United States of America
All rights reserved

To obtain permission to quote, reprint, or otherwise reproduce or distribute material from Ohio University Press/Swallow Press publications, please contact our rights and permissions department at (740) 593-1154 or (740) 593-4536 (fax).

Ohio University Press books are printed on acid-free paper ♾ ™

20 19 18 17 16 15 14 13 12    5 4 3 2 1

Library of Congress Cataloging-in-Publication Data

Congress and the crisis of the 1850s / edited by Paul Finkelman and Donald R. Kennon.
  p. cm. — (Perspectives on the history of congress, 1801–1877)
Includes bibliographical references and index.
ISBN 978-0-8214-1977-9 (hc : alk. paper) — ISBN 978-0-8214-4399-6 (electronic)
 1. United States—Politics and government—1815–1861. 2. United States. Congress—History—19th century. 3. Slavery—United States—Extension to the territories. 4. Slavery—Political aspects—United States—History—19th century. 5. Slavery—United States—Legal status of slaves in free states. 6. Fugitive slaves—Legal status, laws, etc.—United States. 7. Slavery—Law and legislation—United States—History—19th century. 8. Sectionalism (United States)—History—19th century. I. Finkelman, Paul, 1949- II. Kennon, Donald R., 1948- III. United States Capitol Historical Society.
 E415.7.C76 2011
 973.5—dc23
                    2011036823

# Contents

*Paul Finkelman*
Introduction: A Disastrous Decade     1

*Michael F. Holt*
Politics, Patronage, and Public Policy: The Compromise of 1850     18

*Paul Finkelman*
The Appeasement of 1850     36

*Matthew Glassman*
Beyond the Balance Rule: Congress, Statehood, and Slavery, 1850–1859     80

*Amy S. Greenberg*
Manifest Destiny's Hangover: Congress Confronts Territorial Expansion and Martial Masculinity in the 1850s     97

*Spencer R. Crew*
"When the Victims of Oppression Stand Up Manfully for Themselves": The Fugitive Slave Law of 1850 and the Role of African Americans in Obstructing Its Enforcement     120

*Martin J. Hershock*
"Agitation Is as Necessary as Tranquility Is Dangerous": Kinsley S. Bingham Becomes a Republican     143

*Jenny Wahl*
*Dred*, Panic, War: How a Slave Case Triggered Financial Crisis and Civil Disunion     159

*Brooks D. Simpson*
"Hit Him Again": The Caning of Charles Sumner ............ 202

Contributors ............ 221

Index ............ 223

Congress and the Crisis of the 1850s

Paul Finkelman

# Introduction

*A Disastrous Decade*

It was a remarkable period, unlike any other in American history. It was the long decade of the 1850s. It began in 1848 with the end of the Mexican War and the presidential election. It ended in 1860 with the election of Lincoln and the secession of South Carolina. It began in crisis and ended in catastrophe. The crisis was rooted in the dramatic success of American forces in the Mexican War (1846–48). The war added massive amounts of new land to the nation—all or most of the present-day states of Arizona, California, Nevada, New Mexico, and Utah—and parts of Colorado, Oklahoma, Texas, and Wyoming. This enlargement of the nation created a deeply divisive debate over the status of slavery in the new territory. Compounding this were extravagant claims of Texas for much of New Mexico, southern demands for a new fugitive slave law, and growing northern dissatisfaction over the presence of slavery in the national capital. The gold rush of 1849 exacerbated the crisis, as tens of thousands of settlers and prospectors poured into northern California, making it eligible for statehood almost overnight.

Five presidents held office from 1848 to 1860. James K. Polk, the lame-duck, expansionist, proslavery Tennessean, had little influence on the events at the end of his administration. He had aggressively started a war with Mexico that led to overwhelming American victories. But he was unable to control events leading to peace and was forced to accept a treaty when he really wanted to continue the war to secure even more land. Meanwhile, he failed to create a political solution for the status of the newly acquired territory. His successor, Zachary Taylor, was a southerner with substantial northern support and a slave owner who opposed the spread of slavery into the new territories. As a soldier he had commanded northerners and southerners and had lived substantial portions of his life in both sections. As the hero of the Mexican War he was the only president in this period who might have solved the crisis. Tragically, he died just sixteen months after taking office. Each president following Taylor—Millard Fillmore, Franklin Pierce, and James Buchanan—was worse than his predecessor.[1] None was able to successfully deal with the complexities that faced the nation, and all three in the end shamelessly appeased the most aggressive proslavery southerners while utterly ignoring the interests and needs of the North. Congress meanwhile passed two major pieces of legislation—the Compromise of 1850 and the Kansas-Nebraska Act, in 1854—but both only made the crisis worse. In *Dred Scott v. Sandford* (1857)[2] the Supreme Court tried to solve all the nation's problems in a single stroke. But Chief Justice Roger B. Taney's bold move backfired and his decision is considered the most notorious in our history.

Just as the constitutionally created institutions of government—the executive branch, the Congress, and the courts—failed the nation, so too did the political parties. Both major political parties fractured under the stress. The Whigs won the presidency in 1848 but quickly squandered their victory. Henry Clay, who had desperately wanted to be president, petulantly did everything in his power to undermine President Taylor's administration because he was angry at not getting the Whig nomination in 1848.[3] Rather than working with the president of his own party to solve the crisis, Clay opposed Taylor in a vainglorious attempt to make himself the head of the party and the de facto leader of the nation. The result was his proposed "omnibus bill" for dealing with slavery in the territories and other issues, even though his own party's

---

[1] Two, James Buchanan and Franklin Pierce, are consistently listed as among the five worst, with Buchanan ranked as the worst or the second worst, behind Andrew Johnson. Millard Fillmore's place in the worst ten is secure, but I would argue he deserves better, as the fourth or fifth worst president. See Paul Finkelman, *Millard Fillmore* (New York, 2011).

[2] 60 U.S. (19 How.) 393 (1857). The literature on *Dred Scott* is vast. See generally Don E. Fehrenbacher, *The Dred Scott Case: Its Significance in Law and Politics* (New York, 1978); Paul Finkelman, Dred Scott v. Sandford: *A Brief History* (Boston, 1995); and David Thomas Konig, Paul Finkelman, and Christopher Alan Bracey, eds., *The* Dred Scott *Case: Historical and Contemporary Perspectives on Race and Law* (Athens, Ohio, 2010). For a discussion of Chief Justice Taney's goals, see Paul Finkelman, "Was *Dred Scott* Correctly Decided? An 'Expert Report' for the Defendant," *Lewis and Clark Law Review* 12 (2008): 1219–52.

[3] See generally Michael F. Holt, *The Rise and Fall of the American Whig Party: Jacksonian Politics and the Onset of the Civil War* (New York, 1999).

president, Taylor, objected to the bill and was prepared to veto it. Taylor's death, in early July 1850, left a vacuum of leadership as Taylor's utterly obscure vice president, Millard Fillmore, stepped into the White House. On his first day in office Fillmore fired every member of the cabinet, the only accidental president to behave in this way. This left him without advisers and administrators while Congress debated Clay's compromise measures. By the time Fillmore left office the Whigs were in shambles. Fillmore's utter incompetence was underscored by his failure to win the 1852 nomination because his own secretary of state, Daniel Webster, blocked his nomination. In 1852 the party suffered the worst defeat of the century, and by 1856 the Whigs had simply disappeared.

The Democrats failed to capitalize on the ineptitude of their opponents. They won a huge victory in 1852 but bungled their control of Congress and the White House. Illustrative of the failure of the Democrats was the election of Nathaniel Banks as Speaker of the House, in 1855. He had been elected in 1852 to the Thirty-Third Congress as a Democrat, as part of the massive Democratic landslide that put Franklin Pierce in the White House. But in the wake of the Kansas-Nebraska Act, Banks left the Democrats, and in 1854 he won reelection on the Know-Nothing ticket. He became Speaker of the Thirty-Fourth Congress on a plurality vote. By 1856 Banks was a Republican. That year the Democrats barely won the presidential election against the Republicans, a brand new party running a presidential candidate for the first time. After the Democrats won the presidency in 1856 they were able to elect James Orr of South Carolina as Speaker, but in 1858 the Republicans took control of the House, electing William Pennington of New Jersey, a former Whig, as Speaker for the Thirty-Sixth Congress.

Between 1852 and 1856 the Democrats so alienated northern voters that James Buchanan became the nation's first "sectional" president. All previous winners of the presidential election carried a majority, or a near majority, of both sections.[4] Buchanan carried fourteen of the fifteen slave states,[5] but won only five northern states, even though he was from Pennsylvania. Buchanan then managed to alienate northern Democrats so badly that the

---

[4] John Quincy Adams ran second in the electoral and popular vote and gained the presidency when Congress chose him after the 1824 election, when no candidate had a majority of the Electoral College.
[5] Fillmore, running as the candidate of the anti-Catholic, anti-immigrant Know-Nothing Party, carried Maryland.

party split in two. The Democrats lost control of the House in 1858, and were unable to even agree on a single presidential candidate in 1860. That year the Democrats failed to carry a single northern state. For Democrats, Buchanan's legacy was a catastrophe. It would take nearly three-quarters of a century for the party to recover. From 1800 through 1860 the Democrats won every presidential election but three and almost always controlled Congress. But from 1860 until 1932 the party would win the presidency only four times and would rarely control both houses of Congress.

Throughout the 1850s lawlessness and violence also shaped political developments. In the North, average, otherwise law-abiding citizens confronted federal marshals while resisting the enforcement of the Fugitive Slave Law of 1850. In the South, the governor of Texas sent the state militia to invade the New Mexico Territory, threatening to go to war with the United States in an attempt to seize half of New Mexico. In Kansas proslavery and antislavery settlers fought a mini–civil war, with deaths on both sides. In Congress, Representative Preston Brooks of South Carolina brutally attacked Senator Charles Sumner of Massachusetts, sneaking up on him from behind while he was seated at his desk and beating him insensible with a cane. One of Brooks's southern colleagues stood by on the floor of the Senate with a drawn pistol to prevent anyone from stopping the attack. As a final coda to the decade, in 1859 John Brown and eighteen fellow abolitionists seized the federal armory at Harpers Ferry, Virginia, in an attempt to begin a war against slavery. His hanging, in December 1859, turned him into a martyr for liberty in the North, while his raid made him the embodiment of evil in the South.

## Slavery and American Constitutional Politics

The cause of this turmoil was of course slavery. Since the Revolution slavery had bedeviled American politics. As early as 1776 slavery had threatened national unity and undermined national public policy. At the end of July 1776, less than a month after the Continental Congress agreed to the Declaration of Independence, the delegates debated whether to tax slaves as well as free people in order to support the new nation. Taxation was to be based on population, not property. Northerners insisted that slaves contributed to the economy just like free people and thus should be counted when assessing taxes. Samuel Chase of Maryland complained that slaves were "wealth," not people, and should no more be taxed than "Massachusetts fisheries." He argued that old and young slaves were "a burthen to their owners." James Wilson of Pennsylvania sharply responded that in the southern colonies slaves were taxed just as free people. This led Thomas Lynch of South Carolina to utter the first (but not the last) threat of secession from that state, declaring that if Congress "debated whether their slaves are their property" then there would be "an end to the Confederation." He blustered, "Our slaves being our property, why should they be taxed more than the land, sheep, cattle, horses, &c.?" Benjamin Franklin, unimpressed by Lynch's arrogance, replied that there was "some difference between" slaves and sheep because "sheep will never make a revolution."[6]

Congress got past this issue, and did not focus on slavery again until the Revolution was over. By then two states (Massachusetts and New Hampshire) had ended slavery in their new constitutions while three others (Pennsylvania, Connecticut, and Rhode Island) had passed laws to gradually end slavery. In the South there was never any serious movement to end slavery, and policymakers utterly ignored the occasional southerner who proposed even the mildest emancipation scheme, such as Virginia's St. George Tucker.[7] However, in 1782 Virginia did allow masters to manumit their slaves within the state if they wished, and many thousands, who took the revolutionary rhetoric seriously, did so.

In July 1787, while delegates in Philadelphia were drafting the U.S. Constitution, the old Congress passed its only significant legislation on slavery. In the Northwest Ordinance, Congress prohibited slavery in the federal territory north of the Ohio River. This 1787 ordinance was the first national regulation of slavery. It prohibited "slavery or involuntary servitude" in the area but provided no enforcement mechanism. Few slaves were actually emancipated by this law, and settlers in present-day Indiana and Illinois who came there before 1787 continued to hold people in bondage until decades

---

[6]Worthington C. Ford, ed., *Journals of the Continental Congress*, 34 vols. (Washington, D.C., 1904–37), 6:1079–80.

[7]St. George Tucker, *A Dissertation on Slavery: With a Proposal for the Gradual Abolition of It, in the State of Virginia* (Philadelphia, 1796). Tucker reprinted the *Dissertation* in an appendix in his edition of Blackstone's Commentaries. St. George Tucker, "On the State of Slavery in Virginia," in Tucker, *Blackstone's Commentaries: With Notes of Reference, to the Constitution and Laws, of the Federal Government of the United States; and of the Commonwealth of Virginia*, 5 vols. (Philadelphia, 1803), vol. 2, app., pp. 31–89. For a discussion of how Tucker was ignored, see Paul Finkelman, "The Dragon That St. George Could Not Slay: Tucker's Plan to End Slavery," *William and Mary Law Review* 47 (2006):1213.

after the passage of the ordinance. In 1820 the Indiana Supreme Court ruled that under the state constitution of 1816—*not* the Northwest Ordinance—all slaves in the state were free.[8] Slavery lingered in Illinois into the 1840s, nearly sixty years after the adoption of the ordinance. In 1845 the Illinois Supreme Court ruled that the children of slaves born after statehood were free, but the justices were uncertain about the status of slaves born before statehood.[9] The court implied that slaves born in Illinois before the adoption of the Northwest Ordinance did *not* gain their freedom by that act.[10]

While the Confederation Congress debated the Northwest Ordinance, the Constitutional Convention drafted a document that recognized and protected slavery in a variety of ways. Most famously, the delegates agreed to count slaves for representation, but only with a three-fifths ratio. Ironically, in 1776 southerners in Congress like Thomas Lynch had insisted that slaves were property and should not be counted as people for purposes of taxation. However, eleven years later, when debating the allocation of representatives in the new Congress, southerners at the convention suddenly insisted that slaves were people and should be counted just as free people were counted. The final result—the three-fifths clause—gave the South extra voting power in the House of Representatives and also extra votes in the electoral college. Without the votes in Congress created by counting slaves, a number of important pieces of legislation, such as the Missouri Compromise and the Fugitive Slave Law of 1850, might never have passed. Similarly, without the electoral votes created by counting slaves for representation, the slaveholding Thomas Jefferson would not have defeated the nonslaveholding John Adams in the crucial election of 1800.[11]

In addition to giving the South extra political power for its slaves, the Constitution provided a number of other guarantees to slavery. The Constitution empowered Congress to use the military to suppress "domestic insur-

---

[8] *State v. Lasselle*, 1 Blackf. (Ind.) 60 (1820). It is not clear whether this led to the emancipation of the existing slaves in the state. Archivists at the Indiana State Archives have recently discovered documentation suggesting that blacks were held in bondage in Indiana into the 1830s or 1840s. This material is mostly in French and not yet published, but discussions with these archivists lead me to conclude that our understanding of the process of abolition in Indiana is far from complete.

[9] *Jarrot v. Jarrot*, 1 Gilman (Ill.) 1 (1845).

[10] For a discussion of the persistence of bondage in both states, see generally Paul Finkelman, *Slavery and the Founders: Race and Liberty in the Age of Jefferson*, 2d ed. (Armonk, N.Y., 2001), pp. 37–80.

[11] U.S. Constitution, art. I, sec. 2, cl. 3 and art. II, sec. 1, cl. 2. For a complete discussion of slavery and the Constitution, see Finkelman, *Slavery and the Founders*, pp. 3–36.

rections," which for southerners meant slave revolts. In another clause the Constitution required that the national government protect the states from "domestic violence," which also included slave revolts. The fugitive slave clause provided that masters could recover their slaves if they ran away to other states, although it did not spell out the mechanisms for doing this. There was no significant debate over the fugitive slave clause at the convention, and during the ratification process no northerners seem to have noticed it. Southern federalists, however, praised it in their ratification conventions. The return of fugitive slaves would become one of the most divisive political and sectional issues in the 1840s and 1850s.

While the Constitution gave Congress plenary power over all "Commerce with foreign Nations, and among the several States," the delegates in Philadelphia modified this power to protect slavery by prohibiting Congress from ending the African slave trade (or the domestic slave trade) before at least 1808 and prohibiting both Congress and the states from ever levying export taxes. Southerners insisted on this clause to prevent an indirect tax on slavery by taxing the products of slave labor such as tobacco, rice, and later sugar and cotton.[12] In addition to the clauses directly related to slavery, three other provisions of the Constitution—dealing with the federal territories, the national capital, and the commerce power—would affect the debate over slavery in the 1840s and 1850s.

The Constitution gave Congress the right to "dispose of and make all needful Rules and Regulations respecting the Territory" of the United States. The application of this provision was naturally affected by slavery as settlement moved west. This obvious conclusion is underscored by the fact that the Confederation Congress sitting in New York City was legislating about slavery in the Northwest just as the convention was debating the powers of Congress. Following the ratification of the Constitution, Congress spent significant amounts of time dealing with slavery in the territories. Every time a new state entered the Union the issue lurked in the background. Territorial acquisitions from France, Spain, and later Mexico raised the question as well. So too did the creation of new territorial governments. Once the Constitution was in place, Congress reenacted the Northwest Ordinance with its prohibition on slavery, and then enacted the Southwest Ordinance, which allowed slavery in the territories that became Tennessee, Alabama, and Mississippi.

---

[12]U.S. Constitution, art. I, sec. 8, cl. 15 (insurrections); art. IV, sec. 4 (domestic violence); art. I, sec. 8, cl. 3 (commerce); art. I, sec. 9, cl. 1 and art. V (slave trade); art. I, sec. 9, cl. 5 and sec. 10, cl. 2 (export taxes).

The Louisiana Purchase, in 1803, set the stage for other decisions on slavery. When Missouri sought to enter the Union as a slave state, in 1819, congressmen from the North objected, arguing that Missouri was north and west of the southern terminus of the Ohio River, and thus, under the Northwest Ordinance, slavery should not be permitted there. Southerners saw this as a contrived antislavery argument that made little sense. Slavery was an ongoing institution in Missouri when the territory became part of the United States through the Louisiana Purchase. Since 1803 no one in Congress had ever claimed that the ordinance applied to Missouri or that slavery should be prohibited there. Southerners also noted that since the Ohio River ended at the Mississippi River, Missouri, which was on the western side of the Mississippi, could not possibly be considered north of the Ohio River. The northern majority in the House of Representatives was more powerful than either of these two arguments, and thus for a year the Missouri question paralyzed Congress. Finally, Henry Clay of Kentucky brokered a successful compromise which provided that Missouri would enter the Union as a slave state, but slavery would be prohibited in all the remaining territories north and west of Missouri. Under this agreement, known as both the Missouri Compromise and the Compromise of 1820, slavery was prohibited in most of the existing federal territories. The compromise promised that in the future more free states would enter the Union than slave states, and slavery itself would be restricted to existing slave states plus the future states of Arkansas and Oklahoma.

The future, however, did not play out this way. The Missouri Compromise turned out not to be the beginning of the restriction of the spread of slavery, but rather, it was the last time Congress would restrict the spread of slavery until the Civil War. The acquisition of Florida in 1821 and the annexation of Texas in 1845 added huge amounts of land where slavery was legal and would flourish. In 1850 Congress allowed slavery in most of the territory acquired in the Mexican War. Only in California was slavery banned, and that was not accomplished by Congress but was a result of the demands of the people of the Golden State when it entered the Union. In the Kansas-Nebraska Act of 1854 Congress repealed the ban on slavery in most of the remaining territory that had been part of the Louisiana Purchase. And in *Dred Scott v. Sandford* (1857) the Supreme Court held that Congress had no power to prohibit slavery in *any* federal territories. Thus, the expectations of 1820—that slavery would have little space to spread—were undermined by constant acquisitions of new land, congressional backtracking on the settlement of the slavery issue in the Missouri Compromise, and eventually the Supreme Court. In the long decade of the 1850s the debate over slavery in the territories would fracture the political parties and the nation.

Congress also had the power to "exercise exclusive Legislation" over the national capital, what became the District of Columbia.[13] The national capital would eventually be carved out of land ceded by Maryland and Virginia —states where slavery remained legal until the Civil War. Slavery was present at the founding of the national capital, and indeed most of the early public buildings were constructed with the use of slave labor.[14] From the beginning most of the prominent residents of the district were slave owners; and slaves staffed hotels and restaurants, drove carriages, provided skilled labor, and served as domestic servants throughout the city. Southern politicians, government officials, and military officers brought slaves to the district as domestic servants, carriage drivers, cooks, and sometimes paramours. While southerners considered it their right to take slaves into the District of Columbia, northerners found the presence of slaves in the national capital deeply distasteful. They argued that in a nation of free people it was particularly troublesome to have slaves in the seat of government.

Tied to the question of slavery in the capital was the issue of commerce in slaves. More aggressive opponents of slavery wanted to use the commerce power of Congress to prohibit the interstate slave trade. Surely Congress had the power to do this under its power to regulate commerce "among the several states." Agitation for this could get little traction in Congress because southerners were adamant that they *must* have the right to sell slaves in any state where slavery was legal. A ban on the interstate slave trade would have been a direct assault on the entire system of slavery, and would certainly have led to disunion. Thus, Congress never seriously considered such a ban. A prohibition on the public sale of slaves in the District of Columbia and on transporting slaves through the district for sale elsewhere was more realistic. The sight of slave coffles marching past the national Capitol was overwhelmingly offensive to northerners. Even some southern members of Congress may have been uncomfortable with the visible reminder of the most problematic and troublesome aspect of slavery. Most slave owners disliked the trade and considered professional traders to be socially beneath them, even

---

[13]U.S. Constitution, art. IV, sec. 3, cl. 2 (territories) and art. I, sec. 8, cl. 17 (national capital).
[14]See Paul Finkelman, "Slavery in the Shadow of Liberty: The Problem of Slavery in Congress and the Nation's Capital," in Finkelman and Donald R. Kennon, eds., *In the Shadow of Freedom: The Politics of Slavery in the National Capital* (Athens, Ohio, 2010), pp. 3–15.

if they knew that at some point in their life most masters would have to sell slaves to raise cash, settle estates, dispose of troublesome slaves, or relieve themselves of slaves they no longer needed for their farms or plantations. Thomas Jefferson, for example, denied that he participated in the slave trade, even as he ordered his overseers to sell slaves to raise cash.[15] James Madison refused to sell slaves for most of his life and did so only when he had more than he could use, or even feed, on his small landholdings. After the Revolution, George Washington simply did not sell slaves. He was adamant that he would never either buy or sell slaves, "as you would do cattle at a market." Thus, the demand for an end to the slave trade in the district was the one antislavery measure Congress acquiesced to in the 1850s. The ban on the trade in the district was essentially symbolic; it did not harm slavery as an institution, or even masters in the district. They could always take their slaves across the river to Alexandria, Virginia, where commerce in slaves survived.[16]

While white Americans debated the status of slavery in the west or the continuation of the slave trade (or even slavery itself) in the District of Columbia, individual slaves increasingly sought their own liberty by running away. Fugitive slaves created a constant irritation for national politics. For southerners, a runaway slave was a rebel who threatened the security of southern society while diminishing the assets of a slave owner. In *Somerset v. Stewart* (1772) the highest court in England ruled that slaves who reached Great Britain were free because there were no statutes establishing slavery there, and according to Lord Chief Justice Mansfield "so high an act of dominion" as holding someone as a slave could only be established by positive law.[17] This precedent was applicable to the free states of the North, such as Massachusetts and New Hampshire, where slavery had been abolished by the time of the Constitutional Convention. In response to fears based on this precedent and growing opposition to slavery in New England and some of the Middle States, the convention gave masters the right to recover runaway slaves

---

[15]Finkelman, *Slavery and the Founders*, pp. 184–85.

[16]George Washington to Alexander Spotswood, Nov. 23, 1794, in Washington, *The Writings of George Washington from the Original Manuscript Sources, 1745–1799*, ed. John C. Fitzpatrick (Washington, D.C., 1931–44), p. 47; Fritz Hirshfeld, *George Washington and Slavery: A Documentary Portrayal* (Columbia, Mo., 1997), p. 16; Henry Wiencek, *An Imperfect God: George Washington, His Slaves, and the Creation of America* (New York, 2003), p. 188; A. Glenn Crothers, "The 1846 Retrocession of Alexandria: Protecting Slavery and the Slave Trade in the District of Columbia," in Finkelman and Kennon, *In the Shadow of Slavery*, pp. 141–68.

[17]*Somerset v. Stewart*, 98 Eng. Rep. 499 (G.B., 1772).

through the fugitive slave clause. This clause was vague in its wording and opaque as to how it would be implemented. In 1793 Congress passed a law that provided for enforcement by either state or federal officials, with only limited procedural protections to prevent the kidnapping or removal on mistaken identity of free blacks. In response most northern states passed statutes, known as personal liberty laws, to insure that free blacks were not taken south as slaves.[18] In *Prigg v. Pennsylvania* (1842) the U.S. Supreme Court held that these state laws were unconstitutional because Congress had the exclusive power to regulate the return of fugitive slaves. While upholding the federal law of 1793, Justice Joseph Story, speaking for the Court, held that the states *ought* to help enforce the law, but they did not have to do so. In response to this, many states took a hands-off approach to the return of runaway slaves, prohibiting their judges from hearing fugitive slave cases and closing their jails and other facilities to slave catchers. Because there were few federal judges and marshals, this situation made it virtually impossible for masters to recover their slaves in the North.[19]

In response to *Prigg*, southerners demanded a new fugitive slave law that would provide a significant federal involvement in the capture and return of fugitives. Many northerners acknowledged the southern grievance over this issue. However, even some northerners who were not actively antislavery were also repelled at the very idea of slave catchers roaming their states, grabbing blacks who lived and worked in their communities and were often spouses or parents of free black residents and citizens of the northern states. The issue of returning fugitive slaves was deeply emotional for people in both sections. At the Constitutional Convention and during the ratification struggle, there had been almost no debate over the fugitive slave clause, but by the 1840s southerners saw the clause as a key component of the constitutional compromises over slavery. Southern masters saw the return of fugitives as a matter of moral and constitutional obligation as well as property rights. In southern eyes, northerners who failed to help capture fugitive slaves were little more than thieves, who helped deprive masters of their property. For increasing

---

[18] Thomas D. Morris, *Free Men All: The Personal Liberty Laws of the North* (Baltimore, 1974); John Hope Franklin and Loren Schweninger, *Runaway Slaves: Rebels on the Plantation* (New York, 1999).

[19] *Prigg v. Pennsylvania*, 16 Pet. 539 (1842). On *Prigg*, see Paul Finkelman, "*Prigg v. Pennsylvania* and Northern State Courts: Anti-Slavery Use of a Pro-Slavery Decision," *Civil War History* 25 (1979):5–35; and Finkelman, "Story Telling on the Supreme Court: *Prigg v. Pennsylvania* and Justice Joseph Story's Judicial Nationalism," *Supreme Court Review*, 1994, pp. 247–94.

numbers of northerners the return of fugitive slaves was equally a moral issue. Fugitive slaves embodied the spirit of the American Revolution—they bravely took great risks to gain their liberty. Many had lived in the North for years or even decades. Some were landowners; others were parents of northern-born children; some were voters. Dragging such people to the South, especially without even a fair trial, struck many northerners as deeply immoral.

## The Crisis of the 1850s

All these issues coalesced in the 1850s. During and immediately after the Mexican War, Congress persistently debated the status of slavery in the territory that formed the fruits of victory. In the House the northern majority passed the Wilmot Proviso, which prohibited slavery in all the new territory. The Senate, where the South had a two-state majority during all but the last months of the war, defeated the proviso. The admission of Iowa to the Union, in December 1846, and of Wisconsin, in May 1848, gave the North parity in the Senate, but there were always a few northern Democrats willing to vote with the South to defeat the proviso. This led to a stalemate, even as nearly one hundred thousand people poured into California during the gold rush. Nothing could be done about the territories because neither side could win and neither side would compromise on the spread of slavery into the region. That is where the issue stood when President Zachary Taylor died, in July 1850.

Northern demands to end slavery in Washington, D.C., annoyed southerners, although there was no chance such a law would pass the Senate, or even the House. Southern demands for a new fugitive slave law similarly angered northerners, who did not want to become slave catchers doing the bidding of southern masters. Southern hotheads talked about secession, although they had little following in the South and most northerners did not take them very seriously. After all, since Thomas Lynch's outburst in 1776 southerners had been threatening to leave the Union. Meanwhile, the governor of Texas was planning an invasion of the New Mexico Territory to seize more land for what was already the largest state in the Union.

In response to all these issues, Congress crafted the Compromise of 1850 in an attempt to defuse the interstate conflicts. The compromise destroyed the Missouri Compromise line by opening Nevada and Utah to slavery; created a federal law enforcement presence in every county in the North to help catch fugitive slaves; gave Texas a substantial amount of land that had been part of New Mexico; bailed out Texas by paying off the debt it had accumulated while an independent republic; brought California into the Union as a free state; and banned the public slave trade in the District of Columbia.

The Compromise of 1850 solved nothing. In the North anger persisted over the opening of new territories to slavery, while in the South armed adventurers, known as filibusters, invaded Cuba, hoping to seize that island from Spain to create still more land for slavery. Senator Albert G. Brown of Mississippi explained the Caribbean land grab and a future of more land grabs. "I want Cuba, and I know that sooner or later we must have it." But that was hardly enough for the seemingly insatiable southerners. Brown went on, "I want Tamaulipas, Potosi, and one or two other Mexican States; and I want them all for the same reason—for the planting and spreading of slavery."[20]

The next land grab was more local. In 1854 Congress repealed the ban on slavery west of Missouri, opening up all or parts of the future states of Kansas, Nebraska, South Dakota, North Dakota, Wyoming, Colorado, Montana, and Idaho to slavery. In the space of four years the vision of a free United States had been replaced by a nation where slavery could spread across the nation, and where the free states could become a minority. In Kansas northerners resisted this onslaught of bondage by trying to outnumber southern settlers. Congress had provided that the issue of slavery in Kansas would be determined democratically, through "popular sovereignty." But when Free-Soil settlers began to outnumber southerners, the Pierce administration stepped in to support undemocratic elections that favored slavery. As violence turned the Kansas Territory into Bleeding Kansas, Pierce and his successor, James Buchanan, used the military to favor southerners. When the proslavery men sacked the free-state capital at Lawrence, President Pierce did nothing to seek out the culprits.

The failure of the national administration to prosecute proslavery violence in Kansas mirrored other national policies. The Pierce administration refused to seek an indictment against Congressman Preston Brooks after he attacked Senator Charles Sumner with a cane, beating him insensible. Similarly, when filibusters invaded Cuba in violation of federal law and a

---

[20] James McPherson, *Battle Cry of Freedom: The Civil War Era* (New York, 1988), p. 106.

presidential proclamation, President Fillmore did not seek any prosecutions. In fact, he used federal money to bring the invaders back to the United States, after they were captured and sent to Spain for trial. Proslavery violence, in Kansas, on the Senate floor, or in Cuba, went unnoticed by American presidents.

Not so with antislavery activities. Fillmore, Pierce, and Buchanan all authorized vigorous prosecutions of northerners who helped rescue fugitive slaves from their masters or from federal custody. In 1851 fugitive slaves in Christiana, Pennsylvania, resisted an armed attack by a Maryland master, which ended with the slave owner being killed. The runaway slave who actually killed his master escaped to Canada, but President Fillmore personally authorized the largest treason prosecution in American history, as he tried to punish whites and blacks who had not actually participated in the event but rather had simply refused to help the slave owner capture his slave. While southerners in Kansas were never charged by the federal government for shooting and even killing northerners, the national government vigorously proclaimed the abolitionist John Brown a wanted man because he had defended Free-Soilers in Kansas and helped slaves escape from Kansas and Missouri.[21]

Conflicts over fugitive slaves in many ways defined the decade. In 1851 there were three spectacular riots that prevented the return of fugitive slaves from Boston; Christiana, Pennsylvania; and Syracuse, New York. The failed rescue of Thomas Sims in Boston also garnered headlines. The Fillmore administration aggressively, but ultimately incompetently, prosecuted numerous people for these rescues but obtained only one conviction, of a black man from Syracuse, who died while his case was on appeal. In 1854 the Pierce administration proved it could enforce the law in Boston, using federal troops, state militia, scores of special deputies, and a coast guard cutter, and spending perhaps as much as $100,000 to remove Anthony Burns to Virginia, where he was sold for about $900. The political cost of the removal was even greater than the financial cost, as the event exposed the impotence of the federal government to enforce the law and demonstrated to the whole North the utter unfairness of the 1850 law. Both the Pierce and Buchanan administrations relentlessly prosecuted Sherman Booth for leading the rescue of a

---

[21]Brown directed the killing of proslavery settlers at Pottawatomie, but the national government did not know of his involvement in that event and did not try to arrest him for it. See generally Robert E. McGlone, *John Brown's War against Slavery* (New York, 2009).

slave in Wisconsin, which led to one of the few convictions of a slave rescuer.[22] Similarly, in 1858 the Buchanan administration arrested scores of antislavery students and professors at Oberlin College, as well as residents of the town, but won only two convictions, and for the rest of the rescuers had to settle for plea bargains with token fines, many of which were never paid. While three administrations futilely tried to prove the efficacy of the fugitive slave law, northerners read countless stories of rescuers and autobiographies of fugitives, including a new version of Frederick Douglass's autobiography, *My Bondage and My Freedom* (1855). More important, northerners read and reread the greatest best seller of the century, Harriet Beecher Stowe's *Uncle Tom's Cabin* (1852), a novel that was mostly about fugitive slaves. Translated into numerous languages, the book was read everywhere in the world, except the American South, where it was banned. Queen Victoria sent Stowe a personal note, praising the book, but southerners reacted with horror at a novel that gave people around the world a sense of the humanity of slaves and brought into the homes of northerners the deep anguish caused by the sale of slaves and the desire of bondsmen and bondswomen to be free.

The last few years of the decade witnessed a flurry of events that drove the nation toward civil war. Chief Justice Taney's opinion in *Dred Scott* (1857) shocked northerners, who were suddenly told that blacks, even if born free in the North, could *never* be citizens and had *no rights* that whites had to respect.[23] Even more shocking was the chief justice's conclusion that Congress had no power to prohibit or even regulate slavery in the federal territories. This meant the Missouri Compromise (1820), the Compromise of 1850, and the Kansas-Nebraska Act (1854), as well as numerous other laws passed to create or regulate territories, were all unconstitutional. The decision was an invitation to the Republican Party to disband, because it had emerged in opposition to the Kansas-Nebraska Act and the spread of slavery in the territories. But of course the Republicans did not disband; by

---

[22]Paul Finkelman, "The Treason Trial of Castner Hanway," in *American Political Trials*, ed. Michal Belknap (1981; rev. ed., Westport, Conn., 1994), pp. 77–96; Thomas Slaughter, *Bloody Dawn: The Christiana Riot and Racial Violence in the Antebellum North* (New York, 1991); Finkelman, "Legal Ethics and Fugitive Slaves: The Anthony Burns Case, Judge Loring, and Abolitionist Attorneys," *Cardozo Law Review* 17 (1996):1793–1858; H. Robert Baker, *The Rescue of Joshua Glover: A Fugitive Slave, The Constitution, and the Coming of the Civil War* (Athens, Ohio, 2006); Stanley Campbell, *The Slave Catchers: Enforcement of the Fugitive Slave Law of 1850* (Chapel Hill, 1968).
[23]See Fehrenbacher, *The Dred Scott Case*; Paul Finkelman, *An Imperfect Union: Slavery, Federalism, and Comity* (Chapel Hill, 1981); and Konig, Finkelman, and Bracey, *The Dred Scott Case*.

1858 they controlled the House of Representatives and in 1860 they won the White House.

The one great intervening event between *Dred Scott* and the 1860 election was John Brown's raid at Harpers Ferry in October 1859. Brown had been a committed opponent of slavery for most of his life, but was never closely connected to any antislavery organizations. He moved to Kansas in 1856 to help his sons, who had relocated there to make that territory a free state. Brown quickly became a leader of free-state forces. His Kansas adventures led him to conclude that some dramatic action was necessary to challenge slavery.[24] He focused on guerrilla activities, believing he could help slaves escape from the South by taking them north through the Appalachian Mountains. His first strike was at the U.S. arsenal in Harpers Ferry, Virginia (present-day West Virginia). There he planned to seize weapons and then fade into the mountains. In October 1859, with a small band of men—his adult sons and sons-in-law, veterans of Bleeding Kansas, naive abolitionist dreamers, free blacks, and some fugitive slaves—he quickly and easily seized the armory, but then either by design, through a failure of judgment, or because of an emotional collapse, he remained at the armory and the next day was captured. He was tried in early November and hanged on December 2, 1859.

Almost all northerners were appalled by Brown's violence. But, many were also charmed by his audacity and his willingness to bravely confront slavery and even die for freedom. He condemned slavery at his trial and during the last month of his life he wrote hundreds of letters from jail and gave numerous interviews. Brown self-consciously—and successfully—shaped himself as martyr. The transcendentalist philosopher Ralph Waldo Emerson called Brown "the new saint awaiting his martyrdom" and concluded he "will make the gallows glorious like the cross." The pacifist abolitionist William Lloyd Garrison predicted that hanging Brown would be a "terrible losing day for all Slavedom." Rev. Henry Ward Beecher, whose sister had written *Uncle Tom's Cabin,* declared that the "cord and the gibbet would redeem" Brown and turn the disastrous raid at Harpers Ferry into "a heroic success." Brown agreed, telling a colleague, "I am worth inconceivably more to hang than for any other purpose." Northern politicians generally condemned Brown and his violence, but in the end, his act altered northern politics.

---

[24]The best study of Brown is McGlone, *John Brown's War against Slavery.* See also Evan Carton, *Patriotic Treason: John Brown and the Soul of America* (New York, 2006).

Many agreed with the Republican governor of Massachusetts, John A. Andrew, that while violence was wrong, and the raid itself was an absurdity, "John Brown himself is right."[25]

Southerners asserted a connection between Brown and the Republican Party, but of course none existed. Southern senators launched an investigation of the raid that became a partisan extravaganza aimed more at the 1860 election than at Brown or his activities. In 1860 Democrats referred to Lincoln as the candidate of the "John Brown Republicans," even though Lincoln and the Republican platform roundly condemned the raid. By the end of 1860 southerners had convinced themselves that Lincoln would make war on slavery, even though he lacked any constitutional power—and had no desire—to do so. Lincoln personally hated slavery—"If slavery is not wrong, then nothing is wrong," he wrote.[26] But he also understood that the Constitution protected slavery and he had no power to touch it.[27] However, extremist southerners, whether they believed Lincoln or not, used his election to lead their section out of the nation. In December 1860, South Carolina left the Union and in the first months of 1861 ten other southern states followed. The 1850s had ended in disaster and civil war.

---

[25] Quotations in Paul Finkelman, "Manufacturing Martyrdom: The Antislavery Response to John Brown's Raid," in *His Soul Goes Marching On: Responses to John Brown and the Harpers Ferry Raid*, ed. Paul Finkelman (Charlottesville, Va., 1995), pp. 42, 43.

[26] Abraham Lincoln to Albert G. Hodges, Apr. 4, 1864, in Roy P. Basler, *The Collected Works of Abraham Lincoln*, 9 vols. (New Brunswick, N.J., 1953–55), 7:281.

[27] Paul Finkelman, "Lincoln, Emancipation, and the Limits of Constitutional Change," *Supreme Court Review*, 2009, p. 349.

Michael F. Holt

# Politics, Patronage, and Public Policy

*The Compromise of 1850*

Worked out in fractious debates and seemingly endless roll call votes that lasted from early December 1849 until late September 1850, passage of the Compromise of 1850 is one of the most famous episodes in congressional history. It was necessitated by and helped resolve an increasingly rancorous sectional quarrel about whether slavery could be extended to the lands acquired from Mexico as a result of the Mexican War. That quarrel was ignited fully eighteen months before the actual acquisition of the Mexican Cession by ratification of the Treaty of Guadalupe Hidalgo, in March 1848.

War with Mexico began in May 1846. On August 8 of that year Pennsylvania's freshman Democratic representative David Wilmot introduced his famous proviso that would bar slavery from any lands taken from Mexico as a result of the war. The Wilmot Proviso immediately polarized both Whig and Democratic congressmen along sectional lines, and it would continue to do so over the next four years every time a bill incorporating congressional prohibition of slavery from the territories came up for a vote. By the end of 1849, fourteen of fifteen northern state legislatures had instructed their U.S. senators and requested their U.S. representatives to impose the proviso on any formal territorial governments that Congress established in the Mexican Cession. By then many southerners vowed to secede should the proviso

---

This chapter relies heavily on my previously published work, and the documentation for what I say here can be found in those works. See Michael F. Holt, *The Political Crisis of the 1850s* (1978; reprint ed., New York, 1983), pp. 67–99; and Holt, *The Rise and Fall of the American Whig Party: Jacksonian Politics and the Onset of the Civil War* (New York, 1999), pp. 383–552.

ever be enacted into law, and in late 1849 Mississippi issued a call to all slave states to send delegates to a slave-state convention in Nashville, Tennessee, in June 1850 to devise a common regional response to the threatened enactment of the congressional ban on slavery extension. This was the crisis that the first session of the Thirty-First Congress would have to address.

During the presidential election of 1848 both the Democrats and the Whigs had tried to paper over their divisions over the proviso. Democrats did so by nominating Senator Lewis Cass of Michigan, a champion of a doctrine known as popular sovereignty. This doctrine would remove any decision about slavery in the territories from Congress itself and instead allow the actual residents of the territories to decide whether slavery would be permitted in them. Northern and southern Democrats could agree on this formula because they were intentionally ambiguous about precisely when the residents of a territory could make this decision. Northern Democrats insisted that the first elected territorial legislature could decide, and it, they promised, was almost certain to bar slavery. Southern Democrats, in contrast, insisted that only when there was a sufficiently large population to justify admission to statehood could the residents make the decision when they wrote the new state's constitution. Until then, southern Democrats declared, slavery would be legal during the territorial phase. Since Cass also vowed to veto the proviso should it pass Congress while he was president, his nomination satisfied almost all southern Democrats as well as most northern Democrats.

Whigs, in contrast, nominated General Zachary Taylor, a hero of the Mexican War and a large southern slaveholder. The beauty of Taylor as a candidate was that his views on public policy were utterly unknown. Taylor, indeed, had never voted in any prior election, let alone affiliated with either political party. In the spring of 1848, shortly before the Whigs' national nominating convention, however, Taylor did publicly avow his commitment to a fundamental Whig principle: presidents must never veto any law passed by Congress unless it was clearly unconstitutional.

Taylor's nomination allowed the Whigs, too, to run a Janus-faced campaign, saying one thing in the North and another in the South. Northern Whigs seized on Taylor's pledge never to veto constitutional legislation to promise that Taylor would sign the proviso, which northern Whigs remained determined to pass, while Cass would veto it. The best way to stop slavery expansion, they contended, was to elect northern Whig congressmen, who would pass the proviso, and Taylor, who would sign it. Southern Whigs, in contrast, did not promise that Taylor would secure slavery extension into the Mexican Cession. Like Taylor himself, most southern Whigs did not believe that slavery could ever exist profitably in that area. (No one at the time could envision that California would ever become the leading cotton and rice producing state in the nation.) Instead, southern Whigs argued that no one who owned over a hundred slaves, as did Taylor, would ever betray his fellow southerners by signing the hated proviso into law.

Anger at the Whig and Democratic nominations led directly to the formation of the Free-Soil Party in August 1848. Its platform called not only for congressional prohibition of slavery from all federal territories, but also for an absolute ban against the admission of any more slave states into the Union. Free-Soilers ran former Democratic president Martin Van Buren as their presidential candidate, and Van Buren's incursion into the traditional Democratic vote in certain northern states, most notably New York, allowed Taylor to win the election.

By the end of 1848, however, nothing had been decided about the Mexican Cession, and no civil governments had been organized anywhere in it. Formal authority rested with United States army officers. Then, during 1849, some eighty to one hundred thousand gold seekers rushed to California, swamping the small detachment of troops there, many of whom in fact deserted and joined the pell-mell hunt for gold. To bring order to this burgeoning population, a civilian government of some kind had to be created for it. The Thirty-First Congress, which first met in December 1849, it appeared, would once again have to confront the proviso question and its sectionally explosive ramifications.

Within weeks of his inauguration, in March 1849, in fact, President Taylor and his secretary of state, John M. Clayton, a Delaware Whig, devised a plausible solution. They would finesse the divisive quarrel over the proviso by skipping a formal territorial stage in the Mexican Cession altogether. Instead, they sent emissaries to both California and New Mexico to urge their residents to write constitutions and apply for statehood by the time Congress met in December. No one questioned the right of a state to prohibit or legalize slavery within its borders. The proviso applied only to congressionally organized *territorial* governments. Nor did Taylor ignore the Mormons, who had settled around the Great Salt Lake earlier in the 1840s. He sent a separate agent to them who asked them to become part of the new state of California, and, surprisingly, the Mormons agreed. Thus Mormon delegates to the expected California constitutional convention set off for the arduous overland trek across the desert and the Sierra Nevada. By the time they reached the West Coast, however, the California constitution had long since been written and ratified. This created a free state with its modern eastern boundary along the crest of the Sierra.

Taylor, in fact, fully expected both California and New Mexico to bar slavery in their constitutions, although he carefully instructed his emissaries to take no stand on the slavery question. Northerners of all parties, he believed, would gladly accept two new free states, as might southern Whig congressmen, who had pushed a plan in February 1849 to organize the entire Mexican Cession into a single free state. Southern Democrats might demur, but they could be outvoted. Better still, both the Wilmot Proviso and the new Free-Soil Party would be rendered obsolete.

Despite the failure of his hopes of incorporating the Mormon settlement into California, Taylor sent messages to Congress in December 1849 and again in January 1850 touting his plan. California would soon submit a constitution, he wrote, and Congress should admit it as a state as soon as the official document arrived without any attempt to change its provisions concerning slavery. Then Congress should wait until the application for statehood from New Mexico arrived and admit it, too, as a state. In the interim, Taylor stressed in both messages, Congress must make no attempt to organize territorial governments in the cession, for such attempts would only lead to dangerously rancorous sectional strife over the proviso. Taylor's intent, again, was to avert such strife by avoiding the formation of territorial governments.

In his January message Taylor also addressed one other aspect of the looming crisis, one that by the summer of 1850 would become its single most dangerous aspect. The slave state of Texas, with the official blessing of ex-president James K. Polk, claimed all the land east of the Rio Grande, including the trading center of Santa Fe, as part of Texas. Many northerners, certainly all northern Whigs and Free-Soilers, like Taylor himself, believed this claim was outrageous. Taylor, indeed, had sent his emissary, who urged New Mexicans to apply for statehood to Santa Fe. Yet almost all southern Democrats vowed to defend Texas's grandiose land claim. The reason is easily understood. Slavery was legal on every square foot of Texas soil. To boot, as Daniel Webster reminded the Senate in his famous Seventh of March speech, according to the congressional resolution by which Texas was annexed in

1845, as many as four additional states could be carved out of Texas and future Congresses must admit them as slave states if their residents so desired. To allow any relocation of Texas's western boundary therefore struck most southern Democrats as a fatal surrender of southern political power.

New Mexicans, in turn, insisted that Texas's western boundary was where it had been when Texas was a Mexican state, hundreds of miles east of the Rio Grande. In his January message Taylor argued that the best way to settle this boundary dispute was to admit New Mexico as a state and then let the Supreme Court resolve the dispute. In the meantime, he added, the unorganized portions of the cession would still be governed by Mexican laws, one of which had abolished slavery in those areas.

This, then, was the so-called Taylor Plan for the Mexican Cession. It would give the North the substance of free soil and spare the South congressional imposition of the hated Wilmot Proviso, which many northerners had demanded since 1846. It was, in short, a compromise aimed at keeping the sectional peace. Yet it was not the compromise that Congress finally passed in September 1850. Instead the ultimate Compromise of 1850 admitted California as a free state with its modern boundaries; organized the remainder of the cession into the Utah and New Mexico Territories on the basis of the Democratic formula of popular sovereignty; reduced Texas to its modern boundaries and paid it $10 million in compensation, half of which was to be paid to the holders of bonds Texas had issued when it was an independent republic, most of whom were northern investors, not southerners, let alone Texans; enacted a much more rigorous fugitive slave law that occasioned far less debate in Congress than any other part of the package; and abolished the public slave auctions, but not slavery itself, in the District of Columbia.

These developments raise two questions that are the focus of the remainder of this chapter. First, why did Taylor's plan, which avoided the proviso, fail and a different congressional compromise plan, which flouted his insistence that territorial governments not be organized, pass? Second, what explains the unprecedented pattern of roll call votes on the compromise measures in the House and the Senate and the deviations from the overall pattern? In short, why did some people vote for, and others against, the compromise? Congressional votes on Texas annexation had been largely partisan, not sectional, while votes on the Wilmot Proviso had been sectional, with northerners united across party lines against southerners united across party lines. In 1850, however, both partisan and sectional affiliations shaped the voting alignments. The great majority of northern Whigs in both chambers opposed the compromise, whereas almost all southern Whigs supported it. Conversely, the large majority of northern Democrats supported the compromise, while most southern Democrats bitterly opposed it. Each party split along sectional lines, yet each section's congressional delegation split along party lines. How can we account for this extraordinary pattern?[1]

### Pattern of Congressional Votes on the Compromise of 1850

|  | *Whigs* | *Democrats* |
| --- | --- | --- |
| North | anticompromise | procompromise |
| South | procompromise | anticompromise |

As to why some men supported and others opposed the compromise measures,[2] let me begin by rejecting one seemingly obvious but deeply erroneous explanation. This is that supporters of the compromise were more patriotic and more devoted to the preservation of the Union than were its opponents. Anyone who knows anything about Zachary Taylor or William Henry Seward, New York's freshman Whig senator and the leader of the northern anticompromise Whigs, knows how wrongheaded this canard is.

Instead, my argument is based on the following: (1) political developments that threatened both northern and southern Whigs between Taylor's election, in November 1848, and the meeting of Congress in December 1849; (2) the Pavlovian tendency of rival party politicians from the same state, and factional rivals within one party from a state, to take a position on public policy different from that of their rivals in order to mobilize popular support in elections or party nominating conventions; and (3) the U.S. Senate's control over confirming or rejecting many presidential nominees for patronage

---

[1]These assertions are based on statistical analyses of roll call votes in the first session of the Thirty-First Congress in Joel H. Silbey, *The Shrine of Party: Congressional Voting Behavior, 1841–1852* (Pittsburgh, 1967); Thomas B. Alexander, *Sectional Stress and Party Strength: A Computer Analysis of Roll-Call Voting Patterns in the United States House of Representatives, 1836–1860* (Nashville, 1967); and Mark J. Stegmaier, *Texas, New Mexico, and the Compromise of 1850: Boundary Dispute and Sectional Crisis* (Kent, Ohio, 1996). Stegmaier is especially good in establishing the internal cohesion of the odd anticompromise coalition, for northern Whigs and southern Democrats opposed the compromise for diametrically different reasons.

[2]Some of the measures clearly advantaged the North and others the South—California statehood and a new fugitive slave law, for example. Hence support for or opposition to the compromise refers primarily, though not exclusively, to how one voted on the territorial bills and the redrawn Texas–New Mexico boundary line.

jobs in the federal government. In 1850 the most important of these patronage holders were U.S. marshals, U.S. attorneys, customs collectors, postmasters, naval yard inspectors, ambassadors, judges, territorial officials, and Land Office officials. It was on the confirmation or rejection of these forgotten men that passage of the Compromise of 1850 ultimately hinged.

Democrats in both sections were frightened and infuriated by Taylor's victory, which they attributed to the insufficiency of Cass's popular sovereignty formula compared to the Janus-faced campaign Whigs had run in the North and South. Southern Democrats in particular ranted that it had offered no defense against Whig taunts that their candidate was a slaveholder whereas the Democrats' was a Yankee. Taylor had carried eight of the fifteen slave states and had come strikingly close to carrying three traditional Democratic bastions—Alabama, Mississippi, and Virginia. Immediately after the election, therefore, southern Democrats jettisoned popular sovereignty and demanded equal access for slaveholders to all of the Mexican Cession. At the same time, they warned southern voters, Taylor and the Whigs would betray the South on the proviso since Taylor, as northern Whigs had asserted, would sign it into law. Only Democrats could provide adequate protection to slaveholders' rights.

Southern Democrats' case against southern Whigs, who for most of 1849 still boasted that Taylor would never betray the South, was reinforced by two developments that year. Only two of the forty-eight southern Whigs signed a belligerently antinorthern Southern Address that Calhoun wrote and issued to the southern press in February. Thus Calhoun's address seemed a southern Democratic Party manifesto, even though many Democrats also refused to sign it. Democrats could cite Whigs' refusal to sign as evidence of southern Whigs' unreliability as defenders of what were called Southern Rights. Then, in late August and September, word reached the South that President Taylor had told an audience in northwestern Pennsylvania that they need not fear slavery's further expansion. Slavery would never be extended to the Mexican Cession and the need for the Free-Soil Party would soon be obviated. Here, shouted southern Democrats, was irrefutable evidence that Taylor indeed intended to sign the obnoxious Wilmot Proviso.

The political impact of these developments on southern Whigs' political fortunes in 1849, when sixty House seats as well as seven governorships would be filled, was calamitous. In 1847 Whigs and Democrats had split the sixty House seats evenly, thirty to thirty. In 1849, Democrats won forty-one compared to the Whigs' nineteen, thereby assuring Democratic control of the House as well as the Senate when the new Thirty-First Congress met in December. In addition, Democrats swept all seven governorships, four of which were in slave states Taylor had carried a year earlier.

By the end of 1849, in short, southern Whigs were on the ropes. Standing by Taylor as the South's faithful tribune no longer sufficed. To survive politically they needed a new stance on the slavery extension issue. By the same token, gleeful southern Democrats attributed their triumphs to their new, hard-line stance on slavery extension into the Mexican Cession. Any retreat from the position that slaveholders must be allowed equal access to the Mexican Cession would be politically stultifying. Little wonder, then, that most southern Democrats in the Thirty-First Congress fervently opposed both Taylor's plan and Congress's Compromise of 1850, for both California's admission as a free state and the reduction of Texas infuriated them.

Whig setbacks in 1849 in the North, where Taylor had carried seven of fifteen states, including the two biggest, New York and Pennsylvania, were almost as severe, even though far fewer House seats were at stake than in the South. Northern Democrats also blamed their 1848 losses on the inadequacies of popular sovereignty as well as Cass's pledge to veto the proviso. Thus in state after state they abandoned popular sovereignty as the party's position on slavery extension, reembraced the proviso or, even more tellingly, formed open coalitions with Free-Soilers in Connecticut, Illinois, Indiana, Massachusetts, Ohio, Vermont, and Wisconsin. Elsewhere, as in New York, the free-soil Barnburners reunited with the pro-Cass Hunker Democrats to score spectacular gains in the 1849 state elections. State after state that Whigs had carried for Taylor fell to Democrats or Democratic–Free-Soil coalitions.

In 1849 the most successful Democratic–Free-Soil alliances appeared in Connecticut and Ohio. In the former, the coalition carried three of four House seats, all of which had previously been held by Whigs. In the latter, Democrats in the Ohio state legislature readily agreed to dump incumbent Democrat William Allen from his U.S. Senate seat to replace him with the Free-Soiler Salmon P. Chase. In return Free-Soilers helped Democrats capture control of both houses of the state legislature, a prize state-level Democratic politicos deemed considerably more valuable than a U.S. Senate seat.

This Democratic or Democratic–Free-Soil resurgence in 1849 convinced northern Whig representatives in the Thirty-First Congress, almost all of whom had been elected in 1848, of two things. First, they must insist on the legal prohibition of slavery from any territories Congress formally organized in the Mexican Cession in order to stop further Democratic–Free-Soil incursions into their electorate when their seats were up for election in 1850. Second, they needed a new position on the territorial/proviso question to differentiate themselves from their Democratic and Free-Soil foes. They could never one-up them on commitment to the proviso itself, as they had in 1848. Hence, northern Whigs would embrace Taylor's plan with its free-soil implications. And to embrace Taylor's plan meant opposing the compromise proposals that Taylor despised because Congress ignored his advice about not organizing formal territorial governments and which, in any event, organized the Utah and New Mexico Territories without the proviso.

Ultimately even more important than their impact on northern Whigs, northern Democratic state parties' abandonment of popular sovereignty in 1849 and open alliances with Free-Soilers in some northern states infuriated five powerful northern Democrats in the Senate. These men were deeply committed to the popular sovereignty principle, and they regarded the Free-Soilers as dangerous and divisive sectional agitators. They were equally upset by recently passed legislative instructions that they support the proviso, instructions that Whigs and Free-Soilers had often adopted with the support of a minority of Democrats over the protests of their loyalists among Democratic state legislators. What especially worried them, however, was the fate of their former colleague William Allen, for if Ohio Democrats were willing to dump Allen to curry favor with Free-Soilers, they too might suffer a similar fate.

This crucial bloc of northern Democratic senators included Daniel Sturgeon, of Pennsylvania; Jesse Bright, of Indiana; Stephen A. Douglas, of Illinois; Lewis Cass, of Michigan, the party's standard bearer in 1848; and Daniel S. Dickinson, leader of New York's anti–Van Buren Hunker faction and the single most influential man in the Senate, where Democrats enjoyed a clear majority. As soon as they reconvened in Washington, in December 1849, these five men determined to recommit the northern Democratic Party to popular sovereignty. Orders went out to that effect in January 1850—the evidence is quite explicit about that. Platforms on slavery extension must be changed back to the 1848 position, and where possible legislative instructions about imposing the proviso must be repealed. And in state after northern state those instructions were heeded. To defy the Free-Soilers, moreover, these five men were determined in this first session of the Thirty-First Congress to organize territorial governments in the Mexican Cession on the basis of popular sovereignty. Hence they, like most northern Democrats in the House and Senate, rejected Taylor's plan because it opposed the organization of territorial governments and supported the compromise measures once they incorporated the Democratic formula of popular sovereignty.

The exceptions among northern Democrats during that congressional session, that is, the men who opposed prosouthern parts of the compromise like the organization of territorial governments without the proviso and a western boundary for Texas, which they believed still gave too much land to slavery, hailed from congressional districts or states like Wisconsin, where Free-Soilers had made especially strong showings in 1848 and 1849, often at the expense of Democrats. In short the men who deviated from the dominant northern Democratic position on the compromise considered it political suicide to abandon the Wilmot Proviso.

The five northern Democratic senators I've identified were crucial for another reason, one that ostensibly had nothing to do with slavery extension or the four-year deadlock over Wilmot's proviso. They chaired the key Senate committees (Dickinson, for example, chaired Finance, which oversaw all customs collectors) that would recommend rejection or confirmation of most of Zachary Taylor's nominees for federal patronage jobs. And they would wield that power to pressure northern Whigs to support passage of the compromise measures or at least acquiesce in that passage by abstaining rather than casting negative votes. Early in the session, indeed, a caucus of Senate Democrats decided to postpone any action on appointees until the summer, September as it turned out for most, when they could maximize pressure on northern Whigs who sought the confirmation or rejection of particular men.

In point of fact, for reasons I have explained at great length elsewhere, Taylor and his cabinet's dispensation of federal jobs between March and December 1849 had infuriated most congressional Whigs and, just as important, Whigs from congressional districts and states without Whig representation in Congress. Three blocs of Whigs were especially incensed. Midwestern Whigs west of Ohio complained bitterly that Ohio's Thomas Ewing, the only midwesterner in Taylor's cabinet, had steered most of the plums to his state or his personal friends in other states. By the fall of 1849 a coalition of Whig newspaper editors from Indianapolis, Detroit, Chicago, Des Moines, Milwaukee, and other midwestern cities was demanding that Taylor fire Ewing and the rest of the cabinet. Almost all southern Whigs, in turn, complained that Taylor's cabinet had foolishly retained too many Democrats in office rather than replacing them with those southern Whigs' friends. Finally, supporters of conservatives like Kentucky senator-elect Henry Clay, Massachusetts senator Daniel Webster, and Vice President Millard Fillmore, a New Yorker and longtime rival of New York's anticompromise senator Seward, believed, correctly in most cases, that Taylor's administration had excluded them from the best federal jobs. As Clay, who was returning to the Senate for the first time since 1842, wrote upon his arrival in Washington in December 1849, "There is a great and bitter complaint against the Administration from all the Whigs, or almost all."[3]

At least two Whig senators, Maryland's veteran James Pearce and Pennsylvania's freshman James Cooper, had vowed in public speeches in the fall of 1849 that they would secure Senate rejection of Taylor's appointees in their respective states when they came before the Senate. To do so, of course, they needed the help of Senate Democrats. Pearce would become a fervent supporter of the congressional compromise plan, as opposed to Taylor's, yet he also played a key role in shaping the final legislation for the redrawn Texas–New Mexico boundary, which most southern Whigs supported and most southern Democrats opposed.

Pennsylvania's long-since-forgotten James Cooper is a far more interesting case. Before his election to the Senate by Pennsylvania's legislature in the winter of 1849, he had previously served in the House and as Pennsylvania's state attorney general, and he was regarded as a staunch antislavery, antislavery extension man, as were most Pennsylvania Whigs. But after the election of William F. Johnston as Pennsylvania's Whig governor, in October 1848, Cooper soon got into a quarrel with Johnston, who had appointed him as state attorney general. Johnston, a very recent defector from the Democratic Party, opposed Cooper's election as U.S. senator, and once Cooper prevailed in the legislature, he and Johnston then engaged in a titanic, yet one-sided, battle for control of Pennsylvania's federal jobs dispensed by Taylor's cabinet. Johnston won everything; Cooper and his friends got zilch.

Thus Cooper vowed to secure the rejection of Pennsylvania's as-yet-unconfirmed appointees when he went to Washington in December 1849. Yet to do so in a Senate controlled by Democrats, the freshman Cooper was utterly dependent on the aid of his senior Democratic colleague Daniel

---

[3] Henry Clay to Thomas B. Stevenson, Washington, Dec. 21, 1849, Thomas B. Stevenson MSS, Indiana Historical Society Library, Indianapolis.

Sturgeon, one of those key northern Democratic senators who was determined to organize territorial governments in the Mexican Cession on the basis of popular sovereignty, not the Wilmot Proviso to which virtually all northern Whigs, including Cooper, had previously pledged themselves. Thus, to the consternation of his proproviso Whig constituents in Pennsylvania, throughout the very long first session of the Thirty-First Congress Cooper voted identically to Sturgeon on every bill or motion relevant to slavery. No northern Whig in the Senate, including Daniel Webster, supported the congressional compromise measures so loyally as he. For Cooper, sadly, this compromise of his antislavery principles did no good. The Senate confirmed virtually all the men he had come to Washington publicly pledged to defeat.

To recapitulate this fascinating, if tangled, story, when Zachary Taylor sent his plan for the Mexican Cession—statehood for California and New Mexico and no territorial governments—to Congress in December 1849 and January 1850, only most northern Whigs, along with Delaware Whigs loyal to Secretary of State John M. Clayton, supported it. Northern Democrats would admit California as a free state, but they demanded the organization of territorial governments in the rest of the cession on the basis of popular sovereignty. Hence they opposed Taylor's plan. Southern Democrats denounced Taylor's proposals as outrageously unfair to the South, as the Wilmot Proviso in disguise, they harrumphed. Relenting on their previous insistence that slavery be legalized in all of the Mexican Cession, they now insisted that the 1820 Missouri Compromise line barring slavery north of 36°30', be extended to the Pacific Coast, where it would have hit in the middle of what is now the Pebble Beach golf course. In short, southern Democrats refused to allow California's admission as a free state under the terms its constitution requested. Furthermore, whereas the Missouri Compromise line had left the status of slavery ambiguous south of it, southern Democrats now demanded that it be legalized in the Mexican Cession south of it. That is, they demanded a federal slave code legalizing slavery in lands south of that line. In all those areas, it must be stressed again, existing Mexican laws had absolutely prohibited slavery. Thus, one part of southern Democrats' legislative agenda in 1850 was to replace Mexican antislavery statute law with proslavery American statute law. Faced with the challenge from the upstart Free-Soil Party, neither northern Whigs nor northern Democrats could possibly acquiesce to this unconscionable demand, which, in the parlance of the day, vividly represented an aggression by the so-called Slave Power.

Nonetheless, southern Democrats' savage attacks on Taylor's plan were so cogent that southern Whigs in Congress, fully aware that their party had been creamed in the South's 1849 elections, dared not support it, for to do so would render them unreliable on the slavery extension issue. They looked to Congress itself to devise a more politically palatable alternative to Taylor's plan. The most famous of these alternatives was the scheme that Henry Clay presented to the Senate in a series of resolutions on January 29, 1850, eight days after Taylor's second message to Congress had arrived. Clay himself later boasted, and too many historians have mistakenly written, that his proposals on January 29 later became the Compromise of 1850. Nothing could be further from the truth. For one thing, Clay only outlined a series of resolutions about how the Senate should proceed on various matters involving slavery. He did not at that time offer bills for actual legislation. For another, while Clay on January 29 and in a much longer speech in early February dubbed his proposals as a sectional compromise in which he was asking northerners to make the greatest concessions, Clay's fellow southern senators instantly recognized that his resolutions advantaged the North at the South's expense. As soon as Clay sat down on January 29, nine southern senators—eight Democrats and the Georgia Whig John M. Berrien—sprang to their feet to denounce Clay's purported compromise as poison to the South as a whole and to slaveholders in particular.

Their outrage is understandable. Clay, echoing Taylor, also called on Congress to admit California as a free state with the boundaries it claimed in its constitution, boundaries, it must be stressed, that would eliminate any potential slave state port on the Pacific Ocean. For most southern Democrats, admitting California as a free state and thus upsetting the balance of free and slave states in the Senate was reason enough to reject Clay's plan. Nonetheless, what most incensed southerners in the Senate were Clay's proposals for redrawing the Texas–New Mexico boundary and for organizing territorial governments in the rest of the Mexican Cession. At the same time, however, those very provisions for territorial governments, no matter how unacceptable to southern Democrats, turned most northern Whigs and Zachary Taylor against Clay's initial proposals. And from the perspective of Clay and northern Whigs, the proposals for territorial governments only grew worse as the congressional session proceeded.

Clay's original proposal for redrawing the boundary between Texas and New Mexico was to extend it eastward along the thirty-second parallel from

El Paso in the west to the Sabine River, which divided Texas from Louisiana, in the east. Clay would make everything south of that line a new state of Texas. All the area north of it, an area that included Dallas, Fort Worth, and some twenty thousand slaves, would be given to New Mexico, from which, Clay insisted, slavery was prohibited by existing Mexican law.

Indeed, in calling for northerners to abandon their insistence on imposing the proviso on any territories organized in the remainder of the cession, Clay explicitly argued that it was unnecessary because both climate and the existing Mexican law would bar slavery from those territories. And his initial resolutions called on Congress to make no provision about slavery, that is, no provision replacing the existing Mexican antislavery statute, when they organized territorial governments. Once again, the case that southern Democrats made against these proposals was so cogent that southern Whigs dared not support Clay's original proposals. Initially, in fact, only Pennsylvania's Cooper and northern Democratic senators supported Clay, but, as we have seen, those northern Democrats insisted that popular sovereignty be incorporated into the territorial bills.

To make a very long story short, what happened essentially during the agonizingly long first session of the Thirty-First Congress was that Senate Democrats hijacked Clay's plan and turned it into a Democratic version of compromise. This gave Texas far more land than Clay had originally proposed and opened up the possibility of replacing Mexican law in the two territories Congress organized with popular sovereignty provisions. It was Democrats who forced Clay in May to bundle all the proposals for the Mexican Cession into a single "omnibus" bill. It was Democrats who amended the territorial bills reported by Douglas from his Senate Committee on Territories with a distinctively prosouthern clause. Douglas's bills already gave territorial legislatures authority over all "rightful subjects of legislation"—that is, slavery—but southern Democrats added a clause that said all states formed out of Utah and New Mexico *must* be admitted by future congresses with or without slavery as their constitutions prescribed at the time. Northern Democrats loved this intentional slap at Free-Soilers' pledge to bar the admission of any more slave states. And so did southern Whigs because it made support for the reformulated compromise package much safer politically, especially since most southern Democrats continued to oppose it for admitting California and reducing the size of Texas. In short, by the late spring, the procompromise coalition of southern Whigs and northern Democrats had taken shape.

Nonetheless, they lacked the votes in the Senate to pass the omnibus because the anticompromise coalition—composed of all northern Whigs except Cooper and Webster, Delaware's two Whig senators, the Senate's two Free-Soilers, and southern Democrats—held amazingly firm. The wings of this coalition opposed the compromise for diametrically different reasons. Northerners believed it gave the South far too much; southerners attacked it as a betrayal of Southern Rights. Led respectively by New York's Whig Seward and Mississippi Democratic senator Jefferson Davis, who in fact became close personal friends despite their opposite views on slavery, this coalition could stop passage of the compromise package as long as they held together.

But Whig support for it hinged in part on Zachary Taylor's firm opposition to the compromise, and on July 9, 1850, Taylor died. Taylor's death changed the entire political dynamic in Washington. Vice President Millard Fillmore, a longtime rival of Seward within the New York Whig Party, became president and within twenty-four hours asked for the resignations of Taylor's entire cabinet. Among other things this meant the exile of Delaware's Clayton and thus the end of his ability to pressure Delaware's two Whig senators to adhere to the anticompromise coalition. Since the beginning of Taylor's administration Fillmore, and especially his New York Whig allies, had nursed grievances about its allocation of most federal jobs in New York to Seward's friends. Because Seward headed the anticompromise coalition, therefore, it might seem inevitable that Fillmore would throw his support to the procompromise men. Unlike most other historians, however, I do not think Fillmore was committed to the compromise package when he was sworn into office, on July 10.

But he decided to do so within ten days of assuming the presidency, and I think two things changed his mind. First, as vice president he had sought the procompromise Democrat Dickinson's help in securing Senate rejection of the Sewardites Taylor had named to federal jobs, and even though he could replace those as-yet-unconfirmed men with his own conservative supporters as president, he continued to believe he needed Dickinson's help in securing their rejection. And support for the compromise package was clearly the price of Dickinson's help. Second, and far more important, within a few days of assuming the presidency, Fillmore found a letter that Texas governor Peter H. Bell had sent to Taylor in June. In this letter Bell fumed that U.S.

army officers posted in Santa Fe had rebuffed an attempt by Texas to establish a Texas county that included it. In response Bell pledged to call a special session of the Texas legislature in August, the sole purpose of which was to authorize an expedition of Texas militia to seize Santa Fe from U.S. authorities by armed force. What is more, southerners in Washington and elsewhere had learned of this letter even before Taylor died, and from Virginia to Louisiana came pledges to send their own militias to aid Texans in the assault.

The Nashville convention in June had fizzled, largely because of the promise that a compromise might pass, thereby scotching the threat of imminent secession. Instead, the prospect of a shooting civil war between the United States army and southerners over Santa Fe now loomed on the near horizon. Fillmore believed that only a boundary acceptable to Texas drawn by Congress could avert this showdown, and the best chance to get a new boundary was to get the omnibus bill passed into law. Thus Fillmore decided to throw his support to the procompromise men, an intention he signaled by naming Daniel Webster as his secretary of state. By late July, Fillmore and especially Webster, who now gained control of patronage decisions for New England, were pressuring northern Whigs to allow the omnibus to pass.

That pressure failed to stop the anticompromise coalition from breaking up the omnibus bill at the end of July, much to the dismay of compromisers. Yet on that very day the Utah Territory bill passed the Senate by a vote of 32–18, despite the opposition of the two Free-Soilers and every northern Whig still on the floor. The reason is clear: southern Democrats were perfectly willing to accept the organization of a territory on a popular sovereignty basis if they did not have to accept the reduction of Texas and California statehood as part of the bargain.

On August 6, Fillmore sent the Senate a message pleading for the passage of a Texas–New Mexico boundary that was acceptable to Texas in order to avert an armed showdown at Santa Fe. The Maryland Whig Pearce and Douglas devised a new boundary that both Texas senators endorsed. Despite protests from Seward that it still gave Texas far too much land, it passed the Senate 30–20 on August 9. Astonishingly, eight northern Whigs who had steadfastly opposed the omnibus failed to do so now. Six New England Whigs, indeed, were in the majority, while both New Jersey Whigs intentionally abstained to allow the bill's passage. Both Delaware Whigs, now that Clayton was no longer in the cabinet, also joined the majority. Passage of the Texas bill opened the way for Senate passage of the other compromise measures. When the New Mexico Territory bill passed 27–10 on August 15, twenty-three senators went unrecorded. Some like Seward and Clay had left Washington, but among the abstainers were five northern and one Delaware Whig who had opposed the compromise measures so long as Taylor was alive.

It is clear that the prospect of a violent military encounter at Santa Fe influenced those anticompromise Whigs who switched positions. But it is just as clear that they were moved by threats from the new administration and northern Democrats to replace or reject patronage nominees they wanted confirmed. It was hardly a coincidence that Fillmore waited to send the names of seventy-eight nominees for New England to the Senate until after all the compromise bills had been passed and signed into law. The fate of those men and many others depended on passage of the compromise.

Administration threats about patronage took an even greater toll on northern Whigs in the House. There the key vote was on passage of a combined Texas–New Mexico boundary bill that passed 107–99 on September 6. Twenty-six northern Whigs, who had sworn never to allow the organization of territorial governments without the proviso and who clearly had the votes to kill that measure, instead abstained to allow its passage. Similarly, seventeen northern Whig abstainers allowed the Utah Territory bill to pass 97–85. Thus did pressure from northern Democratic senators and Webster regarding the fate of as-yet-unconfirmed customs collectors, marshals, U.S. attorneys, and postmasters facilitate passage of the Compromise of 1850.

But intraparty factional divisions and expedient political calculations also shaped how a few men voted on the compromise measures. A very few southern Whigs, for example, never supported the package, quite unlike most southern Whigs. Without exception these men had been elected with the help of dissident Democrats or were seeking Democratic help in future elections. Hence they voted like most southern Democrats, just as James Cooper voted as Sturgeon did. More important were southern Democrats like Mississippi senator Henry Foote, Alabama senator Jeremiah Clemens, and Georgia's Howell Cobb, the Speaker of the House, who did all they could to facilitate passage of the compromise. Foote was the archrival of Mississippi's other Democratic senator, Jefferson Davis, who led the southern Democratic anticompromise bloc, and indeed in 1851 Foote as the Union candidate would defeat Davis as the Southern Rights candidate in Mississippi's gubernatorial election. Clemens had been put in the Senate by a coalition of dissident

Democrats and Whigs over the choice of the majority of Democrats in the Alabama legislature. Hence he voted as most southern Whigs did. Cobb, whose district in northwestern Georgia was populated primarily by nonslaveholders, had long been at odds with extreme proslavery elements in the Georgia Democratic Party known as the Chivalry.

Thus did factional rivalries, calculations of political advantage, and concerns over patronage shape this famous piece of public policy, the Compromise of 1850. Northern Democrats and southern Whigs happily posed as saviors of the Union and accused their Whig and Democratic rivals in their respective sections of endangering it by blocking the compromise. Northern Whigs and southern Democrats retorted that their partisan rivals were betraying sectional interests. These entrenched positions had produced a stalemate that only threats concerning the fate of patronage nominees and the possibility of a shooting war over Santa Fe had broken.

Paul Finkelman

# The Appeasement of 1850

THE COMPROMISE OF 1850 has always been seen as a classic moment of American political history. Historians wax eloquent about the brilliance of the debate, the selfless dedication to the Union of some of the participants, and particularly the heroic role of Henry Clay in coming out of retirement to craft a compromise in 1850, as he had done in 1820. The traditional works also acknowledge the other "heroic" men of the age who worked with Clay, especially Daniel Webster and John C. Calhoun. Thus the historian Robert Remini has argued in his recent book on the compromise that "once the great men of the antebellum era passed away—men such as Andrew Jackson, Henry Clay, Daniel Webster, and John C. Calhoun —the nation lacked individuals in positions of power who were passionately devoted to the Union." Remini argues that the crisis of 1850 was averted "because there were a number of men in Congress who were willing to compromise—and not simply on one issue, like slavery, but on many related issues that divided North and South, such as congressional control over the territories, the admission of California, the New Mexico boundary, and the Texas debt."[1]

This heroic analysis of the compromise is problematic. Remini argues that the Compromise of 1850 prevented the American Union from being "irreparably smashed" and says the compromise "is a prime example of how close this nation came to a catastrophic smash-up" and that his heroes in

---

[1] Robert Remini, *At the Edge of the Precipice: Henry Clay and the Compromise That Saved the Union* (New York, 2010), pp. xi–xii.

Congress "avoided that disaster—just in time."² But of course, the catastrophic smash-up in fact occurred anyway, with a cost of 625,000 or so lives and hundreds of thousands more wounded and damaged, and property costs in the billions of dollars. The Union was not "irreparably smashed" when the Civil War began, but the legacy of that conflict still haunts the nation as we mark the war's sesquicentennial. Remini implicitly concedes that the compromise was in the end a failure, and having praised Congress and its leaders, he then retreats to saying the real success of the compromise was that it "gave the North ten years to build its industrial strength and enable it to overpower the South when the war finally broke out." He asserts that it was in this decade that the North expanded its industrial capacity but that when the war began the South "did not have a railroad system by which to move men and material to the areas where they were most needed." He further claims that the compromise also gave the North "ten years to find a leader who could save the Union."³

These arguments are, in the end, not persuasive. Remini's list of men "passionately devoted to the Union" includes John C. Calhoun, who left Jackson's administration over nullification and in 1850 asserted that the Union was expendable. He opposed any compromise and had a long record of defending the constitutionality and the expediency of secession. A true Unionist believed that secession was *always* unconstitutional and unacceptable. In 1850 Southern senators like Clay, Thomas Hart Benton of Missouri, and Sam Houston of Texas believed secession could *never* be on the table. They were slave owners who despised abolitionists, but they did not believe in breaking up the Union. Similarly, northern senators like William Henry Seward of New York, Salmon P. Chase of Ohio, John P. Hale of New Hampshire, and Hannibal Hamlin of Maine were passionately opposed to slavery but were also passionately devoted to the Union. They opposed the compromise because it was overwhelmingly proslavery, but they did not return to the North and campaign for secession. But southern Senators who had been acolytes of John C. Calhoun, like Henry S. Foote of Mississippi, R. Barnwell Rhett of South Carolina, James M. Mason of Virginia, and David Levy Yulee of Florida, were still talking about secession after the compromise, even though they won almost everything they wanted in the compromise. Rather than

---
²Ibid., p. xi.
³Ibid., pp. xiii, 158.

stifle secessionist talk, the compromise emboldened southern nationalists to push for more concessions for slavery, while also stimulating them to push their disunion agenda.

The final compromise was, as I argue below, overwhelmingly proslavery. It was an appeasement of the most radical proslavery men, and gave virtually nothing to the North or to freedom. But in its wake no northern political leaders suggested secession. The only politicians considering secession after the compromise were southern followers of the late John C. Calhoun, who were decidedly not passionately devoted to the Union. In the North the only secessionist claims came from a small band of radical abolitionists who followed William Lloyd Garrison, and they did not even vote or participate in politics.[4]

By any measure, the Compromise of 1850 failed to achieve its major goal—to defuse sectional conflict over slavery. The compromise stimulated a decade of confrontations between northerners and the federal government over the fugitive slave law and even led to states' rights arguments by *northern* public officials in opposition to that law.[5] The compromise also failed to settle the issue of slavery in the territories. In 1854 Congress revisited the issue, passing the Kansas-Nebraska Act, which led to a mini–civil war in Kansas and the creation of the first nationally viable antislavery political organization, the Republican Party. The Supreme Court then weighed in on the issue in *Dred Scott v. Sandford* (1857). The presidential elections of 1856 and 1860 were mostly about the issues that the Compromise of 1850 supposedly settled.

Despite Remini's claim that there were many issues troubling Congress, there was, with one minor exception, just a single issue: slavery. Southerners objected to California's admission because it was entering the Union as a free state; northerners worried about the regulation of the territories because Henry Clay wanted to allow slavery in *all* of them. The New Mexico

---

[4]Elsewhere I have argued that the Garrisonian disunionist position was sensible because the U.S. Constitution was proslavery and precluded a democratic response to slavery. The Garrisonians, of course, could not anticipate that the end to slavery would come through a war started by the slaveholders themselves. See Paul Finkelman, "The Founders and Slavery: Little Ventured, Little Gained," *Yale Journal of Law and the Humanities* 13 (2001):413–49.

[5]The most famous example took place in Wisconsin, where the state supreme court declared the federal law unconstitutional. See *In re Booth and Rycraft*, 3 Wis. 157 (1854), which was overturned by the U.S. Supreme Court in *Ableman v. Booth*, 62 U.S. (51 How.) 506 (1859). For a history of this case, see H. Robert Baker, *The Rescue of Joshua Glover: A Fugitive Slave, the Constitution, and the Coming of the Civil War* (Athens, Ohio, 2006).

boundary was an issue because northerners hoped the territory would eventually enter the Union as a free state, and thus giving substantial parts of it to Texas would only increase the land controlled by the slave power. Only the Texas debt—the easiest and least controversial aspect of the compromise—was not directly connected to slavery. Remini's summary of the issues in his heroic analysis of the compromise oddly ignores the single most divisive aspect of the compromise—the Fugitive Slave Law of 1850. Nor does his short list note that by settling the territorial issue as it did, Congress actually eviscerated the Compromise of 1820, which Clay had brilliantly crafted three decades earlier.

The argument of Remini and other scholars that the compromise bought time for the North to become stronger is also problematic. First, it is important to understand that the compromise was not designed to buy time to prepare for a future war. It was designed to avoid secession and war, and in that sense it failed. But even if we accept the argument that an unintended consequence of the compromise was to buy time, it is not clear whether that favored the North. Economic data suggests just the opposite: that the rate of industrial growth in the South actually exceeded that in the North during this period.

The North was clearly more industrialized than the South both in 1850 and in 1860, but by 1860 the South was catching up.[6] Southern railroads "underwent remarkable transformations in the 1850s." In that decade "southerners began committing more money to railroads and an explosion of mileage resulted." For example, between 1850 and 1860 railroad mileage doubled in Pennsylvania and New Jersey and nearly doubled in New York. There were even greater expansions in the Midwest. On the other hand, in New Hampshire railroad mileage grew by only 50 percent, and in Massachusetts it grew by just 20 percent. Many southern states more than matched these growth rates. In Georgia mileage more than doubled; it more than tripled in Alabama, South Carolina, Virginia, and North Carolina; and in Louisiana it more than quadrupled. But these rates were dwarfed in other slave states. While Ohio's railroad mileage grew by about 500 percent, neighbor Kentucky's mileage grew by over 700 percent. Indiana's tracks increased by about 900 percent, but Mississippi topped that with nearly a 1,200 percent growth and Florida topped them both with a 1,900 percent growth. Illinois's mileage

---

[6] Fred Bateman, James D. Foust, Thomas J. Weiss, "Large-Scale Manufacturing in the South and West, 1850–1860," *Business History Review* 45 (1971):1–17.

grew by about 2,500 percent. Wisconsin topped the North with a 4,525 percent growth, but Tennessee easily beat both with a 13,922 percent growth rate. Three slave states (Arkansas, Missouri, and Texas) had no railroads in 1850 but more than 1,150 miles in 1860, while only two northern states (California and Iowa) had no miles in 1850, but they still had only 688 miles in 1860.[7] These figures demonstrate that Remini's arguments about the compromise buying time for the North to increase its railroad capacity are simply wrong. If anything, the compromise gave the South more time to build up its railroads, which it used effectively in the war.

The percentage growth of southern railroads in the 1850s should not be misunderstood. Because of the low starting base, the percentage growth is exaggerated. Tennessee, for example, had only 9 miles of railroads in 1850, so its percentage increase is huge (about 14,000 percent). But its absolute mileage growth of 1,244 miles in the decade was greater than all but four northern states. So too was Virginia's expansion from 481 miles to 1,731 miles. The point here is not that the South was suddenly the industrial equal of the North, but rather that the South's "extraordinary expansion during the 1850s"[8] severely undercuts the notion that the industrial growth between the compromise and the Civil War favored the North.

Railroad receipts underscore the closing gap between the sections. They illustrate not only the growth of railroads but also the growth of commerce and other industrial development in the South. In New England receipts doubled from 1849 to 1859, and in the Middle Atlantic they tripled. But in the South they quadrupled, and in the Southwest they were eighteen times larger in 1859 than in 1849.[9] As with the growth in tracks, the percentage growth in revenue is skewed by low starting bases. But the absolute growth is significant. The Central Railroad of Georgia earned over $269,000 in 1850 from its upfreight operations (freight carried into or across the state). In 1860 this figure was over $637,000. Downfreight usually accounted for even more earnings. Upfreight revenue on the Charlotte and South Carolina Railroad went from over $11,000 in 1851 to over $156,000 in 1858. Other southern railroads recorded similar growth.[10]

---

[7] Aaron W. Marks, *Railroads in the Old South: Pursuing Progress in a Slave Society* (Baltimore, 2009), p. 5.
[8] Ibid., pp. 5–6.
[9] Ibid., p. 4.
[10] Ibid., pp. 117, 123. For other railroads, see pp. 115–25.

Railroad mileage and railroad receipts are crude measures, but they illustrate the growing industrialization of the South in the 1850s. The more dramatic southern growth underscores the general low level of industrialization in the South before 1850. But this dramatic growth shows that Remini is simply wrong in stating that the compromise allowed the North to gain an industrial advantage by 1860. On the contrary, in the 1850s the South was catching up with the North, and thus relative to where it was in 1850, the South may have been better off in 1860.

Remini's argument about leadership is of course utterly impossible to prove or disprove. We can never know if a leader might have emerged in the early 1850s to oppose southern secession, if it had occurred then. We might imagine a young Stephen A. Douglas leading the North in 1852 in fighting to preserve the Union. The staunchly Unionist Sam Houston, a nationally known heroic figure, might also have been the leader of the moment. Like Andrew Jackson in the 1830s, he would have been a southern slaveholder and a military leader standing up to southern hotheads. Missouri's Thomas Hart Benton had similar stature as a staunch slaveholding southern Unionist, although without the military experience of Houston or Jackson.

It is equally important to understand that there is also no way to know if any southern states would have in fact seceded in 1850 if a substantially different set of laws had been passed. There were some secessionist sentiments bandied about in 1850, but two secessionist conventions that year were comical failures. One took place and then collapsed before the compromise was passed; the other met and failed after the compromise had passed. The compromise surely undermined the second secessionist convention, but we cannot know if a more reasonable and less one-sided compromise would not have worked just as well. Moreover, as David Potter points out in his Pulitzer Prize–winning study of the decade, "widespread prosperity" and high cotton prices also undermined the secessionists. Potter notes, "There was too much contentment for a secession movement to take root."[11]

Indeed, we might easily turn Remini's argument on its head. The Compromise of 1850 bought time for the secessionists to gather support, encourage southern industrial growth, and find leadership. The death of Calhoun left the secessionists and extreme southern nationalists groping for a leader.

---

[11] David M. Potter, *The Impending Crisis, 1848–1861*, completed and ed. Don E. Fehrenbacher (New York, 1976), p. 126; see also Michael Holt, *The Rise and Fall of the American Whig Party: Jacksonian Politics and the Onset of the Civil War* (New York, 1999), p. 608.

Not till well after the compromise did Jefferson Davis emerge as a logical successor to Calhoun. Meanwhile, it took a decade under the utterly proslavery compromise for southern nationalists to gain strength and foster hostility to the Union. They could do this because the compromise was so one-sided that it emboldened southern nationalists to make new demands for more concessions to slavery, while the outrageous fugitive slave law led to open northern hostility, which in turn played into the hands of the southern nationalists.

It was during this decade that southerners also seriously began to create their own institutions, ones that would support a southern nation. Georgia's chief justice Joseph Henry Lumpkin teamed up with his son-in-law, Thomas R. R. Cobb, to create the Lumpkin Law School, to teach southern men how to practice a "southern" version of law. At the end of the decade Cobb published his treatise on the law of slavery—the first ever written by a southerner.[12] Southern defenses of slavery proliferated on the heels of the compromise, while in the 1850s southern leaders pushed for an expansion of education throughout the South, reflecting James DeBow's assertions that southerners should "cherish and *give preference to our own institutions of learning and native instructors.*" DeBow argued that "life, habits, thoughts, and aims are so essentially different" in the South "that here a different character of books, tuition, and training is absolutely required, to bring up the boy to manhood with his faculties fully developed." These of course would be "faculties" that reflected southern values and ideology. As an 1856 convention in Savannah noted, sending southern children north for an education was "fraught with peril to our sacred interests."[13]

After the compromise was passed, "military education" in the South "took on a more serious aspect," as traditional schools, like LaGrange College, were turned into military schools and Virginia put more resources into Virginia Military Institute.[14] During the 1850s private military companies proliferated in the South, with state governors urging greater attention to military training. By the mid-1850s "anxieties of some citizens of the upper South regarding

---

[12] Thomas R. R. Cobb, *An Inquiry into the Law of Negro Slavery in the United States of America* (Philadelphia and Savannah, 1858). See Paul Finkelman, "Thomas R. R. Cobb and the Law of Negro Slavery," *Roger Williams Law Review* 5 (1999):75–115.

[13] John Hope Franklin, *The Militant South* (Cambridge, 1956), pp. 136–37; emphasis in original.

[14] Arthur C. Cole, *The Irrepressible Conflict: 1850–1865* (New York, 1934), p. 289.

their militia bordered on hysteria." But the Deep South was equally concerned. For example, in 1858 Alabama incorporated seven new militia companies, while others formed without the benefit of any statutory authority. The growth of militia companies all over the South followed the compromise.[15] Thus, just as the South used the compromise to buy time to build up its railroad infrastructure, the South also expanded in intellectual infrastructure and military preparedness.

Fresh from their victory in claiming the entire Mexican Cession for slavery, except California, the southern nationalists hungered for more. This led to the Kansas-Nebraska Act, in 1854, and then the *Dred Scott* decision, in 1857. These events finally led to the creation and success of the Republican Party, the first political force in the nation's history able and willing to stand up to the endless demands of the slaveocracy. The fear of Republicans galvanized secessionists, as southern demagogues used northern politics to claim that the Republicans were about to make war on the South. Meanwhile, the Fugitive Slave Law of 1850 outraged the North because it was so antithetical to American values of justice, fairness, and due process. Northern opposition to the law infuriated southerners and played directly into the hands of the southern hotheads. Each southern victory encouraged secessionists to demand more, fostering northern opposition. After 1850 every act of northern resistance to the compromise measures and the subsequent proslavery laws and decisions also played into the hands of the secessionists, giving them rhetorical ammunition for their cause. Absent the Compromise of 1850, none of this might have happened.

## The Crisis

The crisis that faced the nation in 1850 had a number of components but was not terribly complicated. During the Mexican War northern members of Congress tried to ban slavery from any territory acquired from the conflict. The first attempt to do this was an amendment to an appropriations bill known as the Wilmot Proviso, after Pennsylvania Congressman David Wilmot. The proviso passed the House but failed in the Senate, where the South had a majority until late 1848 and afterward could always find a few

---

[15] Franklin, *Militant South*, pp. 188–89.

northern Democrats to vote against the proviso. After the war the United States acquired a huge land mass, comprising all of present-day California, Utah, and Nevada, most of Arizona and New Mexico, and parts of Colorado, Wyoming, and Texas. In addition—and this is ignored by most historians of the war—the peace treaty also settled the border of Texas by ceding huge amounts of what is now West Texas and South Texas to the United States. At the time of Texas independence (1836) the southern and western boundary of the Mexican state of Tejas was the Nueces River. Thus the war also settled the ownership of portions of what is today western Texas and eastern New Mexico.[16] Immediately after the war the entire nation recognized that the land south of the Nueces River to the Rio Grande—what is today South Texas—belonged to Texas. But the land west of the Nueces—some fifty thousand square miles—was clearly not part of Texas. As the leading history of Texas notes, "the Nueces was traditionally viewed as the western boundary of Texas."[17] When Texas entered the Union, neither Texas nor the United States had actually defined the western boundary of the state, and the resolution of annexation merely said that "all questions of boundary that may arise with other governments" would be "subject to the adjustment by this government."[18] This covered the contingency of diplomacy with Mexico to settle where the western boundary of the United States ended and Mexico began. But this provision did not anticipate the acquisition of *all* the territory from the Nueces River to the Pacific Ocean.

Thus, with the exception of the Rio Grande valley, in South Texas, the question for Congress—and the nation—was how to organize these territories. About half the land was north of the Missouri Compromise line (36°30'N). One option was to simply extend the line across the rest of the nation, opening up present-day New Mexico, Arizona, and southern California to slavery and leaving northern California, Utah, Nevada, and Colorado free. Northerners rejected this because they did not want any new slave

---

[16] Most maps of the Mexican Cession exclude eastern New Mexico and West and South Texas, but all this land was also ceded to the United States as a result of the treaty. One might argue that Texas was also ceded, since Mexico had never recognized Texas independence, but that argument would not make much sense since all of Texas north and east of the Nueces River was in fact incorporated into the United States in 1845. The United States did not, however, have any political control or even military control over the territory west and south of the Nueces until the war.

[17] Rupert N. Richardson, Adrian Anderson, Cary D. Wintz, and Ernest Wallace, *Texas: The Lone Star State*, 10th ed. (New York, 2009), p. 128.

[18] Ibid., p. 129.

states; southerners opposed this solution because they wanted to spread slavery to all the new federal territories. While this issue festered, the California gold rush brought about one hundred thousand settlers there, making California eligible for immediate statehood. With fewer than a thousand blacks in California—most of whom were not slaves—the settlers there demanded admission to the Union as a free state. Further complicating the organization of the new territories were the increasing demands from Texas that most of New Mexico be ceded to that state. There was no historical or legal basis for this, nor had Texans actually settled the area, which was mostly scrubland and desert.

The territorial issue virtually paralyzed Congress in the last three years of the 1840s. As settlers poured into California, Congress was incapable of passing legislation to provide a working government for the territory. Iowa (1846) and Wisconsin (1848) entered the Union, but Congress could not pass laws to organize the new territories, even though by 1849 both California and New Mexico had enough settlers to justify statehood. Meanwhile, as the territorial question festered, other issues, mostly connected to slavery, further bedeviled Congress.

Beyond the territorial question were three other issues, one of which would become a central focus of political debate in the 1850s. The easiest of the three involved the debt of Texas. From 1836 to 1845 Texas had been an independent republic. When it entered the Union, in 1845, Texas was deeply in debt. Texans argued, with some justice, that the national government should bail out the state. One piece of the Compromise of 1850 would settle this matter in favor of Texas. Less easy to settle were two issues related to slavery. Northerners wanted to end slavery in the District of Columbia. More realistically, they wanted to end the public sale of slaves in the District of Columbia.[19] This would not harm slavery or the system of slavery but merely end the embarrassment of having slaves marched through the national capital in chains or publicly auctioned off in the shadow of the White House and Congress. Northerners were deeply offended by this (as were some diplomats), but everyone understood that the ban was merely symbolic, since slave owners in the district could easily take their slaves to Virginia for sale, or sell them privately. Southerners almost universally opposed ending

---

[19] For a discussion of these issues see Paul Finkelman and Donald R. Kennon, eds., *In the Shadow of Freedom: The Politics of Slavery in the National Capital* (Athens, Ohio, 2011).

the trade, not because it would affect the system of slavery—because it clearly would not—but as a matter of proslavery principles. Ending the D.C. slave trade would be an admission that buying and selling slaves was morally wrong —which southerners would not admit, and most did not believe.

While northerners wanted to end the slave trade in the district, southerners had a more practical demand, although one that was deeply symbolic as well. They wanted a new fugitive slave law that would require the federal government to become involved in the process of capturing runaway slaves and returning them to the South. The practical value of this was obvious, since there were perhaps ten thousand or more fugitive slaves in the North (and more escaping every year) worth millions of dollars. Southerners wanted this property returned to them. Since northern states refused to cooperate in hunting runaway slaves, southerners wanted the national government to do the job. In the face of growing northern noncooperation on the return of fugitive slaves, southerners also wanted an emphatic reaffirmation by Congress of their right to recover their runaways and that the federal government supported that right.

With these issues festering, General Zachary Taylor, who had spent almost his entire adult life in the military, was elected president. In March 1849 he took office. The following December the new Congress met, hoping to finally settle the issues of the moment. One of the newest members of Congress, and thus one with no seniority, was in fact the most senior politician in the nation, Senator Henry Clay of Kentucky. Clay was first elected to the Senate in 1806, when he was a few months shy of the constitutionally required age of thirty to sit in that body. Since then Clay had been in the House or Senate for most of his life. He was in the Senate in 1806–7, 1810–11, and continuously from 1831 to 1842. He also served in the House of Representatives from 1811 to 1821 and 1823 to 1825. Six times he was elected Speaker of the House of Representatives. It was from that post in 1819–20 that he guided the Missouri Compromise through Congress. This was his greatest accomplishment. The Missouri Compromise had allowed for sectional peace over slavery in the territories for three decades. Had there been no war with Mexico the compromise might have continued to hold up, and the whole conflict over slavery in the territories could have been avoided. After his successful negotiation of the Missouri Compromise, Clay ran for president in 1824 but lost. He then served as secretary of state under John Quincy Adams. He ran unsuccessfully for president in 1832 and again in

1844. In 1848 he expected to run one more time but lost the Whig nomination to the hero of the Mexican War, Zachary Taylor, who then won the election. With this career of fame, success, and ultimate disappointment, Clay returned to the Senate in 1849.

## Clay's Return to the Senate

The seventy-two-year-old junior senator from Kentucky returned to the Senate after an absence of seven years. Clay was still deeply bitter about losing the presidency. In 1844 he had come so close. He lost New York by about five thousand votes. Had Clay carried New York, he would have been president. Clay and other Whigs (including the new vice president, Millard Fillmore, who lost the New York governorship that year) blamed the loss on the abolitionists, fifteen thousand of whom voted for the Liberty Party. It was of course unrealistic and even foolish to believe that committed opponents of bondage would have voted for Clay. Moderate opponents of slavery may have seen him as the lesser of two evils when compared to Polk, but for abolitionists there was no meaningful difference between the slaveholding Clay, who waffled on Texas annexation, and the slaveholding Polk, who more directly supported Texas annexation. In 1848 Clay felt he deserved the Whig nomination, after his years of service to the party and his incredibly narrow loss in the previous election. The year seemed to belong to the Whigs, and Clay wanted to lead the party to victory and finally get to live in the White House. Instead, the party shunted him aside for a general who had never held elective office and had never even voted in an election. Taylor's victory only increased Clay's disappointment, since in his mind it should have been *his* victory.

In 1849 Clay claimed to be uninterested in going back to the Senate, but he also agreed to serve if elected by the Kentucky legislature.[20] This was a common pose of nineteenth-century politicians, coyly denying interest in the offices they hungered for. In this pose Clay was ready to make the great "sacrifice" of serving the people, if they chose him for office. Given the politics of Kentucky at the time, Clay's response effectively guaranteed his election. If Clay had really not wanted to serve again, he certainly was a skillful enough politician to avoid getting elected to a position he did not want.

---

[20] Remini, *Edge of the Precipice*, pp. 37–38.

Clay also claimed he would only return to the Senate "if I could be persuaded that I could materially contribute to the proper adjustment of the momentous question which has grown out of the acquisition of New Mexico and California."[21] In other words, he was ready to ride back to Washington on a white horse to save America, as he had done in 1820. Although bruised by three presidential losses and a final failure even to be nominated, Clay's ego was still strong. He was ready to be America's savior. He was also ready to save the Whig Party from the impending catastrophe, as he saw it, of the Taylor presidency. Taylor was no politician and while a lifelong Whig (and a lifelong supporter and admirer of Clay), Taylor talked about being a president above party. Clay was *never* above party, and wanted to redeem the Whig Party and the nation by returning to the Senate. While he was old, and not in great health, he doubtless still dreamed of one more run for the White House. Thus, he happily accepted his election to the Senate, even as he modestly claimed he was uninterested in the job.

Once in the Senate, Clay decided that he, and not President Taylor, should be the leader of the Whig Party. To accomplish this, he would propose a new compromise, replaying his heroic role of 1820. Clay would create the compromise, guide it through Congress, and save the nation. It would make him a hero once again, and maybe, finally, president. To do this he had to oppose a president of his own party.

Taylor did not want a dramatic sweeping bill to solve all the problems of the nation with the stroke of a pen. The methodical, careful general wanted to fight one political battle at a time. He insisted that California, with nearly one hundred thousand residents, enter the Union immediately. Then he would turn to the other issues. He was the only leader in Washington who had actually been to New Mexico. He did not believe slavery could be profitable there, and thus he was not willing to expend a great deal of energy, or political capital, on the issue. Indeed, he wanted to bring New Mexico into the Union as a free state after California was admitted. There were no slaves in New Mexico because under Mexican law slavery had been illegal. The residents of New Mexico did not want slavery but were demanding statehood. New Mexico's population was greater than the free population of Florida, the most recent slave state to enter the Union. Thus, Taylor hoped to bring

---

[21]Ibid., p. 38.

New Mexico in right after California. This would settle the Texas boundary issue and also avoid a debate over the Wilmot Proviso. With California and New Mexico admitted, it would be easier to organize the rest of the Mexican Cession without any reference to slavery, because Taylor believed there would be no support for slavery in the Utah Territory. Then he could turn to the Texas debt, fugitive slaves, and if necessary the slave trade in the District of Columbia. His nondramatic, piecemeal approach might have worked. But that left no role for Clay—no chance for the Kentucky senator to become the hero of the nation and maybe, finally, the president. Thus, Clay plotted his own solution.

## Clay's Compromise

On what was literally a dark and stormy night in late January 1850, Henry Clay surreptitiously visited Daniel Webster to discuss the compromise. In 1830 Webster had famously debated Senator Robert Hayne of South Carolina, powerfully asserting that no state could nullify or defy federal law. His closing statement—"Liberty and Union, Now and Forever, One and Inseparable"—made him a patriotic icon and a hero in the North for his willingness to tie Liberty to Union. The two giants of the Whig Party secretly agreed to cooperate to push through a compromise that they believed would save the Union. The plan was designed to outflank southern nationalists, like John C. Calhoun, who were trying to create a "southern" party that would force slave-state Whigs to align with them, and force a fundamental restructuring of American politics. The plan would also outflank and marginalize President Taylor, forcing the Whig president to accept the leadership of Clay and Webster, rather than having them follow Taylor's lead.

On January 29, 1850, Clay presented his eight resolutions to the Senate.[22] His goal was to have a single bill that would attract votes from both sections. He did not present the details of the laws, but only sketched out their direction. In his Pulitzer Prize–winning book on the coming of the war, David Potter argues that "Clay's proposals gave most of the material concessions to the North." Potter argues that California would enter the Union as a free

---

[22] *Congressional Globe*, 31st Cong., 1st sess., 1850, pp. 244–52.

state but the South gained nothing from the rest of the Mexican Cession because it "was supposedly unsuited to slavery."[23] This traditional analysis is simply wrong. Clay's compromise and the final legislation passed that fall were overwhelmingly favorable to the South, while giving the North almost nothing of value.

At the outset it is important to understand that the land acquired from Mexico was in fact quite suitable for slavery. In 1850 southern slaves were used in mining and metal industries,[24] and could easily have been adapted to mining in what later became the states of Colorado, Nevada, Utah, Arizona, and New Mexico.[25] This was consistent with traditional uses of slave labor in antiquity and in Spanish America. In the colonial period slaves were used as herdsmen and could have been used in the same way in the Southwest. Ultimately, of course, irrigation would open the southwest to mass crop production (including cotton). Southerners fought to open the Mexican Cession to slavery because, contrary to Potter's assertion, they emphatically did not believe that the area was "unsuited to slavery." They knew there were no "natural limits" to slavery, only limits on the production of particular agricultural produce. With this understanding, a careful examination of Clay's proposals is in order.

Five of Clay's eight provisions directly benefited the South. He offered the South a new fugitive slave law. This would be the most divisive aspect of the compromise, and one that made the entire series of laws seem to be a complete capitulation to the demands of slavery. The proposals also called for the organization of all of the new territories "without the adoption of any restriction or condition on the subject of slavery," federal assumption of the debt that the Republic of Texas had when it entered the Union, an ironclad proclamation that Congress could never end slavery in the District of Columbia without the support of the people of the district and the state of Maryland, and finally another resolution affirming that Congress would never interfere with the interstate slave trade. Two resolutions favored the North, or at least Clay claimed they did. His plan would immediately admit

---

[23]Potter, *Impending Crisis*, pp. 100–101.
[24]Ronald L. Lewis, *Coal, Iron, and Slaves: Industrial Slavery in Maryland and Virginia, 1715–1865* (Westport, Conn., 1979); Robert S. Starobin, *Industrial Slavery in the Old South* (New York, 1970); Charles B. Dew, *Bond of Iron: Master and Slave at Buffalo Forge* (New York, 1994).
[25]The use of Chinese "coolie" labor to build western railroads is yet another example of how slavery could have easily been profitable in the Rocky Mountain West.

California as a free state and prohibit the public sale of slaves in the District of Columbia. The eighth resolution would settle the Texas boundary dispute somewhat, but not wholly, in favor of New Mexico. Clay believed this was also a resolution that favored the North. But in fact it was of no value to the North, or freedom, when coupled with the provision that organized the new territories without any restriction on slavery. Under the Clay proposals, the boundary settlement merely shifted land from one slave state (Texas) to a slave territory (New Mexico).

The great gain for the North was the admission of California as a free state. However, with nearly one hundred thousand people in the territory, almost no slaves, and a population expanding at a record pace, it was impossible to imagine any other outcome. Southerners eyed California, where slaves could be used in mines and in the region's fertile valleys. In its first decade of statehood there would be a number of attempts to bring some form of slavery into California.[26] But, in 1850 only about 1 percent of the population was black and many of those blacks were free. Whatever southerners might have wanted, California clearly would not be a slave state. Thus, the compromise "gave" to the North what it already had: the free state of California.

Historians traditionally see California statehood as a huge victory for the North because it gave the free states a permanent majority in the Senate. But this is the wisdom of hindsight. With most of present-day Arizona, New Mexico, Utah, and Nevada, as well as portions of Colorado, Oklahoma, and Wyoming open to slavery, there was still room for many new slave states. (The Kansas-Nebraska Act of 1854 would of course create even more territory that could turn into slave states.)

The fallacy of California statehood and a permanent free-state majority in the Senate is also based on a misunderstanding of the process of creating new states as it had been practiced since 1791. At a number of times before 1850 both the North and the South had had a majority in the Senate. Most historians write about the "pairing" of free and slave territories in admitting new states. This in fact rarely happened. After the ratification of the Constitution by the first thirteen states there were five "free" states where slavery was either already abolished (Massachusetts and New Hampshire) or in the

---

[26]For a discussion of attempts to bring slaves into California, see Paul Finkelman, "The Law of Slavery and Freedom in California," *California Western Law Review* 17 (1981):437–64.

process of gradual abolition (Pennsylvania, Rhode Island, and Connecticut), two northern slave states (New York and New Jersey) and six southern slave states (Delaware, Maryland, Virginia, North Carolina, South Carolina, and Georgia).

This created a Union of seven northern states and six southern states. But it also created a Union of five free states and eight slave states. In 1791 Vermont entered the Union as a free state, but by 1796 Kentucky and Tennessee had come into the Union, creating eight northern and eight southern states, but ten slave states and six free states. In 1799 New York passed a gradual abolition statute, which meant that now there were seven free states and nine slave states. Ohio statehood, in 1803, gave the north a majority of the states—nine to eight—but there was still a majority of slave states until 1804, when New Jersey finally joined the rest of the North with its own gradual emancipation statute. This was the last state to end slavery before the Civil War. From 1804 until 1812 (when Louisiana entered the Union) there was a free-state majority. After that slave and free states entered the Union at different times with apparent pairing, but in each instance there was a short period when the free states had a majority: Indiana (1816) and Mississippi (1817); Illinois (1818) and Alabama (1819); Maine (1820) and Missouri (1821). In 1836 Arkansas entered, giving the South a majority, but then parity was regained with Michigan statehood, in 1837.

In the 1840s this apparent pairing stopped. Florida and Texas both entered in 1845, giving the South a two-state majority, which fell to one state in December 1846 with the admission of Iowa. Parity was not regained until May 1848 when Wisconsin entered the Union. Thus, when the Mexican War began the South had a two-state majority and during the crucial debates over the Wilmot Proviso the South had a one-state majority. It is also important to understand that until 1850 no territory where slavery had been allowed had ever entered the Union as a free state. The lesson of the previous sixty-three years—since the adoption of the Northwest Ordinance, in 1787—was that once slavery was planted in a territory, only slave states would grow there.

Thus, when California entered the Union, in 1850, there was no reason to believe that this would create a permanent free-state majority. This was especially true since Clay's resolutions allowed slavery in New Mexico and Utah, with nearly four hundred thousand square miles between them, to be divided into slave states.

Clay also proposed to ban "the slave trade, in slaves brought into" Washington, D.C., "from states or places beyond the District, either to be sold as merchandise or to be transported to other markets without the District of Columbia." This law only removed a visible irritant that tended to fan antislavery sentiment, but it would have absolutely no effect on slavery itself. Masters could still buy and sell slaves privately "by one neighbor to another,"[27] and they could still ship them out of the district for sale further south. Alexandria, Virginia, which was just across the Potomac from Washington, had a slave market that remained open to residents of the district. Thus, this piece of the compromise did not harm slavery or undermine its viability in the district. Indeed, a shrewd defender of slavery might have concluded that the proposal would actually reduce the growth of antislavery sentiment by removing an aggravating practice that was always in the face of antislavery members of Congress without actually harming slavery in the nation's capital or anywhere else. This analysis was especially powerful when coupled with Clay's resolution that Congress would *never* end slavery in the district without the consent of the residents there and in Maryland.

Clay believed that his proposal for the settlement of the New Mexico boundary was also a boon to the North because it defeated the most aggressive aspects of Texas's seemingly insatiable appetite for land. But in fact his proposal (and the final settlement passed by Congress) was also of dubious benefit to the North. The proposal offered Texas less land than it wanted, which would prevent the further growth of slavery in Texas sometime in the future. But the land that did not go to Texas would simply remain part of the New Mexico Territory, where, under Clay's proposal, slavery would be allowed. If the Wilmot Proviso had been adopted, then slavery would have been banned in the new territories, which would have made the debate over the New Mexico boundary more important. Under the Wilmot Proviso every acre not given to Texas would remain free soil.

However, for opponents of slavery Clay's proposal on the Texas–New Mexico boundary was simply a sleight of hand because it did not include any ban on slavery in the new territories. He offered to only add a little land to Texas, which would presumably please the North. But, Clay then opened all of New Mexico to slavery. Implicitly, this meant that slavery would be allowed in the new territories, and southerners surely expected these places

[27]Clay, quoted in William W. Freehling, *The Road to Disunion: Secessionists at Bay, 1776–1854* (New York, 1990), p. 495.

would become slave states. This of course contrasts dramatically with President Taylor's goal of immediately admitting New Mexico as a free state.

Had the Civil War and the actual compromise not intervened, Clay's proposed settlement of the Texas–New Mexico land issue might actually have helped slavery. Texas wanted about half of present-day New Mexico. If this had occurred then the remaining territory would probably have come into the Union as one single slave state. But, by guaranteeing that the New Mexico Territory would be very large—consisting of most of present-day Arizona and New Mexico and possibly some of present-day West Texas—Clay's proposed settlement of the border dispute actually benefited the South. With about two hundred thousand square miles, this territory was nearly four times the size of the most recent state (Wisconsin) to enter the Union and thus might have provided three or more slave states. The remaining compromise measures wholly benefited the South.

In *The Impending Crisis*, David Potter argues that the territorial settlement "contributed nothing to the strength of the 'slave power'" because the land was "already covered by the Missouri compromise."[28] This analysis is simply wrong, both as a matter of history, and, more significantly, as a matter of geography. Clay's compromise did more than just take the Wilmot Proviso off the table, which in itself was a major victory for the South. It also substantially undercut the Missouri Compromise. Much of the Mexican Cession—the present-day states of Nevada and Utah, as well as most of Colorado and a bit of Wyoming—lay north of the Missouri Compromise line. Thus, contrary to Potter's incorrect assertions, Clay's compromise actually rejected the Missouri Compromise line by opening over 180,000 square miles of new territory to slavery that was north of the line. This vast space, which became the Utah Territory, was more than four times the size of both North Carolina and Tennessee and six times the size of South Carolina—in other words, large enough to accommodate many new slave states, reaching well north of the Missouri Compromise line. If Clay had been truly interested in a compromise, he would have followed the 1820 line, thus giving some of the new territory to the North and some to the South. Instead, with the exception of California—which was out of his control—he gave all the new territories to the South. And, as already noted, by opening all the new territories to slavery, and thus refusing to apply the Missouri Com-

---

[28] Potter, *Impending Crisis*, p. 100.

promise line to the new territory, Clay completely undermined any value to the free states by settling the Texas–New Mexico boundary in favor of New Mexico.

Just as they have misread the territorial settlement, many historians have misunderstood the importance of Clay's two resolutions on slavery in the District of Columbia and on the interstate slave trade. Potter writes that these were not "tangible advantages" to the South.[29] In fact, their passage would have been major victories for supporters of slavery, especially when seen in light of all of Clay's resolutions. Except for a few outlier abolitionists, most opponents of slavery agreed that Congress had no power to regulate slavery in the states where it existed. Political opponents of slavery, from moderates like Abraham Lincoln to radicals like Salmon P. Chase, agreed that there were essentially five areas where Congress could regulate slavery. The first was the African slave trade, which had been banned in 1808 and was not an issue in 1850.[30] Second was in the territories, where Congress had the power to ban slavery. Of course, Clay's compromise measures would preempt that by opening *all* the remaining new territories to slavery. Third was the regulation of the District of Columbia, where Congress had specific and plenary power under the Constitution to "exercise exclusive Legislation in all Cases."[31] It was under this power that Congress would ban the public sale of slaves in the district, which was one of Clay's resolutions. But, under Clay's other resolution on the district, Congress would have voluntarily ceded its powers over the district to the people who lived there *and* to the state of Maryland. Never before (or since) had Congress promised not to exercise one of its constitutionally enumerated powers without first getting the approval of a single state. The fourth area of congressional regulation concerned the interstate slave trade. The Constitution gave Congress complete power to regulate commerce "among the several States,"[32] which of course included the interstate slave trade. Under Clay's resolution, Congress

---

[29] Ibid., p. 100.
[30] Opponents of slavery complained that Congress never adequately funded the U.S. naval ships operating off the coast of West Africa known as the Africa Squadron, which was charged with suppressing the illegal trade. Meanwhile, in the aftermath of the Compromise of 1850, southern nationalists began to argue for a reopening of the African trade.
[31] "Congress shall have Power . . . To exercise exclusive Legislation in all Cases whatsoever, over such District . . . as may, by Cession of particular States, and the Acceptance of Congress, become the Seat of the government of the United States." U.S. Constitution, art. I, sec. 8.
[32] Ibid.

would promise never to exercise the power that it had. This was an unprecedented abdication of congressional power. Congress always has the option to refuse to exercise a constitutional power. In fact, the failure to regulate the domestic slave trade was an example of this. But, it was one thing for Congress to choose not to exercise a power because Congress felt legislation was unwise or unnecessary. It was quite another to do what Clay wanted, which was for Congress to promise *never* to exercise its power.

Clay's proposals were also a direct assault on political antislavery and antislavery constitutionalism. Clay's compromise was essentially an invitation to political opponents of slavery to give up and disband. If Clay's resolution on the slave trade and slavery in the District of Columbia had been adopted, the legislature would have been on record as saying that any political opposition to slavery was illegitimate. Moreover, the resolutions would have signaled to the nation that the Garrisonian abolitionists were right: the government was in the hands of the slave power.

The fifth area of congressional power concerned the return of fugitive slaves. Many constitutional scholars and jurists had argued that Congress did not in fact have a role to play here, because the fugitive slave provision was entirely directed at the states, and it was in a section of the Constitution that never even mentioned the national government.[33] However, in an overwhelmingly proslavery decision, the Supreme Court settled this issue in favor of congressional power and the South in *Prigg v. Pennsylvania*.[34] Justice Joseph Story's opinion declared that Congress had full authority, and full responsibility, to ensure the return of fugitive slaves. If Congress had plenary power to regulate the return of fugitive slaves, then it could do so in a variety of ways. Clay's resolution did not spell out any details—that came later. But, the eventual law—the Fugitive Slave Law of 1850—would be an enormous legislative victory for "the slave power." It would create the first national system of law enforcement and deny alleged fugitives—including free blacks wrongly claimed as fugitive slaves—fundamental due-process rights.

---

[33] Art. IV, sec. 3, cl. 3 of the Constitution provides: "No Person held to Service or Labour in one State, under the Laws thereof, escaping into another, shall, in Consequence of any Law or Regulation therein, be discharged from such Service or Labour, but shall be delivered up on Claim of the Party to whom such Service or Labour may be due."

[34] *Prigg v. Pennsylvania*, 41 U.S. (16 Pet.) 539 (1842). See generally Paul Finkelman, "Story Telling on the Supreme Court: *Prigg v. Pennsylvania* and Justice Joseph Story's Judicial Nationalism," *Supreme Court Review* (1994):247–94.

## Debating Clay's Bill

From February until July 4 the Senate debated Clay's measures. The debates were some of the most eloquent and memorable in American history. On February 4, Clay with charm and wit set out his plan to resolve the crisis. He was later supported by Sam Houston of Texas and predictably opposed by Jefferson Davis of Mississippi. Speaking for President Taylor, Senator Jacob Miller of New Jersey insisted that California be admitted to the Union immediately and then the other issues could be settled. The only other pressing issue was the absurd demand emanating from Austin that half of New Mexico—all the way to Santa Fe—belonged to Texas. Taylor lost little sleep over the saber rattling of the government in Austin. The former general and war hero was prepared to personally lead the army in New Mexico to stop an invasion of federal territory, just as President Andrew Jackson has been prepared to march to South Carolina to suppress nullification. Thus, from the perspective of the administration, California statehood, followed by New Mexico statehood, would settle most of the territorial issues. Then in a more relaxed atmosphere Congress could craft a new fugitive slave law, organize the Utah Territory, settle the Texas debt question, and if necessary consider the slave trade in the national capital. Taylor's program might have worked, but Clay was not about to defer to a president of his own party and therefore lose his chance at glory and perhaps the White House.

On March 4, John C. Calhoun came to the Senate to oppose Clay's compromise, Taylor's solution, and just about any other legislative solution that could have ended the crisis. By this time Calhoun was fading fast—he would be dead by the end of the month—and was too weak to read his own speech. James Mason of Virginia read it for him. Calhoun's speech is memorable, but often misunderstood. Historians looking for glory and heroism, who talk about the "great triumvirate" of Webster, Clay, and Calhoun, fail to see that in the end Calhoun did not want a solution to the crisis. He wanted an excuse to dissolve the Union, and his whole speech was a threat to do just that, if he could not have *everything* he wanted—including things Congress lacked the constitutional power to grant. His speech in effect acknowledged that slavery and freedom were incompatible within the same Union. His solution was to demand that the supporters of human liberty be silenced and democratic notions of majority rule be undone. Calhoun's speech reflected a lifetime of pent-up anger and frustration, for like Webster and Clay, Calhoun, too, had dreamed of being president. He also dreamed of shaping the country entirely his way.

Much of his speech was based on a history of America that simply did not reflect reality. He complained that the "northern section" had "a predominance in every part of the Government."[35] This claim ignored the fact that nine of the nation's twelve presidents had been southern-born slave owners, including the current incumbent, Zachary Taylor.[36] All the northerners were one-term presidents, while five of the southerners served two terms. Slaveholders had held the presidency for fifty years while nonslaveholders had held it for a mere twelve years. Since Jefferson took office in 1801 *every* president except John Quincy Adams had been either a slaveholder or northern Democrat who was closely allied to the South. Similarly, since the Jeffersonian "revolution" of 1801 there had been twenty-five Congresses, and southerners had been Speaker of the House in all but five of them. None of the four northerners who had been Speaker had shown any hostility to the South or slavery. Similarly, except for a brief period in the 1820s and early 1830s, the Supreme Court always had a southern majority. Equally important, the Democratic Party had dominated American politics since 1800 and southerners had always dominated that party. Thus, many northern Democrats—such as Supreme Court justices Samuel Nelson and Robert Grier and President Martin Van Buren—had consistently supported southern interests. The military had similarly been dominated by slaveholding generals, like Andrew Jackson, Winfield Scott, and Zachary Taylor. Extreme proslavery men, like Calhoun and Abel Upshur of Virginia, had served in presidential cabinets, but no strong antislavery men had ever served in a cabinet.

Calhoun argued that the "cords of Union" could not be broken "at a single blow," but he claimed that "the slavery question has snapped some of the most important" cords and "greatly weakened all the others."[37] He noted that the churches had divided over slavery, and this signaled an end to the Union. But surely Calhoun did not think Congress could bring the Methodists, Baptists, or Presbyterians back together. This was not evidence of the

---

[35] *Congressional Globe*, 31st Cong., 1st sess., 1850, p. 451.

[36] William Henry Harrison, while elected from Ohio, was from a distinguished Virginia planter family and owned slaves most of his life. As territorial governor of Ohio he had attempted to get Congress to modify the Northwest Ordinance to allow slavery there. Paul Finkelman, *Slavery and the Founders: Race and Liberty in the Age of Jefferson*, 2d ed. (Armonk, N.Y., 2001), pp. 58–70.

[37] *Congressional Globe*, 31st Cong., 1st sess., 1850, p. 453.

failure of the political system. But Calhoun was not interested in making distinctions between politics and nonpolitical opposition to slavery. Thus, Calhoun argued the "abolition party" in the North was destroying the Union —even though, except for the minuscule Liberty Party, there was in fact no such "party." But for Calhoun, the "abolition party" consisted of everyone in the North, because Calhoun asserted, "Every portion of the North entertains views and feelings more or less hostile to" slavery.[38]

For Calhoun the key to restoring the Union was entirely in the hands of the North. He wanted Congress to adopt "such measures as will satisfy the States belonging to the southern section that they can remain in the Union consistently with their honor and their safety." But neither Clay's nor President Taylor's proposals would satisfy this, even though both men were southern slave owners and planters. Calhoun demanded southern access to all the territories and a guarantee that fugitive slaves would be returned—which was exactly what Clay was offering. But he wanted more. He insisted that northerners "cease the agitation of the slave question" and pass a constitutional amendment guaranteeing the South "the power . . . of protecting herself."[39] Here then, was the key to Calhoun's solution to the problem: northerners had to recognize the legitimacy and justice of slavery and cease to oppose or denounce it. This was not something Congress could *ever* accomplish, short of a constitutional amendment prohibiting antislavery speech. Thus, while Calhoun pretended to want to preserve the Union, he articulated utterly impossible conditions for that result.

Potter's description of Calhoun as the "the most majestic champion of error since Milton's Satan in *Paradise Lost*"[40] is far more accurate than Remini's claim that he was "passionately devoted to the Union." But both exaggerate the power and logic of Calhoun's speech. Calhoun declared that the Union could be saved only if freedom of speech and press were abolished in the North and that the notion of majority rule in Congress or in the election of the president were abandoned. This was not, despite the claims of Professor Remini, the speech of a lover of the Union. It was a carefully crafted justification for secession and disunion.

Four days later, on March 7, Calhoun returned to the Senate to hear Webster speak on the compromise. Doubtless he expected Webster to support the Wilmot Proviso and to denounce slavery. He probably even wanted

---

[38] Ibid., p. 452.
[39] Ibid., pp. 453, 455.
[40] Potter, *Impending Crisis*, p. 98.

such a speech, because at this point Calhoun was not arguing for a plausible compromise but instead was setting the stage for disunion. But Webster surprised Calhoun and the nation—and lost almost all credibility in his home state—by supporting the compromise. He poignantly told his colleagues: "I wish to speak to-day, not as a Massachusetts man, nor as a Northern man, but as an American. . . . I speak to-day for the preservation of the Union. 'Hear me for my cause.'" His rhetoric was supremely nationalist, but it was also a betrayal of his state, his section, and the assumption of his supporters that he opposed slavery. Webster's speech also redefined nationalism by implying that to be an American one had to accept the spread of slavery into the new territories and support a fugitive slave law that denied even the most fundamental rights of due process to alleged fugitive slaves. Indeed, in the fugitive slave law Congress gratuitously declared that "all good citizens are hereby commanded to aid and assist in the prompt and efficient execution of this law." For Webster, a good citizen was someone willing to participate in shipping blacks to bondage without a trial or any due process hearing.

Staunch opponents of slavery, like William H. Seward, Salmon P. Chase, and Hannibal Hamlin, weighed in against the compromise, but not the Union. They were thoroughly opposed to secession and disunion, but they did not believe that the Union had to be built on a foundation of human bondage. They argued that Clay's proposals were wrong and especially that the proposed fugitive slave law was immoral. Speaking as a man who had defended black rights for his whole career, Seward declared the compromise was "radically wrong and essentially vicious, involving the surrender of the exercise of judgment and conscience." President Taylor was unhappy with the self-righteousness of Seward's speech, but he was not entirely in disagreement with Seward's complaints that the compromise gave too much to slavery and rejected American values of liberty and fundamental justice.[41] Taylor wanted immediate admission of California and New Mexico as well. He did not really believe Texas would force a confrontation over the sands of eastern New Mexico, but Old Rough and Ready ordered troops to New Mexico to be ready, and if necessary, rough, in enforcing American law. Taylor opposed opening the Southwest to slavery, and he had no interest in tying California admission to a new fugitive slave law. Clay nevertheless moved forward in opposition to the president of his party.

---

[41] Elbert B. Smith, *The Presidencies of Zachary Taylor and Millard Fillmore* (Lawrence, Kan., 1988), pp. 119–20.

Webster may have spoken "not as a Massachusetts man, nor as a Northern man, but as an American," but he also spoke as a Whig who was bitter that he had never been his party's presidential candidate and hostile to one of the party's most successful candidates. Clay, like Webster, hoped to save the Union, but now with Webster's support he directly challenged Taylor's leadership. On May 21, Clay openly attacked Taylor saying that the Whig president's plan would not solve the crisis but would lead the country to "bleed more profusely than ever." In his opposition to the Whig president, Clay, the longtime leader of the Whig Party, was in league with the arch-Democrat, Calhoun. Meanwhile, Taylor's vice president, Millard Fillmore, supported Clay and the compromise. He told Taylor that if he had to break a tie in the Senate, he would do so in favor of Clay's bill. Assuming Clay's bill also passed the House, this would force Taylor to veto the compromise, which would have undermined his administration.[42] Thus, a Whig vice president and two leading Whig senators worked to destroy the presidency of the first Whig president to hold office long enough to accomplish anything.[43]

That was where the debate stood when Congress recessed for the July Fourth holiday. A week later Zachary Taylor was dead. Millard Fillmore, the most obscure vice president ever, was now president of the United States.

## President Fillmore and the Compromise

On July 10, 1850, Millard Fillmore went to the House of Representatives to take the oath as president of the United States. Later that day he fired his entire cabinet, something no other accidental president has ever done. Ten days later he sent the Senate nominations for some cabinet positions. His most important nominee was Daniel Webster, who became his secretary of state. This gave Fillmore a much-needed seasoned adviser in his administration, but it also removed an important voice for the compromise from the Senate. Fillmore was unable to immediately find people to serve as secretary of war and secretary of the interior. Thus, as Congress continued to debate the fate of the Mexican Cession and Texas made noises about invading New Mexico, Fillmore had no one in place to run the departments most necessary for both issues.

---

[42]Ibid., pp. 141, 167. See also Paul Finkelman, *Millard Fillmore* (New York, 2011).
[43]In 1840 William Henry Harrison had been elected as a Whig, but he died a month after taking office.

As the Senate continued to debate Clay's omnibus bill, Fillmore faced his first crisis—without the benefit of having his cabinet in place. Just a few days after he was sworn in, Fillmore received a letter from Governor Peter H. Bell of Texas—addressed to the now-deceased President Taylor—demanding that the United States recognize Texas's extravagant claims to much of New Mexico, including Santa Fe, and to disavow the U.S. Army's actions to preserve the integrity of the New Mexico Territory.

Bell's absurdly arrogant communication would probably have bemused Taylor, a commander in chief with vast military experience and a president with a full cabinet in place, including a secretary of war to deal with military issues and a secretary of the interior to deal with territorial questions. Indeed, Taylor was prepared to personally lead the army into New Mexico to stop an invasion of federal territory, just as Jackson had been prepared to march to South Carolina to suppress nullification. Fillmore had no military experience, no secretary of war, no secretary of the interior, and no sense of the impossibility of Texas enforcing its will against a determined American president. Texas had a lot of land, very few people, and huge debts. More than 750 miles of mostly trackless desert and scrublands separated Austin from Santa Fe. Experienced soldiers were stationed in New Mexico, and it is hard to imagine Texas successfully invading New Mexico. In August, Fillmore ordered another 750 soldiers to New Mexico. Despite his understanding that he needed to defend United States territory against an invasion from any source, Fillmore was ultimately unwilling to actually confront the absurd demands of the Texans that, having once been admitted in to the Union, the state could now unilaterally demand that its boundaries be expanded. Taylor had been ready to confront this argument head on. Fillmore vacillated. He sent more troops to New Mexico but then gave Texas almost everything it demanded.

Fillmore might have sent a stern response to Bell reminding him who was commander in chief, who had an army, and who did not. Or he might have sent him a lawyerly explanation of how the U.S. Constitution worked. He did neither. Nor did he move to bring New Mexico into the Union along with California, as Taylor had wanted. This would have preempted the Texas debate and mooted the Wilmot Proviso debate. By this time residents of New Mexico had already held a convention and written a state constitution that was on its way to Washington. Thus, statehood could have been quickly accomplished.

In their proposed constitution, the New Mexicans made extravagant claims for their new state, based on the old Mexican Department of New Mexico, which would have moved the New Mexico boundary deep into what everyone agreed was clearly the state of Texas. Under the U.S. Constitution, no state could be forced to give up its own territory against its will. Admission to the Union preserved the existing borders of Texas. Furthermore, a territory could never define its own boundaries. Only Congress could do that. Thus, the territorial claims of the New Mexico convention had no basis in law, just as the Texas claims to territory acquired by the United States from Mexico were legally baseless.

These constitutional and legal realities created the potential for presidential leadership. A strong president could have firmly, but tactfully, told both sides they were wrong. Texas was in the Union with the boundaries Congress had already set; New Mexico could enter the Union with boundaries that Congress would create. Since New Mexico had a free population greater than Florida's, it was certainly entitled to admission into the Union. There were many variations on this strategy. Fillmore might have offered to support a compromise that would have admitted New Mexico as a free state under the theory of popular sovereignty that Lewis Cass had proposed in the 1848 election. The extreme southern hotheads were all Democrats, and they would have been forced to repudiate the principles of their own party if they objected to New Mexico statehood on this basis. Fillmore then might have simultaneously urged that Congress pay off the bonds of the Texas republic, as Clay had proposed. He might even have offered a compromise on its territorial claims with New Mexico, as Clay also proposed.[44] Or, he might have forcefully sent Congress a concrete proposal for settling the boundary one way or the other.

Instead, Fillmore was so paralyzed by the Texans' saber rattling that he seems to have forgotten that he was both president and commander in chief. Rather than lead on this issue, he moved to appease the Texas legislature by refusing to submit the proposed New Mexico constitution to Congress. He offered no guidance to Congress at this time, beyond supporting Clay's omnibus bill, which was set to open up all the Mexican Cession to slavery—

---

[44]Fillmore might have argued that the Texas debt was similar to the Revolutionary War state bonds that the United States paid off under the programs of Secretary of State Alexander Hamilton. Such an argument would have strengthened a sense of federalism and national power in the South.

despite the clear objections of the residents of New Mexico, and the repudiation of the Missouri Compromise in Nevada, Utah, and Colorado.

With no leadership from the Whig in the White House, on July 24 the Democrats proposed that Congress not actually set the Texas–New Mexico boundary but instead create a commission to do so. On the heels of this, a Georgia Whig, William Dawson, put together a coalition of southerners and northern Democrats to stipulate that, until the commission met, the New Mexico territorial government would have no authority in the disputed area. This was patently unfair to the claims of New Mexico, and it led to a total unraveling of the compromise. A week later, on July 31, another Whig, James Pearce, who was a close ally of Fillmore, proposed that the whole New Mexico issue be removed from the pending bill. A series of other amendments followed, and by the end of the day the compromise was dead.

The compromise had begun with Clay attempting to wrest control of the Whig Party from its own president. Clay envisioned he would once again be the party leader and hero of the nation, as he had been when he guided the Missouri Compromise through Congress, in 1820. It might finally make him president. But it had backfired. In the Senate, the party had become utterly leaderless, with two Whigs—both of whom supported the compromise—amending the compromise to death while Clay looked on helplessly. The old president was dead, and thus there was no need for Clay to dethrone him. The new president, a lifetime Whig, offered no leadership on the nation's pressing issues and had been prepared to work with Clay. But Clay failed to get other Whigs to go along. The aging Kentucky senator, devastated by the collapse of all his work, left Washington even though Congress remained in session.

At this point, the Illinois Democrat, Senator Stephen A. Douglas, put the compromise back together. This was the ultimate irony of Clay's and Fillmore's machinations against Taylor. Designed to promote Clay and regular Whigs, and to undermine Taylor, the compromise ended up catapulting the Democrat Douglas to greater prominence and devastating Fillmore's presidency and the Whig Party.

Douglas broke the compromise into its component parts and pushed them through Congress one at a time, with a small group of southern and northern senators and representatives voting for all, or almost all, the measures, and then picking up the rest of the southerners or northerners for particular issues. This new configuration of the legislation as a series of separate and disconnected laws undermined any pretense of an actual compromise between competing parties. The final outcome overwhelmingly favored the South, because, at most, only two parts of the original compromise—California statehood and closing the public slave trade in Washington, D.C.—had strong northern support or reflected northern interests.

Thus, the final Compromise of 1850 favored the South over the North and slavery over freedom.[45] Potter called it the Armistice of 1850. But, in fact, it might best be seen as the Appeasement of 1850. Southerners blustered and threatened to destroy the Union; Texans threatened to invade New Mexico. A frightened and inexperienced accidental president—only the fourth northerner in the nation's history to hold the office—was easily cowed into giving southerners everything they wanted. Leaderless northerners in Congress caved as well. The South gained everything it wanted, and the North received almost nothing in return. The appeasement was orchestrated with the active support of a northern Whig president working closely with a northern Democrat to defeat the interests of most northerners.

Fillmore's response to the demands of Texas illustrates his failure of leadership and the northern capitulation to southern threats. Fillmore's August 6 special message to Congress on Texas, which one historian has called "a political masterstroke,"[46] was in fact almost cowardly. The president began by correctly pointing out that the boundary dispute was not between New Mexico and Texas but between the government of the United States and Texas. He detailed the way the Constitution operated, noted that he had the power to call out the militia or army under some circumstances, and explained how the disputed land had been acquired by a treaty between the United States and Mexico. The president asserted that if armed Texans entered New Mexico they would be "trespassers" and were to "be regarded merely as intruders."[47] This was odd terminology for what others might have called invaders, rebels, or even traitors. So far, except for his milquetoast description of invaders as trespassers, Fillmore seemed to have learned the lessons of Andrew Jackson and Zachary Taylor on how to deal with renegade states. The message up to this point resembled Daniel Webster's

---

[45]David Potter uses this term in his chapter "The Armistice of 1850," in *Impending Crisis*.
[46]Holt, *American Whig Party*, p. 534.
[47]Message to the Senate and House of Representatives, Aug. 6, 1850, in James D. Richardson, ed., *A Compilation of the Messages and Papers of the Presidents*, 11 vols. (New York, 1911), 6:2605.

great confrontation with Senator Hayne over nullification. Doubtless this reflected the fact that Webster helped Fillmore write the message.

But this initial strong response was just a prelude to Fillmore's total capitulation to the Texans. Astoundingly, he then asserted that the "executive government of the United States has no power or authority" to determine what the boundary line of the United States was *before* President Polk signed the Treaty of Guadalupe Hidalgo. In other words, the president of the United States told Congress that it was not his job to assert what the national boundaries were, even though every president since George Washington had asserted strong plenary power over foreign policy. If this were really the case, then the president did not know where to collect foreign duties or when an invading army had entered the nation. Throughout his life Fillmore had been allied with nativists, and in 1856 he would run for president on the ticket of the anti-immigrant, anti-Catholic Know-Nothing Party. But here he argued that even if the nation chose to regulate or ban foreign immigration, the president was incapable of determining when a foreigner had entered the nation.[48] Having just declared that only Congress could determine what the boundary of the United States had been before 1848, Fillmore compounded his abdication of leadership by adding that "the assent of the State of Texas may be necessary" to decide where the boundary was.[49] Thus, Fillmore and Webster decided unilaterally that Texas should have a veto power—a power of nullification—over the executive branch and Congress. Under Fillmore's bizarre theory, Congress could pass a law deciding what the boundaries of the New Mexico Territory were, and the president could sign that law, but Texas would have the right—the power—to reject the result. Webster had apparently forgotten where he once stood on the question of nullification; Fillmore had apparently forgotten that the Constitution was the "supreme law of the land."

Fillmore's plan was to guide Congress in passing a law that the Texans would accept. The final settlement over the southwest, which passed the Senate on August 9, gave Texas about seventy thousand square miles more than Clay's bill had (and took that territory away from New Mexico), opened up the entire New Mexico Territory to slavery, *and* gave Texas a $10 million

---

[48]The issue of immigration is important, given Fillmore's long-standing alliances with nativists and his final run for the presidency on the anti-Catholic, anti-immigrant, Know-Nothing Party ticket.

[49]Richardson, *Messages and Papers of the Presidents*, 6:2607.

bailout. The politics of this included a fear—perpetuated by Fillmore and Webster—that if the issues were not settled there would be civil war between Texas and the United States of America over who owned the New Mexico desert. Taylor, the general who had served in the region and knew the geography of Texas and New Mexico, would have thought this was preposterous. But Fillmore, without a working cabinet or a secretary of war, and never having seen the vast deserts of the Southwest, was cowed by the idea that Texas could somehow raise an army that would be a match for that of the entire United States! Webster, now seemingly in control of White House patronage, pressured New England's Whig senators to accept the Texas bill. The Senate, led by Douglas, made sure that there would be no vote on California statehood until after the Texas boundary was resolved. Four days after the Texas vote, the Senate voted 34–18 in favor of California statehood. Significantly, two southern Democrats voted for the bill, Sam Houston of Texas and Thomas Hart Benton of Missouri. With the exception of the two senators from Delaware, no southern Whigs supported California statehood. Webster and Fillmore had pressured New England Whigs to support the Texas bill, but they were unwilling or unable to get any southern Whig (except those from Delaware) to support California statehood. This underscores the lack of compromise in the Compromise of 1850.

On August 15 the Senate voted to organize the New Mexico Territory without a ban on slavery, even though by this time everyone was well aware that a convention in New Mexico had written a constitution that would have made it a free state. This was a blunt attempt to force slavery into the territory and in effect to give federal support to turning a free New Mexico into a slave state.

Finally, after passing all the laws allowing slavery in the new territories and admitting California as a free state, the Senate turned to the District of Columbia slave trade bill and the fugitive slave law. As already noted, the slave trade bill was largely symbolic. It removed an irritation that northerners abhorred, but it had absolutely no effect on the system of slavery or even the sale of slaves. Secretary of State Daniel Webster, Senator Stephen A. Douglas, and President Fillmore sold this law to northerners as a fair trade-off for the new fugitive slave law. But that was a mirage.

Each bill had to pass the House as well, where the politics were more complex. Northerners had a huge majority in the House and could have blocked some of the proslavery measures, or at least forced amendments to them.

But in the end that did not happen. On really tough votes, like the fugitive slave law, many northern congressmen simply failed to show up to vote, rather than fight the law. The final vote on the Texas–New Mexico boundary was possible only because Fillmore pressured northern Whigs in the House to support the bill even though most had been elected on pledges that they would never vote to allow slavery in the new territories. Representative Abraham Schermerhorn of Rochester, for example, supported the bill because Fillmore was prepared to do everything in his power to block Schermerhorn's renomination. Schermerhorn came from the heart of New York's antislavery "Burned-Over District" and the home of the nation's most famous black abolitionist, Frederick Douglass, but on this proslavery bill he abandoned his constituents. Using threats and promises of patronage, Fillmore managed to get just enough votes in the House to get each component of the package through Congress.

In September it all came together. On the ninth, Fillmore signed bills on the Texas–New Mexico boundary, California statehood, and the Utah Territory. Slavery was now legal everywhere in all the new territories, including land well north of the Missouri Compromise line. This was a huge victory for the South, especially when paired with the settlement over Texas that gave that slave state more land and ten million dollars. Since 1787 every territory where slavery was allowed had become a slave state. While some politicians, like Clay, Webster, and Douglas, argued that slavery was unsuited for these territories, southerners knew better. As already discussed, slaves had historically been used in mining and in ranching. Indeed, the first cowboys in America were black slaves in South Carolina. If what had just become West Texas was viable slave country—as the Texans insisted—then so too would be the land just over the border in New Mexico and in the mining country of Utah and Nevada.

On September 18, Fillmore signed the Fugitive Slave Law of 1850. Two days later a last crumb was offered to the North as Fillmore signed the bill prohibiting bringing slaves into the District of Columbia for the purpose of sale. It did not prevent the private sale of slaves already in the district. Nor did it prevent people from moving into the district with slaves. It was a symbolic victory for freedom but nothing more.

The abandonment of both the Wilmot Proviso and the Missouri Compromise would lead to a decade of controversy over the status of slavery in the territories. Emboldened by his success in 1850 with the cooperation of a

Whig president, in 1854 Stephen A. Douglas would contrive, with a northern doughface Democrat in the White House, to eviscerate almost all that remained of the Missouri Compromise line, setting the stage for Bleeding Kansas and the final crisis leading to the Civil War. These long-term consequences of the New Mexico and Utah bills were in the future and not readily apparent in the 1850s. What was apparent, from the moment it was conceived, was the potential disaster that the new fugitive slave law would cause. Fillmore's enthusiastic support for this law, and his aggressive enforcement of it, would become the hallmark of his administration, and in the end that support destroyed his administration, the Whig Party, and any chance the "compromise" might have worked.

## The Fugitive Slave Law of 1850

The Fugitive Slave Law of 1850 was one of the most repressive and unfair statutes ever adopted by the United States. It created, for the first time, a national system of law enforcement. In 1793, Congress had passed a fugitive slave law that authorized any judge—federal, state, or local—to hear a fugitive slave case and remand a fugitive to the custody of a master or a master's agent. The law provided very lax evidentiary standards and no guarantees that free blacks would not be taken south as fugitives. To protect free blacks, almost every northern state had passed a personal liberty law to guarantee due process for alleged fugitive slaves. In *Prigg v. Pennsylvania* (1842) the U.S. Supreme Court said these laws were unconstitutional because they interfered with the implementation of a federal law. However, the Court also said that Congress did not have the power to require the states to enforce this federal law. Almost immediately state officials throughout the North refused to enforce the law and a number of states passed legislation prohibiting their judges from hearing fugitive slave cases and prohibiting federal officials or private slave catchers from using state jails to secure alleged fugitive slaves. Southerners complained, with some legitimacy, that these new personal liberty laws made it impossible for them to vindicate their constitutional right to recover fugitive slaves. With only a few federal courts operating in the country and a similarly small number of federal marshals, masters had to pursue their slaves on their own or with professional slave catchers. The 1850 law remedied this situation by providing for the appointment of federal commissioners in every county who were empowered to hear fugitive slave cases and summon sufficient force to secure the return of runaways.

Under the law federal marshals could be fined $1,000 if they failed to "use all proper means to diligently" execute the law. Marshals and commissioners were empowered to call on the militia and the army and to create a posse to enforce the law. The statute gratuitously declared that "all good citizens are hereby commanded to aid and assist in the prompt and efficient execution of this law," although there was no clear remedy if citizens refused to help enforce the law.[50] If these measures failed, however, and marshals were unable to prevent a rescue by a mob, they could be held personally liable for the value of any slave who escaped or was rescued from their custody. No other federal statute had ever provided such penalties for officers who were unable to implement a law.

Any persons who aided or harbored a fugitive slave or interfered with the rendition process, for whatever reason, were subject to a $1,000 fine and six months in jail. In addition, they were subject to civil damages of $1,000 to be paid to the owner of a slave for each slave who was not recovered. Many northerners found these provisions particularly obnoxious because, if literally enforced, a farmer could be fined, sued, or jailed for giving a cup of water to a black person walking down the road. The harsh penalties, and the minimal standards of proof, could force northern whites to assume that all blacks they saw were fugitives, even though in 1850 there were more than 150,000 free blacks living in the North. The new law not only imperiled the liberty of free blacks but also undermined their relationships with their white neighbors. Whites, and even free blacks in the North, might be reluctant to hire a black for fear the person was a fugitive, and the very act of hiring could be a violation of the law. From the perspective of blacks and many white northerners, the act of 1850 had brought the law of slavery into the free states and required northerners to do the bidding of southerners.

These provisions punished free people—white and black—if they helped fugitives. Even more obnoxious were the procedures for returning a slave. Under the law, the alleged slave would get a summary hearing before a fed-

---

[50]Some southerners in fact were contemptuous of the willingness of northerners to participate in the return of fugitive slaves. While the law was being debated, one Kentuckian told Senator Salmon P. Chase that in the South "no man will voluntarily become a negro catcher" and that it would be "gross insult" to ask a southern gentleman to do such a thing. Professional slave catchers were "held in public estimation only secondary to the professional Negro trader, and that is the lowest possible." Edgar Needham to Salmon P. Chase, Feb. 9, 1850, Salmon P. Chase Papers, Library of Congress.

eral judge or commissioner. The court was precluded from even considering a writ of habeas corpus. This was the first time the U.S. Congress suspended the privilege of the writ of habeas corpus, and it was done in violation of the constitutional provision that provided that habeas could be suspended only in response to an invasion or rebellion.

The law required any judge or commissioner to "hear and determine the case" in "a summary manner," without a jury. The slave owner or his agent had only to present "satisfactory proof" that the person claimed was a fugitive slave. This could be done by "deposition or affidavit, in writing . . . certified" before any judge or magistrate in the home state of the slave owner. The potential for fraud, or even mistaken identity, was huge. The claimant might bring any black who fit the description in the "deposition or affidavit" before a judge and demand the right to remove the person as a fugitive slave.

In what was clearly its most unfair aspect, the law provided, "In no trial or hearing under this act shall the testimony of such alleged fugitive be admitted in evidence." Someone could be dragged south as a slave and never be allowed to offer his or her own voice as evidence that he or she was free. As one northern minister complained, "It requires but the collusion of two men to seize a freeman in the streets of New York or Boston, to drag him before a commissioner, to make affidavit of his escape from service and of his personal identity, and in one hour the freeman shall be in the custody of an armed force on his way to the slave coffles . . . to be sold to the rice plantations of the South."[51]

The outrageousness of the testimony provision was matched by the provision for paying the commissioners and judges who heard these cases. If a judge ruled in favor of the alleged slave, thus setting him or her free, the judge was entitled to a $5 fee. If the judge ruled for the master, he got a $10 fee. Most northerners viewed this as a blatant attempt to bribe the courts.[52]

The law needlessly threatened free blacks and unnecessarily trampled on traditional American notions of due process and the fair administration of justice. It was not a bill that could be considered part of a "compromise,"

---

[51] Joseph P. Thompson, *The Fugitive Slave Law: Tried by the Old and New Testaments* (New York, 1850), p. 8, quoted in Paul Finkelman, "The Treason Trial of Castner Hanway," in *American Political Trials*, ed. Michal R. Belknap, 2d ed. (Westport, Conn., 1994), p. 80.

[52] The differential payment was based on the fact that commissioners were paid by collecting fees (rather than a salary), and it took much more time to fill out the paperwork necessary to return a fugitive slave than to set a black free. While the different fees made economic sense, they created the appearance that justice was for sale in the North. The payment scale was a public relations disaster for the national government and the Fillmore administration.

because it was so utterly one-sided. In addition to all the denials of due process and the apparent attempt to buy justice, the law made no provisions to protect free people who might be illegally seized under it. There was no antikidnapping provision that would have ameliorated northern sensibilities, and under the Supreme Court's decision in *Prigg v. Pennsylvania*, the free states were prohibited from providing any protections for their black residents. Under this law a northern white could be fined, jailed, and sued for helping a black person who he thought was free, but a southerner would face no sanction for seizing a free black and fraudulently or mistakenly claiming him or her as a slave.

## The Great Failure and Its Aftermath: The Spread of Slavery

The compromise measures accomplished little, but they deeply damaged the Union and the credibility of the national government. The territorial accommodation did not satisfy the South, but only whetted slaveholders' appetite for more land. In 1850 the southerners, with the aid of Senator Stephen A. Douglas of Illinois, had undermined the Missouri Compromise line. In 1854 Douglas introduced the Kansas-Nebraska Act, which repealed the Missouri Compromise line for most of the existing western territories. This was the logical extension of the 1850 compromise. The doughface president Franklin Pierce dutifully signed the law, making slavery legal in all the federal territories except Minnesota and Oregon (which included present-day Washington and parts of Idaho). Slavery was now legal everywhere else in the West. What followed was Bleeding Kansas and the failure of the Pierce and Buchanan administrations to oversee peaceful settlement or fair and democratic elections in Kansas.

In 1857 the Supreme Court finished this task in the *Dred Scott* case, by striking down the ban on slavery in the Missouri Compromise, and further holding that Congress could *never* ban slavery in the territories. It is impossible to know if the legislation of 1850 and 1854 emboldened Chief Justice Taney to reach such an extreme result, but this seems likely. This was only the second time the Court had ever found an act of Congress unconstitutional. Striking down an act of Congress seemed counter to Taney's Jacksonian jurisprudence, but in light of the legislation of 1850 and 1854 the result was consistent with Taney's general deference to Congress.

Thus the compromise passed in 1850 led to a total collapse of the idea of free soil in America. At the beginning of 1850 slavery was banned from almost all the federal territories. Congress had not yet acted on the status of slavery in the newly acquired lands of the Southwest, so presumably Mexican law still applied, which made slavery illegal there.[53] In almost all of the rest of the West slavery was prohibited by the Missouri Compromise. By the end of the year Congress had reversed the Mexican law, and opened all the new land except California to slavery; by 1854 Congress extended this reversal of decades of American policy by allowing slavery in what would later be the states of Kansas, Nebraska, South Dakota, North Dakota, Montana, and parts of Colorado, Wyoming, and Idaho. By 1857 slavery was legal in all the remaining territories. In seven years a gigantic revolution in American public policy had taken place, all under the guise of a compromise between the North and the South. The compromise was that slavery would be allowed everywhere.

Just as it protected slavery in the territories, the Compromise of 1850 strengthened slavery in the nation's capital. After 1850 there were no longer any public slave markets in Washington, D.C., but that did not limit private sales. Nor did closing the District of Columbia markets harm slavery in the capital. Before 1850 some congressmen, including Abraham Lincoln, had proposed legislation to gradually end slavery there. But after 1850 such proposals disappeared. The ban on the slave trade seems to have shut off debate on the larger issue of slavery in the district. Thus, the law designed to give something to the North had the effect of actually protecting slavery in the district.

## The Great Failure and Its Aftermath: The Fugitive Slave Law

The most important part of the compromise was the Fugitive Slave Law of 1850. Few laws have been so disastrous. The blatant unfairness of the law shocked many northerners, who were otherwise law-abiding citizens. The enforcement of the law stimulated lawless and even violent responses in many northern communities. Early opposition to the law led President Fillmore to

---

[53]William W. Freehling, *The Road to Disunion: Secessionists at Bay, 1776–1854* (New York, 1990), pp. 488–90.

ever more vigorous enforcement, as he sought to vindicate his reputation for supporting the law. He also aggressively enforced the law in order to gain southern support for the 1852 Whig nomination. Meanwhile, Secretary of State Webster, equally anxious for the presidential nomination, joined Fillmore in urging vigorous prosecutions of opponents of the law.

The law undermined Fillmore's presidency, the Whig Party, and the compromise. Northern opposition to the law stemmed from its absurdly unfair provisions and its failure to protect free blacks from kidnapping or mistakenly being sent to the South as slaves. Also troublesome was the fact that many blacks seized under the law had not recently escaped from bondage but were people who had been away from slavery long enough to establish themselves in northern communities. The first fugitive returned under the law, James Hamlet, had been living in New York City long enough to find steady employment, marry, and have two children. His master saw him as a fugitive slave, but New Yorkers saw him as a neighbor, husband, father, and employee. After he was taken back into bondage, New Yorkers raised $800 to buy his freedom and he was met on his return by an integrated demonstration of four to five thousand people.[54]

President Fillmore's obsession with enforcing the law, in conjunction with his other actions as president, illustrates the poisonous nature of the law. Fillmore's biographers claim the law "plague[ed] Fillmore's conscience," and that he found it "repugnant." Thus, "he had delayed signing the bill as long as he could."[55] But the evidence does not support either argument. During the summer of 1850 Fillmore communicated with Congress about the compromise. As noted above, he sent Congress a detailed, but inconclusive, message about the boundary dispute between Texas and New Mexico. Similarly, throughout his administration Fillmore asked Congress to pass legislation on all sorts of things, from building lighthouses on the Great Lakes to establishing a new mint in San Francisco. But in the summer of 1850 Fillmore never once suggested that the fugitive slave bill needed to be altered to guarantee due process. After Clay's Omnibus Bill failed, Fillmore "inten-

---

[54] American and Foreign Anti-Slavery Society, *The Fugitive Slave Bill: Its History and Unconstitutionality; With an Account of the Seizure and Enslavement of James Hamlet, and His Subsequent Restoration to Liberty* (New York, 1850); Paul Finkelman, *Slavery in the Courtroom* (Washington, D.C., 1985), pp. 85–86.

[55] Robert J. Rayback, *Millard Fillmore: Biography of a President* (Buffalo, N.Y., 1959), p. 252; Smith, *Presidencies*, p. 200.

sified his intervention in Congress's proceedings" to secure the compromise and he was "adamant about passing . . . the fugitive slave measure."[56] If he truly had doubts about its constitutionality—if he knew his "conscience" would be bothered by signing a law that was so arbitrary and such an affront to due process—it is surprising he did not mention these concerns in some communication to Congress. If he was bothered by the fugitive slave law, or any of its provisions, we have no evidence of it.

Nor is there evidence that he "hesitated" or "delayed signing the bill as long as he could." The fugitive slave bill passed on the Senate on August 26, without any input from Fillmore. On September 12, the House passed the bill, still without any input or communication from Fillmore, and sent it back to the Senate. On September 16, the presiding officer of the Senate reported that bill had been delivered to the president, who signed it on the eighteenth.[57]

Did this bill plague Fillmore's conscience? The evidence suggests otherwise. More than a month after its passage, Fillmore told Secretary of State Webster "that the law, having been passed, must be executed." He emphatically asserted that "so far as it provides for the surrender of fugitives from labor it is according to the requirements of the Constitution and should be sustained against all attempts at repeal."[58] This was hardly the voice of a man who had any pangs of conscience. He saw nothing unconstitutional or even arbitrary about a law that did not allow a man to speak in his own defense as to whether he should be dragged away from where he was living to some other state to be claimed as a slave. He did not even see how this might undermine the liberty of the tens of thousands of free blacks in the North, including the nearly fifty thousand who lived in his home state of New York. He saw nothing wrong, or even politically unwise, in paying commissioners twice as much money for sending a man to slavery as sending him to freedom. He was only willing to concede that "if there" was a provision that endangered liberty, he would not object to changing the law. In fact, however, he would soon reject even this possibility.

[56]Holt, *American Whig Party*, p. 533.
[57]*Congressional Globe*, 31st Cong., 1st sess., 1850, pp. 1660, 1806–7, 1810; *Senate Journal*, 31st Cong., 1st sess., Sept. 16, 1850, p. 638. *Digest of the Official Opinions of the Attorneys-General of the United States*, 16 vols. (Washington, D.C., 1885), 5:254.
[58]Fillmore to Daniel Webster, Oct. 23, 1850, reprinted in Claude H. Van Tyne, ed., *The Letters of Daniel Webster* (New York, 1902), pp. 436–47.

While Fillmore's biographers claim he was troubled by the law, he enforced it more vigorously than any other federal law on the books. The administration's treatment of filibusters underscores Fillmore's almost fanatical attempts to support the fugitive slave law and prosecute those who refused to help enforce it or actually violated its provisions.

During Fillmore's administration a small army of about four hundred men, led by the notorious filibuster Narciso López, a Venezuelan, sailed from New Orleans to Cuba, where they hoped to seize that Spanish colony. This filibustering expedition violated American and international law and could have forced the United States into a war with Spain. In April 1851 Fillmore issued an official proclamation condemning filibustering expeditions as "wicked schemes," warning that participants in such "adventures for plunder and robbery," would "subject themselves to heavy penalties" of up to $3,000 in fines and three years in prison, and would "forfeit their claim to the protection of this Government."[59] But when López's army sailed for Cuba in August, Fillmore did nothing to stop the invasion force. When these soldiers of fortune were captured and brought to Spain for trial, Fillmore negotiated for their return—at government expense—to the United States. Despite this brazen violation of American law, as well as the president's proclamation against filibustering, Fillmore did not seek any indictments of these lawbreakers. This of course sharply contrasts with Fillmore's response to those who opposed the fugitive slave law.[60]

In his last two years in office Fillmore would expend enormous energy overseeing the enforcement of the fugitive slave law. At no time would he express any doubts about the constitutionality of the law. Privately Fillmore told Webster, "God knows that I detest Slavery."[61] Perhaps the Almighty did know that Fillmore secretly detested slavery, but no human being would have seen this in his policies, his speeches, or the acts of his administration. He told Webster slavery was "an existing evil, for which we are not responsible, and we must endure it,"[62] but in fact he was more than willing to endure and protect it. His notion of compromise was to give everything to slavery

---

[59] "By the President of the United States: A Proclamation," Apr. 25, 1851, in James D. Richardson, ed., *Messages of the Presidents* (New York, 1897), pp. 2647–48.

[60] For a discussion of the filibuster issue, see Finkelman, *Millard Fillmore*, pp. 98–100, 116–28.

[61] Fillmore to Webster, Oct. 23, 1850.

[62] Ibid.

and not even blink at the act's fundamental denials of due process, its harshness, or the way it threatened all northerners.

Throughout 1851 and 1852 Fillmore and Webster teamed up to aggressively enforce the fugitive slave law. Both men hoped for the Whig presidential nomination in 1852, and both believed aggressive enforcement of the 1850 law would secure this for them. Fillmore and Webster both personally intervened with local U.S. attorneys to help secure convictions of opponents of the law. After fugitives successfully resisted capture at Christiana, Pennsylvania, Fillmore ordered the U.S. attorney to charge more than forty men, all of whom had been bystanders in the event, with treason for failing to help the U.S. marshal seize a runaway slave. This led to the largest treason trial in American history, but no convictions. Supreme Court Justice Robert Grier, who was a doughface Democrat and no friend of abolitionists, nevertheless ruled that refusing to help enforce the fugitive slave law, or even resisting its enforcement, was not treason. Rescues and attempted rescues in Syracuse and Boston also led to seemingly endless trials, but only one conviction, and that defendant died of natural causes while his case was on appeal.

Overall, the success of the 1850 law was at best mixed. Between 1850 and 1861 about a thousand blacks would be returned to bondage under the law. Since southerners estimated that more than ten thousand escaped in that time —and many more were already in the North—the law hardly gave the South what it needed. The decade was punctuated by rescues and other kinds of resistance. Fillmore, Webster, Clay, and the others who supported the law never expected white northerners to break the law to protect black freedom, which happened sporadically throughout the decade. In trials northern juries often refused to convict men charged with interfering with the law.

Southerners, and their northern allies in Congress, probably assumed that blacks were irrelevant to the political equation. Doubtless their own racist assumptions made them believe that blacks were not "manly" enough to fight for their own liberty. But they were wrong. In Boston blacks rushed the courthouse to rescue Shadrach Minkins from a U.S. marshal. In rural Pennsylvania fugitive slaves fought for their freedom, killing a master at Christiana. In Syracuse blacks and whites teamed up to rescue the fugitive slave Jerry from federal custody. Throughout the North, blacks, sometimes with white allies, sometimes not, organized self-defense groups. These events, along with resistance organized by blacks and their white friends throughout the North, horrified Fillmore, who saw them as a violation of the fundamental principles of the Constitution. He told Webster, "I mean at every sacrifice and at every hazard to perform my duty." He grandly declared, "Nullification can not and will not be tolerated."[63] But from the perspective of American blacks and many whites, it was absurd to believe that a person who escaped from bondage should peacefully return to slavery. If this was a "nullification" of the Constitution, it was nevertheless an implementation of the Declaration of Independence.

While President Fillmore insisted he would enforce the law at all costs, Frederick Douglass suggested that the best way to deal with the new law was "to make a dozen or more dead kidnappers."[64] In fact, there were only a few dead slave catchers—one at Christiana in 1851, another in Boston during a failed attempt to rescue Anthony Burns in 1854. But they were enough to terrify Fillmore and two subsequent administrations and help derail the compromise.

Most arrests under the law did not lead to confrontations of violence, but enough did to embarrass every administration for the rest of the decade and lead southerners to conclude that nowhere in the North could they expect to vindicate their claims to fugitive slaves. Northerners who were otherwise law abiding and peaceful suddenly found themselves helping rescue slaves from federal marshals or voting to acquit those who did.

Meanwhile the law stimulated Harriet Beecher Stowe to write *Uncle Tom's Cabin* (1852), the most politically powerful text since Thomas Paine's *Common Sense* and the greatest best seller of the century. Stowe's book was a powerful indictment of slavery and the fugitive slave law, and provided a cultural defense of those who protected fugitives and sent them on their way to Canada.

The Fugitive Slave Law of 1850 did not lead to a wholesale breakdown of law and order. But this law, which turned out to be the central component of the compromise, was so unfair, so one-sided, so outrageous, that it could not possibly work. It left southerners arrogantly believing they could demand

---

[63] Ibid.

[64] Frederick Douglass, "Let All Soil Be Free Soil," speech of Aug. 11, 1852, at Pittsburgh, in *The Frederick Douglass Papers*, Series One: *Speeches, Debates, and Interviews*, ed. John Blassingame et al., 5 vols. (New Haven, 1979–92), 2:390.

and win *anything* from the supine North; it then left them furious when average northern citizens proved to be less pliant.

In the end, the compromise failed because it was never a compromise at all. It gave almost everything to slavery and almost nothing to freedom. The only tangible gain for the North was the free state of California, and that was a foregone conclusion. The compromise left southerners arrogant and then angry when their legislative victory turned out to be a mirage. They demanded more, and more, and still it was never enough. In the end, secession was their only solution. That was the fruit of the "compromise" that Henry Clay, Daniel Webster, Stephen A. Douglas, and Millard Fillmore planted in 1850.

Matthew Glassman

# Beyond the Balance Rule

*Congress, Statehood, and Slavery, 1850–1859*

In February 1859 the U.S. House of Representatives voted on S. 239, an Act to Admit Oregon to the Union, which had passed the Senate the previous March by a vote of 35 to 17.[1] At the time of the vote, members of the House knew one crucial piece of information: Oregon was going to be a free state.[2] As part of the referendum on their new constitution in November 1857 and in accordance with the general principles of the Kansas-Nebraska Act, voters in the Oregon Territory had been given a choice on slavery in the future state, and had chosen to be a free state by a vote of 7,727 (75 percent) to 2,645 (25 percent).[3] The admission vote in the House was close, 114 in favor and 103 against. Two days later, President Buchanan signed the bill and Oregon became the thirty-third state.[4]

If you knew nothing about the admission vote, but you knew something about slavery, the balance rule, and politics of the antebellum era, you might assume that the Oregon admission vote was on sectional lines, with north-

---

[1] *Senate Journal*, 35th Cong., 1st sess., May 18, 1858, p. 477.

[2] The Senate knew the same at the time of their vote, the previous March.

[3] Voters were given separate choices on the ballot in which one question asked them to approve or disapprove of the proposed constitution and a second question asked them to vote for or against slavery. The constitution was approved by a similar vote to the slave vote, 7,195 (69%) to 3,215 (31%). A third question on the ballot asked about voting and residency rights of free blacks, and this vote was soundly defeated, 8,640 (89%) against and 1,081 (11%) in favor. See Charles H. Carey, "The Creation of Oregon as a State," *Oregon Historical Quarterly* 26 (1925): 281; Grupo de Investigadores Puertorriqueños, *Breakthrough from Colonialism: An Interdisciplinary Study of Statehood*, 1st ed., 2 vols. (Río Piedras, Puerto Rico, 1984); Earl S. Pomeroy, *The Pacific Slope: A History of California, Oregon, Washington, Idaho, Utah, and Nevada* (Seattle, 1973).

[4] 11 Stat. 383 (1859).

ern representatives supporting it and southern representatives opposing it. You might further conjecture that Republicans were most supportive, southern Democrats most opposed, and northern Democrats mostly supportive, with anti-Lecompton Democrats perhaps more supportive than pro-Lecompton Democrats. You might also assume that a slave state also was awaiting admission.

On all these counts, you would be wrong. The actual vote was: northern members, 73–71 *against* admission, southern members 42–18 *in favor* of admission. The party breakdown was: northern Democrats 56–2 in favor, southern Democrats 42–18 *in favor*, and Republicans 71–15 *against* admission.[5] Heading into the final months of the slave crisis, the southern Democrats defeated the Republicans so that they could *bring a free state into the Union*. The admission also furthered the sectional skew in the Senate: Oregon became the eighteenth free state, and fifteen slave states were in existence. Additionally, its admission came on the heels of the admission of another free state, Minnesota (spring 1858), and the defeat of admission for a slave state, the Kansas Territory, at approximately the same time.[6] No plausible slave state was awaiting admission.

This story illustrates how the so-called balance rule—the informal mechanism of admitting states in pairs, one slave and one free, as a mechanism of maintaining sectional harmony between the North and the South in the U.S. Senate—is an incomplete analytical explanation for the politics of state admissions. In the case of the Oregon Territory, it has almost no explanatory power. There was only one state being considered for admission, the vote positions of the congressional factions cut directly against their positions in the slave crisis, and the admission did absolutely nothing to restore the balance of power in the Senate.

---

[5] *House Journal*, 35th Cong., 2d sess., 1859, pp. 398–99. See also Nolan McCarty, Keith Poole, and Howard Rosenthal, "Congress and the Territorial Expansion of the United States," in *Party, Process, and Political Change: New Perspectives on the History of Congress*, ed. David W. Brady and Mathew D. McCubbins (Stanford, Calif., 2002).

[6] The Kansas Territory was the only plausible place left to carve out a legitimate slave state, but it had soundly defeated its own admission by rejecting the English Bill Constitution in August 1858, in the final moments of the five-year drama that was the Kansas-Nebraska Act and the Lecompton Constitution. While it is plausible that the Senate, which voted on Oregon before the defeat of the Kansas Constitution, thought that Kansas would be admitted along with Oregon, it is highly unlikely. It was not possible in the House, whose vote took place after the defeat of the English Bill Constitution. See David M. Potter, *The Impending Crisis, 1848–1861*, completed and ed. Don E. Fehrenbacher (New York, 1976).

This chapter examines the balance rule within the larger framework of statehood politics in the antebellum era. It argues that the congressional politics of Oregon's admission are best understood by a wider conception of the balance rule. After a brief review of the balance rule theory, the remainder of the essay considers four features of statehood politics that revise our understanding of the relationship between Congress, statehood, slavery, and admission politics. By employing a more textured analytical assessment of statehood politics, a better understanding of both the balance rule and the admissions politics of the 1850s becomes possible.

## The Balance Rule

The balance rule is a relatively well known analytical thesis that explains how state admissions were politically negotiated during the antebellum era. It has three tenets. First, states are admitted to the Union in pairs (or on an alternating basis). Second, the paired admissions are done on the basis of the status of slavery in the new states, with the admission of one free state and one slave. Third, the pairing is done to ensure that the balance of power in the Senate remains unchanged. By balancing slave- and free-state admissions to the Union, neither section can gain a majority in the Senate, and thus neither proslavery nor antislavery policies can dominate Congress.

This logic is so well accepted that most high school history textbooks feature it, usually during a discussion of the Missouri Compromise or the Compromise of 1850. For instance, James West Davidson writes, under the heading "The Missouri Question,"

> The admission of Missouri would upset the balance of power in the Senate. In 1819, there were 11 free states and 11 slave states. Each state had two senators. If Missouri became a slave state, the South would have a majority in the Senate. Determined not to lose power, northerners fought against letting Missouri enter as a slave state. . . . Finally, Senator Henry Clay proposed a compromise . . . admitting Missouri as a slave state and Maine as a free state.[7]

Similarly, academic writing comes to the same conclusion. Barry Weingast has written,

---

[7] James West Davidson and Michael B. Stoff, *The American Nation* (Needham, Mass., 1995), p. 428.

Made explicit during the Missouri Compromise, the balance rule had two components. It held, first, that the North and South would have an equal number of states, and, second, that slave and free states would be admitted in pairs. Sectional balance afforded each section a veto in the Senate, allowing each to prevent the adoption of national policies they deemed onerous.[8]

The balance rule thesis explains admissions during the first half of the nineteenth century almost perfectly: after the admission of Tennessee in 1796, there were eight slave states and eight free or soon-to-be-free states. Over the next fifty years, admissions were either paired or alternated: Ohio and Louisiana, Indiana and Mississippi, Illinois and Alabama, Maine and Missouri, Michigan and Arkansas, and then Texas and Florida coupled with Iowa and Wisconsin.

However, as we have seen, the balance rule does not explain the case of Oregon. Indeed, throughout the 1850s, it falls apart. In the four major episodes of state admission in the 1850s—the Compromise of 1850, the ultimate failure of Kansas statehood, the admission of Minnesota, and the admission of Oregon—the balance rule does not have much explanatory power. Some scholars have argued that this is because of the exceptional circumstances of the 1850s—that the breakdown of the balance rule was due to growing agitation over slavery in the North or growing paranoia on the part of the southerners. In short, something changed historically such that the political calculus of state admissions in the 1850s was different from that of the previous sixty years in regard to statehood politics.

The argument presented here suggests that the perceived breakdown of the balance framework for understanding the admissions of the 1850s is due to its incomplete conception of the relationship between the balance rule and the statehood process itself. In the discussion that follows, four aspects of statehood politics are examined within the concept of this relationship: the inherently controversial nature of statehood without reference to slavery; the multiple stages of state construction, of which admission was only one step; the multiple locations of political action, of which Congress was only one setting; and the continual political contestation during the nineteenth century over the structure of the statehood process itself. A deeper understanding of the statehood process places the balance

---

[8] Barry R. Weingast, "Political Stability and Civil War: Institutions, Commitment, and American Democracy," in *Analytic Narratives*, ed. Robert Bates (Princeton, N.J., 1996), p. 151.

rule in context, and in turn the politics of the 1850s becomes less of an analytical puzzle.

## Statehood as Inherently Controversial

During the nineteenth century, statehood was consequential—and controversial—without regard to slavery. The major episodes of conflict over slavery in the nineteenth century are well known: the Missouri Compromise, the Compromise of 1850, the Kansas-Nebraska Act, the Lecompton Constitution, and so on. And while these are all conflicts over slavery, they are also conflicts over statehood. The traditional balance rule thesis assigns the controversy to slavery, making statehood a catalyst that exacerbated the tension. In the traditional view, slavery is the bonfire, statehood perhaps some extra gasoline thrown on it.

But there are good reasons to believe the opposite is true, that the root conflict in these episodes is not slavery but national expansion, and that the catalyst is whatever interest—such as slavery—happens to be dividing national politics. In this view, statehood itself is a bonfire. This is a satisfying revision in at least one sense: we know that statehood politics was extraordinarily controversial both before the existence of slavery as a major cleavage in American politics and after slavery's demise. It just so happened that slavery was the dominant issue during a significant portion of western state construction.

Since the admission of new states inherently alters the composition of both Congress and the electorate for presidential elections, existing interests already represented in these institutions have an interest in the timing and order of admission. The Founders were keenly aware of, and extremely sensitive to, issues of apportionment at the Constitutional Convention, and the very idea of sharing central power with yet-to-be-constructed western states struck fear into many of the delegates.[9] Gouverneur Morris of Pennsylvania openly questioned whether western states should have equal representation, arguing that "they will ruin the Atlantic interest" if they gained power.[10]

---

[9]Charles A. Kromkowski, *Recreating the American Republic: Rules of Apportionment, Constitutional Change, and American Political Development, 1700–1870* (Cheltenham, U.K., 2002).

[10]Max Farrand, ed., *The Records of the Federal Convention of 1787*, 4 vols. (1911; rev. ed., New Haven, 1966), 1:571.

Elbridge Gerry of Massachusetts made similar comments, arguing that it might be "necessary to limit the number of new states admitted."[11]

Similarly, the potential rebels at the Hartford Convention in 1814–15 held significant grievances about the recent admission of western states, without any regard to slavery. They were upset at the development of a western interest that had begun to take power away from the New England states. Indeed, throughout the nineteenth century, tension over western expansion existed on any number of dimensions that pitted not North versus South in a slavery struggle, but a variety of factions and a variety of interests. In contemporary times, it can be seen in the ideological and partisan struggles over representation for Washington, D.C.

But more important than the controversy, statehood was *consequential*. The admission of new states affected American politics in the nineteenth century in a way almost unimaginable today. Consider the period from 1812 to 1821. The United States went from a seventeen-state union to a twenty-four-state union in just nine years. Indeed, the entire nineteenth century experienced this phenomenon on a smaller scale, as on average three or four new states were added to the Union each decade. The effect of this reapportionment on the national government was profound. The mere passing of time altered the balance of power in Congress as much as any election.

So while typical accounts talk about the balance rule in the context of slavery, its basic features have nothing to do with slavery. It can be generally understood as an informal legislative solution to the institutional problem of reapportionment in the national government. If national power is to be redistributed, how can it be done in a way that is amenable to the existing, conflicting interests? One way is to cancel out opposing interests: thus, paired admissions. This raises a question: If we understand the balance rule as an artifact of the statehood process and not as an artifact of the sectional controversy, what role then do slavery and slave-related interests play in the balancing of state admissions?

I would suggest that slavery occupies no special position in statehood politics beyond that of an extremely important interest. Other interest cleavages (economics, taxation and tariffs, and government spending) are visible in state admissions politics. For instance, congressional representatives from western states had a recurring interest in internal improvements in the nineteenth

---

[11] Ibid., 2:2.

century, and in many instances both free and slave western states supported the addition of other western states regardless of the slave status of the new state.

However, one aspect of slavery made it an ideal issue on which to balance state admissions: it was extremely stable as an interest. Free states did not become slave states; after the final abolition of northern slavery in the early nineteenth century, slave states did not become free. So when congressional factions enacted compromise legislation on the admission of new states, slave and antislave interests could be reasonably sure that the new states would remain in their respective coalitions indefinitely. State admission balanced along other policy cleavages—be it partisan affiliation or tariff policy—were much more likely to result in one side getting burned down the road, as the politics of the new state shifted.

## Statehood as a Multistage Process

Most accounts of statehood politics—and in particular the balance rule thesis—focus on state admissions. But often the consequential moments in the statehood process—and thus the proper place to look for political compromise—are not necessarily the final votes in Congress on admission. As Congress recognized early in the nineteenth century, they had the power to shape the political, economic, demographic, and cultural development of the territories and consequently the power to shape the future states. For instance, the homestead bill proposed by the Republican Party during the 1850s was a direct attempt to shape the West: by offering free plots of land limited to 160 acres, the bill would have undoubtedly encouraged small independent farmers to populate the territories, while discouraging slaveholders who needed larger plots of land to profitably operate a plantation.

The statehood process is largely characterized by *path dependence*. Decisions made early on in the process of forming new western states are likely to have large effects downstream and ultimately come to shape the states long before they achieve statehood. This was largely recognized by politicians in the nineteenth century, and gradually the battle over western slavery as a legal construction shifted from an admissions battle to a territorial-creation battle in Congress between 1820 and 1860. The ability to shape the West at points of development before the admission of new states led to the need for legislative compromise earlier in the statehood process.

The Kansas-Nebraska Act of 1854 is an example. Bills had been introduced in 1851 and 1852 in the House for the organization of Nebraska—defined as all the leftover territory of the Louisiana Purchase—but little had come of it. In December 1852, Representative Willard P. Hall (D-Mo.) introduced a bill for the organization of the Platte Territory, reported out of committee by Representative William A. Richardson (D-Ill.) as the Nebraska Territory.[12] It defined Nebraska as present-day Kansas and present-day Nebraska, extended to the Rocky Mountains. The bill passed the House over southern opposition, 98–43, but was defeated in the Senate, as no accommodation to slavery was contained in the provision, and the southerners joined with some breakaway northern Whigs to block what looked to be just another territory north of the Missouri Compromise line.[13]

In December 1853, Senator Augustus C. Dodge (D-Iowa) introduced a new Nebraska bill, this time defining the territory as the entire unorganized residue of the Louisiana Purchase north of 36°30' N.[14] Still going nowhere in the Senate, the bill was entangled once again in sectional animosity, this time open rhetorical warfare over the continuation of the Missouri Compromise. The bill was recommitted to Stephen A. Douglas's Committee on Territories, for adjustments that could hopefully provide satisfactory on the slavery question and finally organize Nebraska.[15]

The goal in committee, for Douglas, was originally to find language that could appease both sections on the question of slavery. His own view was that the tenets of the Compromise of 1850 should prevail—that Congress has no place in assigning slave status to territories, and that each territory, upon its admission to the Union, could decide the question for itself.[16] Whether or not the southerners would accept this trade-off—the explicit repeal of the Missouri Compromise and the glimmer of hope for future slave states in exchange for the hard reality that the Plains was likely to produce six or more free states and zero slave states—was unknown.

Luckily for Douglas, the answer did not matter, because local politics intervened. In the fall of 1853 prospective settlers from Iowa and Missouri had crossed the rivers and organized themselves, the Iowans in Bellevue and the

---

[12] "A Bill to Organize the Territory of Nebraska," H.R. 353, 32d Cong., 2d sess., 1853.

[13] *House Journal*, 32d Cong., 2d sess., Feb. 10, 1853, pp. 272–73; *Senate Journal*, 32d Cong., 2d sess., Mar. 3, 1853, pp. 321–22.

[14] "A Bill to Organize the Territory of Nebraska," S.22, 33rd Cong., 1st sess. 1853.

[15] Julius Morton and Albert Watkins, *History of Nebraska from the Earliest Explorations of the Trans-Mississippi Region*, rev. ed. (Lincoln, 1918), p. 122.

[16] Ibid. p. 125.

Missourians in Wyandotte.[17] There in assembly, they elected "delegates" to Congress from "Nebraska," Hadley Johnson and Rev. Thomas Johnson. Hadley Johnson then spent the remainder of the fall of 1853 traveling Iowa and ascertaining the wishes of various constituents in the western portion of the state as to their desires for Nebraska. The key demand, as it turned out, was for a territory that was exclusively west of Iowa, as much as was possible. Similar sentiments were echoed in Missouri.[18] In January, Johnson traveled to Washington, seeking an audience with the Committee on Territories and Judge Douglas, in the hopes of convincing him that a partition of the Plains into two territories along the fortieth parallel would be the wisest course of action.

Hadley Johnson's plan was met with gushing support in Washington from the Senate delegations of Iowa and Missouri. They quickly arranged for Johnson to address Douglas and the committee on territories with his proposal. It was at this moment that Douglas saw the writing on the wall. Though the South might balk at a symbolic repeal of the Missouri Compromise that actually yielded zero slave states, the prospect of creating a new territory that might actually have an even chance at becoming a slave state would be too much for them to resist. Douglas brought forth a substitute bill, which included both the formation of two territories—Nebraska and Kansas—and the explicit language of popular sovereignty.[19]

At this point, it was all over except for the shouting, which was considerable. The new bill tied together all the pieces necessary for the center to hold: it purposefully undid the Missouri Compromise while specifically endorsing the logic of the Compromise of 1850; it satisfied the local needs of both Iowa and Missouri, guaranteeing it enthusiastic backers from both sides of the Mason-Dixon line; and it united the eastern and western portions of the nation with organized land that would provide an ocean-bound nation, with an economic center in Chicago, completing the work Douglas set out to do a decade earlier.

The bill passed on May 24, 1854, and was signed by the president on May 30.[20] The hindsight of history produces a view of Kansas-Nebraska necessarily seen through the prism of the slave crisis, Bleeding Kansas, the

---

[17] Raymond E. Dale, *History of the State of Nebraska* (Chicago, 1882), p. 174.
[18] Ibid., p. 177.
[19] Morton, *History of Nebraska*, p. 128.
[20] *Stat.* 277 (1854).

Lecompton Constitution, and the Civil War. At the time, however, Douglas and others almost certainly thought they were completing the work of 1850 and securing once again a temporary peace in the slave conflict. The radicals in the North had shouted before; there was little reason to believe this time would be any different.

While this story almost perfectly represents the logic of the balance rule, it contains none of the details of the balance rule: there are no state admissions, there are no Senate seats at stake. The compromise is purely political: there is virtually no organic political community calling for a territory in Kansas—its creation was almost completely the result of political compromise in response to the demands of pluralism: giving each faction what it needs to secure the passage of the legislation. Even more important, in most balance rule discussions, the whole point of the balance rule is to maintain the sectional parity in the U.S. Senate. But the Kansas-Nebraska Act shows that the prizes awarded as part of statehood compromises are often not Senate seats. In this case, the prizes were a balance of potential Senate seats in the form of new territories, as well as the reversal of a public policy, the Missouri Compromise.

And this was true throughout the nineteenth century: the Missouri Compromise itself, often held up as the textbook example of the balance rule, was actually a larger compromise: one side got a slave state, the other side got a free state and a ban on slavery in most of the remaining west. The same was true of the Compromise of 1850. The North got a free state. The South got two territories organized without reference to slavery and a stronger fugitive slave act.

## Statehood as More Than a Congressional Process

It is popular to think about the statehood process as a congressional process. This is not unreasonable. The Constitution gives Congress complete control over the production of new states. Furthermore, members of Congress have always taken a deep interest in the addition of new states to the Union. This is not surprising. It is, after all, their legislative chambers that are altered by the addition of new member states and their coalitional balances that are upset by such alterations. Any change made to the balance of power in Congress has the ability to affect all public policies, as well as the rules of the chambers. Necessarily, each member of Congress will be concerned with the ramifications of new states, as they will have the potential to affect the issues that are most dear to each individual member of Congress.

Nevertheless, there are theoretical reasons to suspect that western political leaders, both in political communities that exist on unorganized land and in the existing territories, would have just as much, if not more, interest in the institutional change of the western land as the members of Congress. First, the creation of new states alters not just the composition of the central government, but also the actual arrangements of governance in the individual territory or new state. To create a territory or a state is to fundamentally rearrange the institutions of governance in the provincial region: powers that were formerly held by the central government are granted to the territory or state, and the locus of decision-making power over public policy moves accordingly. For western political leaders *not* to take an interest in the politics of state formation would indeed be a strange observation.

Second, information about the West was asymmetric in the nineteenth century. Those who lived in the unorganized lands and territories of the United States were in a better position to understand and judge the realities of life in the developing areas. Members of Congress may have had specific positions, and even objectives, regarding the construction of new states, but their knowledge of the West was severely limited from their vantage point in Washington, D.C. Thus, when it came time to make the crucial decisions about western state construction—particularly issues of boundaries—they were almost completely reliant on the westerners themselves to make sensible decisions on the details of the issues of territorial division and final state boundaries, details that had long-lasting impacts for the development of the western political institutions as a whole.

Third, from the very early days of the Union, it became custom—if not law—that states would not be admitted to the Union against their will. This gave the citizens of western lands—and their leaders—something of a veto over institutional changes to the developing states. Particularly as admission approached, the ability of the westerners to reject statehood gave them leverage in decisions over the final size and boundaries of their new states. This was particularly clear in the cases of Iowa and New Mexico, each of whose territorial citizens rejected statehood plans produced in Congress that would have either reduced (in Iowa) or enlarged (in New Mexico) the size of the state.

As it affects the balance rule thesis, all this is most clear in the admission of Minnesota and the nonadmission of Kansas, in 1857. Minnesota, obviously destined to become a free state, was winding its way toward admission in 1856 and 1857. After moving through constitutional convention, the votes in Congress on final admission (originally scheduled in bill S. 86) were delayed in the months of January and February, 1858. Southern senators were worried about Kansas's admission to the Union (scheduled in bill S. 161) as a slave state, and thus delayed the admission of Minnesota.[21]

In early March an attempt was made by Senator James S. Green (D-Mo.), chairman of the Committee on Territories, to explicitly link the two bills into one, but the amendment failed. After much heated debate, and attempts by Senator Douglas to defeat the measure, the Senate voted to admit Kansas, with the proslavery Lecompton Constitution, on March 23, 1858, by a vote of 33 to 25.[22] The admission, however, was held up in the House, where antislavery forces had control of the chamber, newly named Douglas Democrats joining with Republicans to block the bill.

Meanwhile, Minnesota statehood was moving forward. Having passed the Lecompton admission of Kansas, the Senate voted 49–7 to admit Minnesota on April 7.[23] In the House, a compromise was reached, acceptable enough to pass, on Kansas. The so-called English Bill, admitting Kansas to the Union upon reratification of the Lecompton Constitution, passed the House on April 30 on a party line vote, 112–103, the compromise being enough to draw the northern Democrats back into the fold and support Kansas.[24] Minnesota statehood passed the House on May 11, 157–39, with the main opposition coming from Republicans and American Party members.[25]

Taking stock of what transpired in the spring of 1858, there was either a major miscalculation, or a major reassessment of strategy, by the Democrats. They had effectively admitted another free state, bringing the current ratio of free to slave states to 17:15, on nothing more than the hopes that the people of Kansas could be bought off by the Lecompton Constitution. All signs indicated that this was not going to be the case. Robert S. Stevens, writing to territorial governor James W. Denver in Kansas, thought the English

---

[21]Jonathan Kasparek, "The State of Minnesota," in *The Uniting States*, ed. Benjamin F. Shearer (Westport, Conn., 2004), p. 639.
[22]*Senate Journal*, 35th Cong., 1st sess., Mar. 23, 1858, p. 280.
[23]Kasparek, "State of Minnesota," p. 639.
[24]*House Journal*, 35th Cong., 1st sess., Apr. 30, 1858, pp. 719–20.
[25]*House Journal*, 35th Cong., 1st sess., May 11, 1858, pp. 777–78.

Bill was unimaginably naive on the part of the southerners. "To my mind it is a most foolish plan; as it in fact submits the Lecompton Const. back to the people of Kansas for their acceptance with Slavery; and can it be possible they will take it! My opinion is they will not."[26]

And they did not. Kansas rejected the Lecompton Constitution—and, in effect, slavery—by a vote of 11,300 to 1,788 in the referendum held in August 1858. This did not put them in the Union as a slave state, instead it sent them back to the drawing board for another Constitutional Convention, one that would not see the completion of statehood until after the secession crisis began in 1861. But it did seal the door on the last plausible slave state.[27]

## Contestation over the Statehood Process Itself

The admission of new states to the Union is a process largely governed by a single sentence in the Constitution. Article IV, section 3, clause 1, states, "New States may be admitted by the Congress into this Union."[28] As a structural matter, there are three important features of constitutional statehood. The first feature is irreversibility; unlike most things in the Constitution, the addition of states is not a process that can be undone. This, perhaps, makes statehood unique among Constitutional actions. The second feature of the statehood clause is a surprisingly low threshold for the admission of new states. As noted above, the statehood clause is irreversible when applied and results in a fundamental altering of the political system. Yet the creation of a state is subject only to the same approval mechanism as a federal law: a bare majority in both Houses and the signature of the president.

The third feature of the statehood clause is that it gives Congress extraordinarily wide discretion. It gives almost no guidelines as to how expansion should happen; it directs only that Congress shall be responsible for it. This made the constitutional statehood process the most radical of all plans pro-

---

[26]Robert S. Stevens to Honorable J. W. Denver, May 14, 1858, Robert Wadleigh Smith Stevens Papers, 1856–75, Kansas State Historical Society.

[27]Grupo de Investigadores Puertorriquenōs, *Breakthrough from Colonialism*, p. 481.

[28]There are a few restrictions on the power of Congress to create new states: they cannot be formed within the boundaries of existing states, nor can they be formed by the junction of two or more states or parts of states without the consent of the state legislatures involved. Additionally, one jurisdiction—a future seat of government for the central government—is given special constitutional status.

posed in the 1780s for national expansion. All other plans provided Congress with specific instructions for either the sizing of new states or the factors that would lead to admission, usually a population threshold.

As the political battles over individual instances of territorial development and state admissions intensified during the nineteenth century, a significant number of political actors—hardened by over fifty years of disputes—tried to reform the rules of the game itself. Virtually all attempts made to alter the statehood process shared the same goal: depoliticize the process by removing congressional discretion over the timing and nature of admissions. During the 1850s a number of major legislative efforts were made to revise the statehood process and depoliticize the timing of admissions. Some bills, such as the Douglas plan of the Thirty-Sixth Congress, were introduced that specified the specific size of future states. Others, such as the Haskin plan, set exact population requirements for admission, completely removing final votes on admission.

The most famous bill of the Thirty-Sixth Congress—the Crittenden compromise—was not just a plan for a constitutional compromise on slavery but also a complete restructuring of the constitutional statehood process. In December 1860 two joint resolutions were brought before the Senate. The first and more famous was put forth by Senator John J. Crittenden of Kentucky, and later became known (after a few modifications) as the Crittenden compromise. The second joint resolution was put forth by Senator Stephen Douglas of Illinois. These resolutions are historically famous because of their main intent—they both attempt to alter the Constitution in such a way as to defuse the secession crisis that was brewing throughout the South in the wake of Lincoln's election and that had come to fruition in South Carolina on December 20.

What is often overlooked about both these resolutions is that they go into extraordinary detail about another change they both would make—a change to the fundamental mechanism of adding states to the Union—Article IV, section 3 of the Constitution. As it is written, Article IV, section 3, reads,

> New States may be admitted by the Congress into this Union; but no new State shall be formed or erected within the Jurisdiction of any other State; nor any State be formed by the Junction of two or more States, or Parts of States, without the Consent of the Legislatures of the States concerned as well as of the Congress.

> The Congress shall have Power to dispose of and make all needful Rules and Regulations respecting the Territory or other Property belonging to the United States; and nothing in this Constitution shall be so construed as to Prejudice any Claims of the United States, or of any particular State.

Crittenden's proposal would have added the following relevant text:

> When any Territory, north or south of said line, within such boundaries as Congress may prescribe, shall contain the population requisite for a member of Congress, according to the federal ratio of representation of the people of the United States, it shall, if its form of government be republican, be admitted into the Union on an equal footing with the original States.[29]

Douglas's proposal would have added the following relevant text:

> When such new States shall contain the requisite population for a member of Congress, according to the then federal ratio of representation, it shall be admitted into the Union on an equal footing with the original States. . . . No more territory shall be acquired by the United States, except by treaty, or by the concurrent vote of two thirds of each house of Congress; and, when so acquired, the status thereof in respect to servitude, as it existed at the time of acquisition, shall remain unchanged until it shall contain the population aforesaid for the formation of new States, when it shall be subject to the terms, conditions, and privileges herein provided for the existing Territories. . . . The area of all new States shall be as nearly uniform in size as may be practicable, having due regard to convenient boundaries and natural capacities, and shall not be less than sixty nor more than eighty thousand square miles, except in case of islands, which may contain less than that amount.[30]

All these plans had one thing in common: they sought to define a specific process for the production of new states, and place it beyond the reach of day-to-day politics. Experience had taught many in Congress that statehood was too important, and too controversial, a topic to be safely left in the hands of the legislature, because political opportunism too easily replaced objective decision making.

---

[29] Joint Resolution Proposing Certain Amendments to the Constitution, S.R. 50, 36th Cong., 2d sess. (1860).
[30] Ibid.

## Back to Oregon

The admission of Oregon to the Union in 1859 does not fit well with the traditional balance-rule logic of the antebellum era: no southern state was paired for admission with Oregon, the voting did not go along sectional lines, and the southern Democrats—not the Republican Party—provided the decisive votes for admission.

In reality, the admission of Oregon is somewhat less puzzling. Although it was to be a free state, Oregon was also strongly Democratic in party affiliation and thus was able to capture enough votes from southern Democrats that, combined with virtually every northern Democratic vote, it could be brought into the Union, not as a free state but as a Democratic state. In effect, northern Democrats got the best of both worlds—a new free state that was Democratic in character. More interesting, however, is the trade-off made by the southern Democrats—accepting a free state in exchange for partisan control of it—and the Republicans—attempting to block a free state simply because they would not have partisan control of it. What explains this behavior?

After the admission of Minnesota and the failure of Lecompton, new slave states were essentially dead. No state had been brought into the Union with slavery since Florida in 1846, and all attempts to bring a proslave Kansas into the Union had failed. Thus, when Oregon came up for a vote in 1859, the entire playing field of the admissions compromise game had been changed. The southern Democrats had lost in Congress. They would never again have anything close to a majority in the House of Representatives; they were also two states behind in the Senate, with no slave states on the horizon and at least one free state, Oregon, awaiting admission.

Thus, the decision to push for the admission of Oregon by the southern Democrats was not a decision related to the balance of power in the Senate at all; that had been lost, irrevocably, as far as slavery was concerned. Instead, after Lecompton and *Dred Scott*, the southern Democrats shifted their attention away from the legislature and toward the executive. The real prize being competed for in the spring of 1859 was not the balance of power in the Senate between free and slave states but victory in the 1860 election and, as a secondary matter, partisan control of the Senate.

As David Potter has shown, the heart of southern paranoia in the late 1850s was not the crumbling of legislative power in the federal Congress and the legislating of the abolishment of slavery, although that was a concern. The more immediate fear was that Republican control of the federal bureaucracy —particularly the end of censored mail and the placement of Republican federal officials in the South—could lead to either the rise of an abolitionist element in the South or, worse, a massive slave revolt.[31]

And thus the push for Oregon from the southern Democrats, and the attempt by Republicans to block Oregon statehood, are best understood in the context of the 1860 election, and the three (or possibly four) electoral votes that Oregon would carry. The events of 1856–58—the relative success of the Fremont candidacy in the north, the failure of the Lecompton Constitution and the rise of the Douglas Democrats, the *Dred Scott* decision, and the Lincoln-Douglas campaign—had put everyone on notice that 1860 was going to be a showdown between the forces of slavery and antislavery. Three partisan electoral votes were important enough that the balance of slave power in the Senate was a secondary concern to the parties involved.

The result, while perhaps a bit surprising, does reflect the wider understanding of the balance rule as an example of legislative bargaining over the admissions of states in a pluralistic legislature. And taking this wider view in general—one in which slavery is not the only issue, the balance of power in the Senate not the only concern, the admissions vote not the only point of conflict, and Congress not the only actor—allows us to more clearly examine the congressional politics of statehood and slavery in the 1850s.

---

[31] Potter, *Impending Crisis*, p. 452.

Amy S. Greenberg

# Manifest Destiny's Hangover

*Congress Confronts Territorial Expansion and Martial Masculinity in the 1850s*

How much land is too much land? In the course of a short but devastating war in the late 1840s, Mexico lost about half her territory to the United States. One might imagine that the Mexican Cession, over half a million square miles of land, would satisfy Americans and would satiate the seemingly unquenchable expansionist desire that had governed American international relations since at least the 1830s. How after dismembering Mexico in 1848, and becoming a continental nation, could anyone expect, demand even, that the United States grow yet larger? This seems like a particularly good question given the explosive power of those newly acquired territories, and the issue of slavery in them, to tear the nation in two.

The fact that the territorial growth of the United States was more or less complete in 1848 (with the exception of Alaska and Hawaii) had led most historians to accept what appears to be obvious, that the ideology of Manifest Destiny, the belief that God has singled out the United States to continue growing, spreading her superior social, economic, and political forms to less fortunate peoples in the Western Hemisphere, was fulfilled in 1848 with the Mexican Cession. But such a view is incorrect. Just because the United States failed to gain much more territory in the 1850s, and territorial expansion was the number one factor exacerbating the sectional crisis, does not mean Americans did not try, very hard, to gain more land in the 1850s. Many Americans were as passionate in the 1850s as they had ever been to gain more lands. They believed that America's Manifest Destiny was yet to be fulfilled, and they envisioned the United States not as a continental nation but a hemispheric one, spreading from an annexed Canada in the North, to an annexed Central America and Caribbean, and possibly even an annexed South America. As Texas senator Sam Houston proudly proclaimed in 1848, "the people whom God has placed here in this land," must "spread, prevail and pervade throughout the whole rich empire of this great hemisphere."[1] Senator Stephen Russell Mallory, Democrat of Florida, asserted in 1859 that it was "no more possible for this country to pause in its career than it is for the free and untrammeled eagle to cease to soar," and that "at our present rate of progress this vast continent, every inch of it, must soon be ours."[2]

Nor would the continents themselves limit the spread of the United States. When rumor reached Congress in 1852 that Kamehameha III, king of independent Hawaii, had approached a U.S. diplomat about forming a tighter alliance with the United States, the Senate twice requested information from President Millard Fillmore and twice the Senate was denied. In response, California Democrat Joseph McCorkle demanded the immediate annexation of the islands in an inflammatory congressional speech in August 1852. The following year, after more rumors, congressmen again spoke in favor of annexing the islands.[3]

Why this lust for territory? There were cultural factors at work in the 1850s that drove this ongoing and destructive impulse to ever expand the territorial boundaries of the United States. As economic changes led to increasing economic inequality, as Irish immigrants poured into the country in the potato famine years, as middle-class women began, through the Woman's Rights movement and the emerging ideology known as domesticity, to assert their authority both within and outside the home, norms and practices of manhood in American shifted in response, ultimately coalescing into two competing ideals of white masculinity. Two visions of proper manhood, restrained and martial, battled for supremacy during this period, competing, in part, over how large the nation should be, and what the right way was to go about gaining new territories.[4]

---

[1] "The Great War Meeting," *New York Herald*, Jan. 30, 1848.
[2] *Congressional Globe*, 35th Cong., 2d sess., 1859, p. 1331.
[3] Sylvester Stevens, *American Expansion in Hawaii, 1842–1898* (Harrisburg, Pa., 1945), pp. 43–45; *Congressional Globe*, 32d Cong., 1st sess., 1852, app., p. 1081; Ralph S. Kuykendall, *The Hawaiian Kingdom*, vol. 1, *1778–1854: Foundation and Transformation* (Honolulu, 1957), pp. 409–10.
[4] For a fuller explanation of these economic and social changes and their relation to gender and foreign policy, see Amy S. Greenberg, *Manifest Manhood and the Antebellum American Empire* (New York, 2005), esp. pp. 1–17.

Restrained men, who understood their virtue as men in terms of their business success, family life, and Christian behavior, argued that the United States was plenty large enough and should expand its reach around the globe through commercial treaties and missionary activities. Martial men, on the other hand, largely understood their virtue as men through their ability to dominate others. They were empowered by the lesson of the U.S.-Mexico War, that Americans had the right to take, through force, what should rightfully be theirs. If the inferior peoples of Latin America would not sell their lands to us, then we should take them. It was because of this belief that the post–Mexican War years saw a rash of mercenary activities by American men operating without governmental sanction, men who, at the time, were known as filibusters. Filibusters repeatedly and unsuccessfully targeted Mexico, Central America, and Cuba in the 1850s, and their actions, however illegal, and in our eyes immoral, were upheld by martial men as right and just. Ultimately, although the martial men lost out, in that they managed to annex almost none of the lands they desperately wanted, their vision of violence as a solution to conflict won the day when sectional differences exploded into civil war in 1861. In other words, martial manhood was ascendant during the 1850s, and one issue it thrived on was territorial expansion.

These two visions of manhood, and of America's place in the world, were not held and espoused only by marginal characters; they are clearly evident in virtually every national debate over expansionism from the 1850s, expressed clearly and with conviction by members of Congress. Democratic senator Henry S. Foote of Mississippi, for example, took an extreme martial position when he argued in 1848 in favor of taking all of Mexico as spoils of war. He compared the occupying American army in Mexico to the "children of Israel," who "under the direction of Jehovah himself, acquired what was deemed a good and valid title to all the territory included in the promised land, by force of arms alone." By virtue of our strength we had won the right to take as much of Mexico as we could grasp.[5] Whig congressman Alexander Stephens of Georgia expressed the restrained position when he condemned the U.S.-Mexico war as the self-indulgent exercise of antiquated forms of aggression. He declared the war to be "*downward* progress. It is a progress of party—of excitement—of lust of power—a spirit of war—aggression—violence and licentiousness. It is a progress which, if indulged

---

[5]"The Great War Meeting," *New York Herald,* Jan. 30, 1848.

in, would soon sweep over all law, all order, and the Constitution itself." Note that Stephens was right when he predicted that this "spirit of war" and "aggression" would ultimately "sweep over all law, all order, and the Constitution itself." But Stephens would hardly be an objective bystander when that day came. He was the vice president of the Confederacy.[6]

In sum, martial men argued that America, and American men, proved that they were great by physically dominating others, as the United States had dominated Mexico. Restrained men argued that the United States and American men proved that they were great by restraining their violent impulses, focusing on business (or commercial growth) and setting an example of Christian forbearance for others to emulate. Lust for new territory did not dissipate, because it served so many purposes for so many Americans. It provided the Democratic Party with a platform that they believed could hold their fracturing coalition together, it offered the possibilities of new lands to working men and their allies who were being marginalized in the industrializing economy, and it stroked the egos of Americans who understood their worth and power in terms of their ability to dominate others.

Territorial expansionism was appealing but dangerous, a fact that congressmen recognized at the time. Proexpansionists, and even some antiexpansionists understood that their positions could very well lead to civil war. Congressmen knew how poisonous the issue of territorial growth was during the 1850s, particularly after the Kansas-Nebraska Act of 1854. The act opened up Kansas to slavery, overturning the Missouri Compromise of 1820 and provoking intense wrath among northerners. Congressional debates over new territories frequently devolved into threats of secession after the passage of this act. But some congressmen, and their constituents, found territorial acquisition too addictive to lay aside, regardless of the consequences.

This chapter will consider congressional responses to three of the most significant expansionist episodes of the 1850s, the period of Manifest Destiny's hangover, in order to explore how Congress dealt with the twin problems of territorial expansion and the rise of martial manhood. This essay will first examine the controversy that led to the Gadsden Purchase of 1853–1854 and resulted in the only addition of new territory during the decade. It will then move into the Caribbean and consider the many attempts to gain

---

[6] *Congressional Globe*, 29th Cong., 1st sess., 1847, app., pp. 949–50 (emphasis in original).

FIG. 1. This 1856 map presents the post–Gadsden Purchase United States, with "the comparative area of the free and slave states," featuring Kansas in white. *Courtesy Library of Congress, Prints and Photographs Division.*

Cuba over the course of the decade, and then shift to Central America, in order to explore the congressional debate in 1857 over William Walker, the most famous of the filibusters and one-time president and dictator of Nicaragua. This organization, while not precisely chronological, has the virtue of exploring increasingly violent methods of territorial acquisition, from a legal treaty, to negotiation backed up with a clear threat of violence, and finally outright filibustering or piracy. Despite the obvious problems with further territorial growth in the 1850s, many in Congress were still passionately devoted to the continued growth of the United States, even through force of arms. As a result, territorial expansionism was central to the crisis of the 1850s.

## The Gadsden Purchase

The Treaty of Guadalupe Hidalgo transferred just over half of Mexico's territory to the United States at the close of the war in 1848. Mexico lost her provinces of Alta California, Nuevo Mexico, and parts of Tamaulipas, Coahuila, and Sonora. This territory would become the American states of California, Nevada, Utah, Texas, and parts of Arizona, New Mexico, and Colorado. But the present-day border between the two countries was not finalized until December 1853, when the Gadsden Purchase added an extra 45,535 square miles to the American Southwest, below the Gila River. The Gadsden Purchase was the final solution to problems that emerged out of a failed attempt to map the boundary between the United States and Mexico. Article V of the Treaty of Guadalupe Hidalgo specified that a joint commission of American and Mexican surveyors should meet in San Diego by February 1849 to mark the boundary to the mouth of the Río Bravo del Norte.[7] The commissioners and surveyors were given the power within the treaty to resolve any differences of opinion on the boundary line. Their agreements were to have the force of treaty. But in the uncharted territory of the Southwest things quickly went awry.

After three-and-a-half years of work the boundary commission was disbanded—Congress having rejected the results of the survey, the Bartlett-Conde agreement, as too favorable to Mexico. The results of the commission were repudiated by Congress; the American director of the commission, John Bartlett, was publicly humiliated; and the resulting conflicts resolved through President Franklin Pierce's (and his representative James Gadsden's) brazen intimidation of Mexico into giving up yet more territory with the Gadsden Treaty. The failure of the U.S.-Mexico boundary commission, one of America's first politically sanctioned cross-cultural efforts, was one of the key events in the history of antebellum expansionism. It also greatly exacerbated sectional tensions by highlighting the avarice of southern expansionists hungry for a workable route for a southern transcontinental railroad.[8]

The Mexican commissioner of the boundary survey was General Pedro García Conde, a former military commander of Chihuahua. As boundary

---

[7]"Treaty of Peace, Friendship, Limits, and Settlement, signed at Guadalupe Hidalgo February 2, 1848," Charles I. Bevans, *Treaties and Other International Agreements of the United States of America, 1776–1949,* 13 vols. (Washington, D.C., 1968–76), 9:791–806.

[8]"Treaty of Boundaries, signed at Mexico December 30, 1853," Bevans, *Treaties,* 9:812–16; Deborah Carley Emory, "Running the Line: Men, Maps, Science, and Art of the United States and Mexico Boundary Survey, 1849–1856," *New Mexico Historical Review* 75 (2000):250.

commissioner, García Conde was a superb advocate for Mexican interests, but they were Mexico's interests broadly understood. *Fronterizos,* or residents of the territory in question, many of whom opposed the Treaty of Guadalupe Hidalgo and wanted to continue fighting the United States, were understandably wary of the entire boundary commission.[9]

García Conde's U.S. counterpart and partner in the survey was John Russell Bartlett, a Rhode Island Whig appointed by President Fillmore, who also was a notable scholar of American Indian ethnology. He spent millions of the government's dollars on meandering travels through the region, studying the flora, fauna, people, and land of the new American possessions. Unlike the politically savvy García Conde, Bartlett entered the job with neither surveying nor diplomatic experience. His nepotistic appointments produced a remarkably unqualified and sometimes corrupt body of officers. Many of the problems that plagued the boundary survey during his tenure were outside his control, such as the political squabbling in Washington that held up commission funds, and the difficulty of travel through the deserts and mountains of the region, but other problems were of his own making. The dearth of supplies and their expense was partially due to the simultaneous beginnings of gold fever, but the ineptitude (some said outright corruption) of his brother, appointed to handle those supplies, exacerbated the situation. Difficulties with the Apaches, who had terrorized Mexican residents of the region for decades, were probably inevitable, but in refusing to share alcohol with the tribes, the teetotaler Bartlett helped alienate potential allies. Violence and drunkenness among soldiers is traditionally common, but Bartlett had no clear plan as to how to control and discipline troublemakers, and certainly the number of murders perpetrated against and *by* his soldiers was unusually high. A more experienced traveler would have known to pack enough water to make it through the desert without losing the majority of his livestock. Perhaps a better diplomat would have understood the implications of the fact that the Treaty of Guadalupe Hidalgo was based on an inaccurate map of

---

[9]Joseph Werne, "Pedro García Conde: El trazado de límites con Estados Unidos desde el punto de vista mexicano (1848–1853)," *Historia mexicana* 36 (1986):113–29; Oscar Martínez, ed., *U.S.-Mexico Borderlands: Historical and Contemporary Perspectives* (Wilmington, Del., 1996), p. 18; José Salazar Ylarregui, *Datos de los trabajos astronómicos y topográficos despuestos en forma de diario* (Mexico City, 1850), pp. 8–12. The significance of García Conde's allegiances became clear early on, when he attempted to trade land south of the Gila River for land on the Pacific Coast, essentially selling out the Southwest in the interests of gaining the port of San Diego. William H. Goetzmann, *Army Exploration in the American West, 1803–1863* (New Haven, Conn., 1959), pp. 162–63.

Mexico, one that located a boundary 35 miles north and 175 miles east of its stated location.

When Bartlett and García Conde agreed, in 1852, to split the difference between two radically different views of where the southern boundary of Arizona should be placed, opposition in Congress was immediate and violent. On the eve of an administration and party change, the fact that an antislavery Whig appointee, from Rhode Island no less, might compromise with Mexico over the question of southern territory was too much for Democrats, especially southern Democrats, to bear.[10] Newly elected New Hampshire Democrat Franklin Pierce had run and won on a platform that made territorial expansionism an explicit goal. His administration would "not be controlled by any timid forebodings of evil from expansion," he stated in his inaugural address.[11]

Congressional opposition to Bartlett's treaty revolved around his "unmanly" willingness to compromise with a Mexican. Some in Congress suggested that Bartlett, the political neophyte, had been duped by the "shrewd" García Conde, an insult made all the more painful given the low regard in which many Americans held Mexican men. V. E. Howard, Democrat of Texas, claimed that Bartlett had "allowed the Mexican Commissioner to inveigle them into giving up miles of latitude." While California senator John B. Weller fumed that "the Mexican Commissioner, a very shrewd and intelligent man, who, from a residence of some years in that section of country, was intimately acquainted with all the localities, unquestionably obtained a decided advantage in this settlement."[12]

---

[10] As William Goetzmann has put it, "The Whigs were thus easily labeled the party of the great land give-away and an obstacle in the path of Manifest Destiny." Goetzmann, *Army Exploration*, pp. 188–93. See also Joseph Richard Werne, "Partisan Politics and the Mexican Boundary Survey, 1848–1853," *Southwestern Historical Quarterly* 90 (1987):329–46; John Duncan Haskell, Jr., "John Russell Bartlett (1805–1886): Bookman," Ph.D. diss., George Washington University, 1977, pp. 138–40; Odie Faulk, *Too Far North . . . Too Far South* (Los Angeles, 1967), pp. 39, 58, 74; Emory, "Running the Line."

[11] Robert E. May, *The Southern Dream of a Caribbean Empire* (Baton Rouge, 1973), pp. 46–76.

[12] Weller was actually appointed commissioner before Bartlett and had an ax to grind with the Whigs who replaced him. *Congressional Globe*, 32d Cong., 1st sess., app., pp. 25, 776, 801; on the view that Bartlett had "cowered before the Mexicans," see John Mack Faragher, "North, South, and West: Sectional Controversies and the U.S.-Mexico Boundary Survey," in *Drawing the Borderline: Artist-Explorers of the U.S.-Mexico Boundary Survey*, ed. Dawn Hall (Albuquerque, 1996), p. 10. Historians, however, have agreed that Bartlett and García Conde's compromise position was exactly what the treaty makers of both countries intended. It was a good compromise in keeping with the spirit and law of the treaty. It is also worth noting that Mexicans, especially fronterizos, were also outraged by the compromise, believing it too generous to the United States. Goetzmann, *Army Exploration*, pp. 188–93; Humberto Escoto Ochoa, *Integración y desintegración de nuestra frontera norte* (Mexico, 1949), p. 126; Faulk, *Too Far North*, p. 63.

Bartlett was replaced on the commission with a southern military man, William Emory, whose actions while directing the post-Bartlett boundary survey suggest that he was committed to a southern expansionist position and was willing to adjust his professional opinion in order to support the desires of congressional expansionists who were desperate for a workable southern transcontinental railroad route. Unfortunately, the best possible route ran through land that still belonged to Mexico. The result was the Gadsden Purchase treaty, offering $10 million for the Mesilla Valley of Mexico, which was secretly negotiated by President Pierce's representative. It was presented to Congress at the end of 1853 with no supporting documentation, leading to rumors that Mexico had been threatened into signing it.[13]

The Mexico bill, as it was called, was debated in Congress in the summer of 1854, at the same time as the Kansas-Nebraska bill and a bill to acquire Cuba. In the view of northern critics, already upset over Kansas, the Gadsden Purchase was a prime example of the southern slave power attempting to corrupt the political process to its own end. Support and opposition to this bill crossed party lines, but both sides found common currency in a critique of the manhood of their opponents.

Rufus Wheeler Peckham, Democrat of New York, began his critique of the Gadsden Purchase by explicitly referring to the Nebraska bill. "Insomuch as Nebraska has been introduced into this discussion, I will take that route to this Mexican territory proposed to be ceded, and stop a moment there on the way down." Much as opponents of Bartlett's compromise a year earlier had framed their critique around his unmanly character, Peckham questioned whether President Pierce could be trusted in matters of treaty making. Pierce was "the very man to be easily imposed upon; the very man to be misled, bewildered and deceived." The president's failure to provide any supporting explanation of the manner in which the treaty was negotiated also rankled. "There was dignity and self-respect, there was manhood, though there was error, in the old Federal position that denied the right of the House to any information beyond the treaty. The evasive excuse presented here for the non-production of these papers I will not characterize."[14]

---

[13]In point of fact the official commissioner as of May 1853 was General Robert Blair Campbell of Alabama, but it was Emory "who for all practical purposes directed the entire survey." Goetzmann, *Army Exploration,* pp. 194, 129; Deborah Carley Emory, "Running the Line," pp. 235–36; Oscar Martínez, "Surveying and Marking the U.S.-Mexico Boundary: The Mexican Perspective," in Hall, *Drawing the Borderline,* p. 18.

[14]*Congressional Globe,* 33d Cong., 1st sess., 1854, pp. 1028–31.

New York Free-Soiler Gerrit Smith also rejected the treaty, although he claimed that "the more land we get from Mexico (by righteous means) the better. I would, that the treaty gave us whole provinces; yes, and even all Mexico." Indeed, as long as annexation did not involve violence or the threat of violence, Smith was in favor of "the annexation to us of every other part of North America," particularly Canada. What bothered Smith was the underlying assumption of the treaty that the United States had a *right* to the land. He warned that while the Monroe Doctrine "gratifies our conceit of our courage and power, . . . [w]e are already acting on . . . the maxim, that might makes right." Our nation was "self-deceived" by her pride, and pride was leading us to dangerous places.

For Smith, it was better to embrace a restrained Christian model of manhood. "Liberty—precious boon of Heaven—is meek and reasonable," he claimed, but "the merits of true liberty," "will be known to all, who bow themselves, gratefully and lovingly, to her claims." As for his opponents, Smith had only the harshest words: "Oh, how slow are men to emerge from the brutehood, into which their passions and their false education have sunk them! I say brutehood; for rage and violence and war belong to it, while love and gentleness and peace are the adornments of true manhood." Just in case others did not understand the implications of the struggle at hand, Smith made clear that he would be fine with the South seceding. "It is not for this nation to deny the right either of annexation or secession," he said pointedly. The same brutish actions that would lead people to grab territory would also lead them to violence and war. If they wanted to secede, let them.[15]

Gadsden supporters were ready with a gender critique of their own. Thomas Stanley Bocock, Democrat of Virginia, was a passionate supporter of the Gadsden Treaty, which regained for the United States lands that he accused "Mr. Bartlett" of "surrendering." Opponents of the treaty were only "smarting under a fancied wrong in the passage of the Nebraska bill, which the Administration was said to favor, they have taken this as the first proffered occasion, perhaps, of wreaking upon it their collected and envenomed wrath." If they really wanted to prevent violence they would support the Gadsden Treaty, he argued, because Americans would stop filibustering in the area once it belonged to the United States (suggesting, in effect, that the best way to prevent theft was to give the thief a present). "I wish to pre-

---

[15]Ibid., pp. 1016–17.

serve the Constitution from the danger of violence, induced by the temptation which exists to have a shorter route to our Pacific States," he claimed.

Indeed, to Bocock, Gadsden opponents were nothing less than hypocrites, complaining about legitimate treaties that actually prevented violence. "We might have pursued a different course. Relying on our superior strength, we might have taken from Mexico whatever we wished, and whipped her into quiet if she complained. Would that policy have pleased gentlemen better?" Bocock made it clear that he had no problem with "whipping" Mexico into submission, unlike his opponents. Bocock also saw the threat of civil war lurking behind the treaty negotiations but suggested it would be the anti-Gadsden forces who might precipitate war. If "these gentlemen who oppose" the treaty, he warned, "should succeed in their aims," then "all the wild isms that can be conceived of" (a few in his long list: Free-Soilers, the Liberty Party, the abolitionists, the Woman's Rights' men, the Fourierites) "would burst forth in all their fury, and . . . shake the earth with their strife. . . . All order, authority, and virtue would lie crushed beneath the feet of contending factions, when to rise again!" Unable to keep their women, among others, in line, these weak anti-expansionists would allow anarchy to erupt, which would lead to civil war.[16]

Note that what both Gerrit Smith and Bocock were discussing was a legally negotiated treaty. Yet even this most benign version of territorial expansion raised the specter of civil war, framed in competing gender critiques. Other proposed annexations were far less benign, and provoked even harsher responses.

## Cuba

The status of Cuba was a matter of national concern and repeated congressional discussion throughout the decade. The strategic location, fertility, and wealth (in sugar and slaves) of Cuba made it a natural target for filibusters. Venezuela-born Narciso López gained international attention as he repeatedly tried to liberate the island from Spain in the late 1840s and early 1850s. With the help of a wide variety of American supporters from New York to Natchez and followed by an American volunteer army, López seemed unstoppable, until he and fifty-one American volunteers were captured in Cuba

---

[16]Ibid., pp. 1049–50.

and put to death in the summer of 1851. This hardly dampened American ardor for the Queen of the Antilles, even for some Whigs.[17] Massachusetts Whig Edward Everett, secretary of state under Millard Fillmore starting in 1852, left the question of Cuba's destiny tantalizingly open. Everett asserted that the final destiny of Cuba was an American question, one that Europe had no voice in, and that the eventual annexation of the island "might be almost essential to our safety."[18] Not surprisingly then, filibusters kept their sights on the island.

Among the most prominent of the mid-century would-be filibusters was John Quitman, former governor of Mississippi. It was well known in the South, as well as in Washington, that Quitman was eager to invade Cuba in 1854. Quitman believed that Pierce and his secretary of war, Jefferson Davis, were so keen to take Cuba that they would not prosecute him for violating America's neutrality laws. One southerner actually brought a bill to the floor of the Senate to repeal the neutrality laws that banned filibustering in order to facilitate Quitman's trip, although the bill failed. Quitman was ready to go when the Pierce administration stopped the filibuster, in part, perhaps, because Pierce believed that his diplomats in Europe could gain the island through more peaceful means. The public leak of the result of their "diplomacy," the Ostend Manifesto, was, to say the least, not what Pierce was hoping for.[19]

The Ostend Manifesto was a document drawn up by three of Pierce's European diplomats in 1854, after the minister to Spain, Pierre Soulé of Louisiana, bungled negotiations over the sale of the island. Soulé, along with the minister to Great Britain, James Buchanan, and the minister to France, John Mason, declared in the manifesto that the United States should forcibly take Cuba if Spain refused to sell it. "We shall be justified in wresting it from Spain if we possess the power," the manifesto stated. The outcry against a document that seemed to license outright robbery was overwhelming, and the secretary of state was forced to repudiate it.[20] Not before it was

---

[17] Robert E. May, *Manifest Destiny's Underworld: Filibustering in Antebellum America* (Chapel Hill, 2002), pp. 22–23, 33–35.

[18] Peter H. Smith, *Talons of the Eagle: Dynamics of U.S.-Latin American Relations* (New York, 2000), p. 24.

[19] May, *Southern Dream*, pp. 46–76.

[20] Smith, *Talons of the Eagle*, pp. 24–25; Soulé's limitations as a diplomat are suggested by the fact that while in Spain he fought a duel with the French ambassador over the issue of Mrs. Soulé's "immodest" dress. Janet L. Coryell, "Duty with Delicacy: Anna Ella Carroll of Maryland," in *Women and American Foreign Policy: Lobbyists, Critics, and Insiders*, ed. Edward P. Crapol (New York, 1987), p. 49.

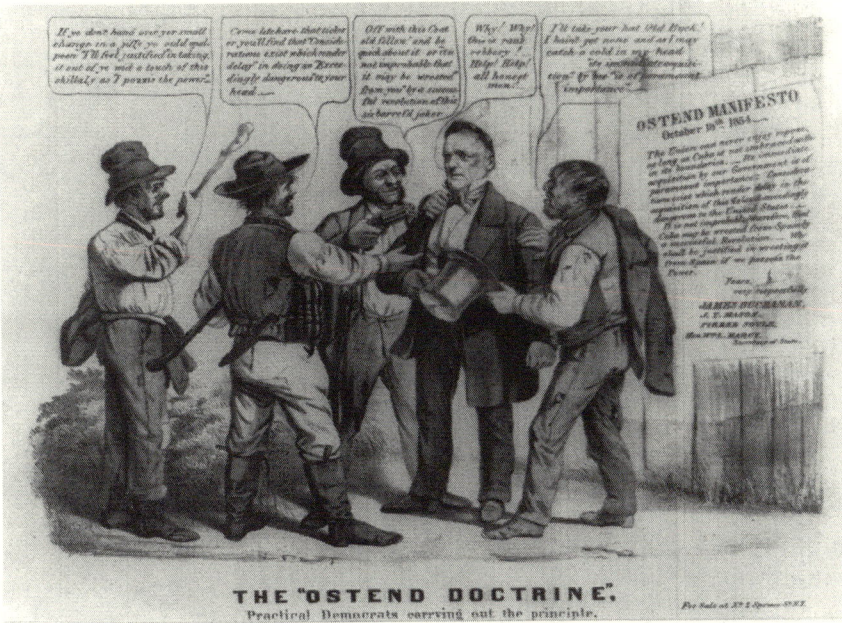

FIG. 2. The Ostend Manifesto as highway robbery: the Irish hooligans robbing James Buchanan are quoting directly from the manifesto. *Courtesy Library of Congress, Prints and Photographs Division.*

debated in Congress, however. Several of the most eloquent opponents of using "force" to acquire Cuba were Democrats from the South and West, suggesting that narratives that explain the territorial lust in this period as a "southern dream" are too simple.[21] Opponents of the Ostend Manifesto drew on a vision of proper manliness just as explicit as the framers of the manifesto, who openly asserted that might made right.

Debate over the Ostend Manifesto overlapped not only with the Kansas-Nebraska Act, but also with the Gadsden Purchase debate. In June 1854 Milton Slocum Latham, Democratic representative of California, admitted that he was at heart a "Cuban annexationist" but that he deplored filibustering. He condemned "those whose love of glory looks to the tented field for a theater of action, 'seeking the bubble reputation, even at the cannon's mouth.'" Using an analogy of nations with men, and echoing the words and arguments of reformers in the period who cautioned young men that sexual activity could lead to premature old age, he argued that precipitous action

---

[21] See, for example, May, *Southern Dream.*

would undermine the manhood of the United States. "We have a continent before us, and the future is ours without dispute.... We ... can afford to let the years roll on which bring us nearer to our full manhood, and *all other nations* whom we are now emulating to old age and decrepitude. All we require is to nurse our health, and to commit no excesses, that we may not be doomed to a premature old age." What excesses might doom the United States to a premature old age? He cautioned against "sophisms which blunt our perceptions of right and wrong, and lend to vice itself the color of reason and justice." He warned that "there is nothing so disastrous to the rising fortune of an industrious man as the anticipation of his income. It begets looseness of expenditure, and a reckless speculation to meet it, which interferes with the profits of his regular business, and frequently involves him in embarrassment and ruin. The same may be said of nations, especially of industrious nations like our own. Sir, our people are preeminently a business people."

In Latham's view, the United States should focus on cultivating what it already owned. "It is said, Mr. Chairman, that we are impelled to these things by 'manifest destiny,' and I more than half believe it," he mused. "We have, no doubt, a proud mission to fulfill; but it does not merely consist in the acquisition of territory, and in the extension of power ... it is not merely power, but our institutions and laws, and our higher civilization which we are bound, in the course of time, to carry to the most remote part of this continent and to its neighboring islands."[22]

In January 1855 another Democrat, from South Carolina no less, also argued against using force to acquire Cuba. William Waters Boyce noted,

> A feverish impatience seems to be seizing upon our people for territorial extension. In some quarters the cry is for the Canadas.... In other quarters the cry is for the Sandwich Islands; some are wishing for another partition of Mexico; others are looking to the regions watered by the mighty Amazon; more are bent upon the acquisition of Cuba, and some have such inordinate stomachs that they are trying to swallow up the entire continent. These are all but various phases of the manifest destiny idea. I must confess, I do not sympathize with this idea. I think our true mission is conservatism, not indefinite extension.

---

[22] *Congressional Globe*, 33d Cong., 1st sess., 1854, pp. 949–54 (emphasis in original). On fears that sexual activity could lead to premature old age, see Helen Lefkowitz Horowitz, *Attitudes toward Sex in Antebellum America* (Boston, 2006).

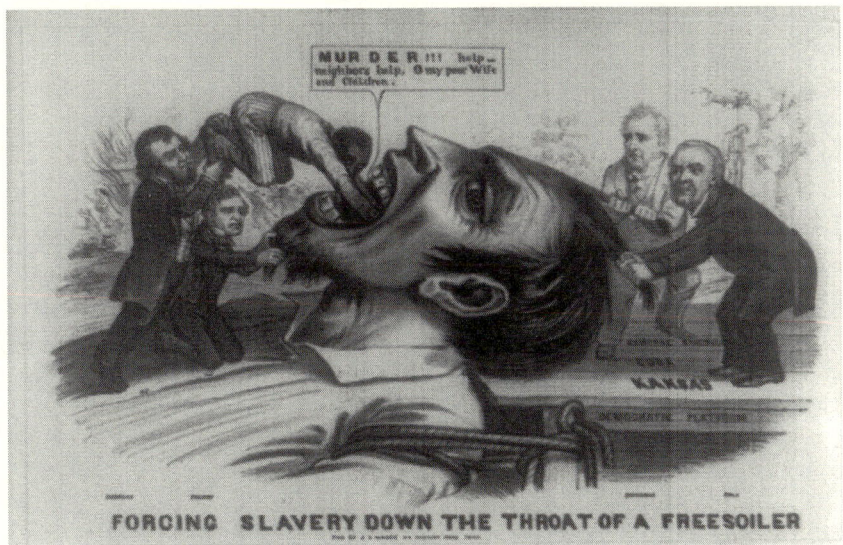

FIG. 3. This 1856 image places the horrors of Kansas in the context of territorial expansion. Buchanan is standing on a platform that reads Central America, Cuba, and Kansas, while the Democrats force slavery down the throat of a Free-Soiler. *Courtesy Library of Congress, Prints and Photographs Division.*

While the Ostend Manifesto equated might with right, Boyce would "act towards Spain with extreme forbearance, for she is weak and we are strong." He trusted that "we shall turn with aversion from the deceitful seductions of false glory" and "turn from the line of vulgar conquerors to the fathers of this Republic, let us learn from them, that the truest patriotism is the preservation of our institutions, the truest wisdom is moderation." In place of "triumphal arches . . . trophies of victory, and boundless domination," Boyce recommended "the conquests of peace . . . Christianity working out, unimpeded, her Divine mission."

Christianity, moderation, forbearance toward the weak, avoiding the seductions of false glory; this was a restrained man. But Boyce offered one more reason why he opposed the Ostend Manifesto:

> Another motive which makes me still more determined not to go to war with Spain for Cuba, is that we of the South are upon the eve of a great struggle with a hostile majority of the North, and we will need all our resources, not to make foreign conquests, but to defend the very ground upon which we stand. I am, therefore, unwilling to weaken our resources, or complicate our

position by an attack on Cuba; others, who hear only the songs of peace in the future, may take a different course.[23]

In 1855 at least one southerner opposed expansion because he was preparing for a war of northern aggression.

Spain clearly did not want to sell Cuba to the United States, Narciso López's filibustering expedition ended in the deaths of twenty-four Americans, and the Ostend Manifesto was a debacle for Pierce. Spain turned down an offer of $100 million for Cuba during the Polk presidency, and an offer of $130 million during Pierce's presidency. But the Cuba issue would not die. The public backlash against the Ostend Manifesto did not prevent one of its authors, Pennsylvania Democrat James Buchanan, from winning the presidency in 1856 on an openly expansionist platform. In a classic equation of expansion and manliness, Buchanan argued that "expansion is in the future the policy of our country, and only cowards fear and oppose it." Buchanan's secretary of state, Lewis Cass of Michigan, was even more enthusiastic, writing that the United States "requires more land, more territory upon which to settle, and just as fast as our interests and our destiny require additional territory in the North, or in the South, or on the Islands of the Ocean, I am for it." Cass authorized the American minister to Mexico to offer $15 million for Baja California and parts of Sonora and Chihuahua, an offer that was repeatedly rebuffed by Mexico. The Buchanan administration also worked toward purchasing Cuba, despite the exploding sectional conflict. In January 1859, Louisiana Democratic senator John Slidell introduced a bill allocating $30 million as a down payment toward the acquisition of Cuba ($130 million was again mentioned as a plausible final price).[24]

One of the bill's supporters was Stephen Russell Mallory, Democrat of Florida. In an extended discourse in February 1859 on why Cuba was "essential to the general welfare of the United States, and to its military defenses," he made clear his view that "this vast continent, every inch of it, must soon be ours." Offering his own analogy of nations to men, he suggested that ambition and glory were a natural condition in the United States, and the fear was not precipitous action leading to old age but stunting the

---

[23]*Congressional Globe*, 33d Cong., 2d sess., 1855, pp. 91–94.
[24]Albert K. Weinberg, *Manifest Destiny: A Study of Nationalist Expansionism in American History* (Chicago, 1935), p. 201; Willard Karl Klunder, *Lewis Cass and the Politics of Moderation* (Kent, Ohio, 1996), pp. 289–90, quote p. 289; Alexander DeConde, *Presidential Machismo: Executive Authority, Military Intervention, and Foreign Relations* (Boston, 2000), pp. 95–97; Elbert B. Smith, *The Presidency of James Buchanan* (Lawrence, Kans., 1975), p. 78.

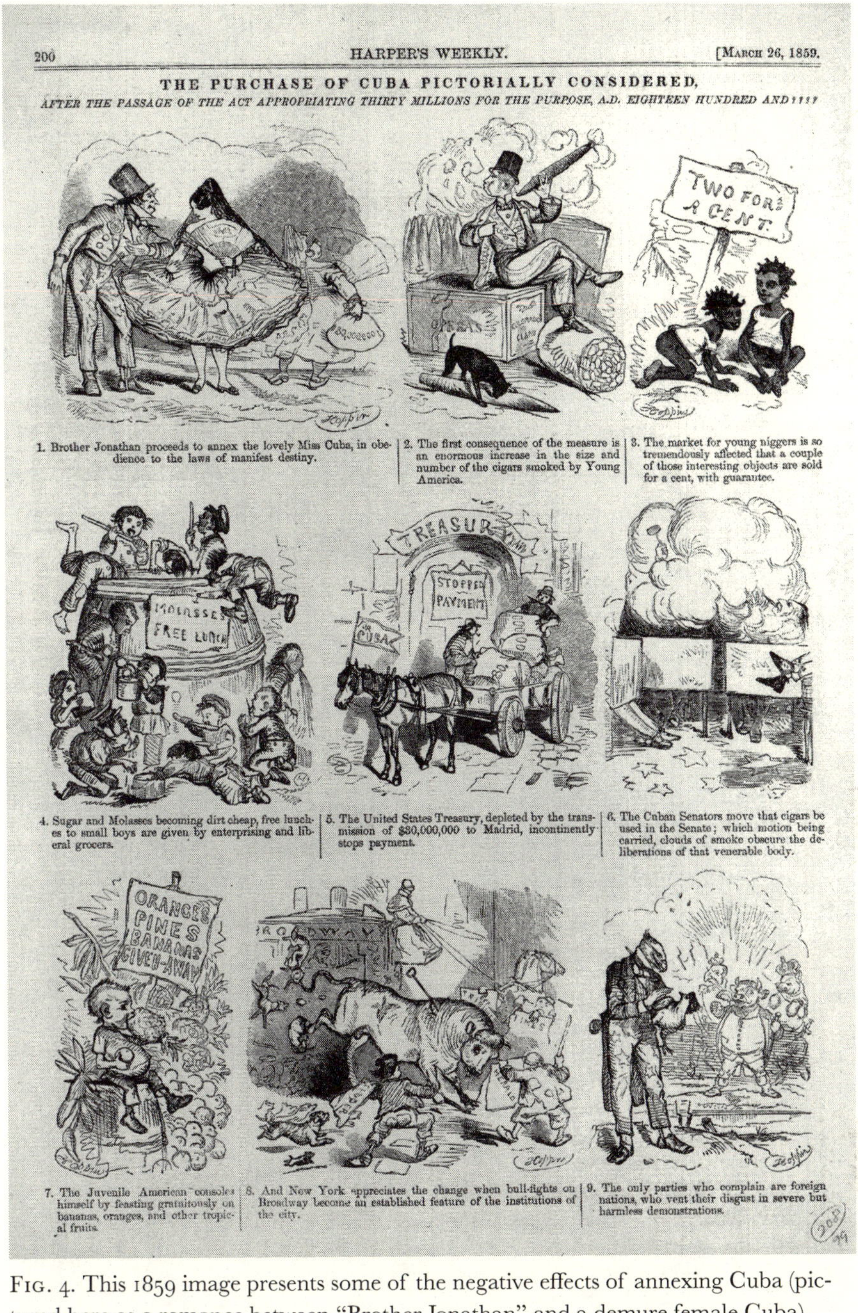
200 HARPER'S WEEKLY. [MARCH 26, 1859.

THE PURCHASE OF CUBA PICTORIALLY CONSIDERED,

*AFTER THE PASSAGE OF THE ACT APPROPRIATING THIRTY MILLIONS FOR THE PURPOSE, A.D. EIGHTEEN HUNDRED AND????*



1. Brother Jonathan proceeds to annex the lovely Miss Cuba, in obedience to the laws of manifest destiny.

2. The first consequence of the measure is an enormous increase in the size and number of the cigars smoked by Young America.

3. The market for young niggers is so tremendously affected that a couple of those interesting objects are sold for a cent, with guarantee.

4. Sugar and Molasses becoming dirt cheap, free lunches to small boys are given by enterprising and liberal grocers.

5. The United States Treasury, depleted by the transmission of $30,000,000 to Madrid, incontinently stops payment.

6. The Cuban Senators move that cigars be used in the Senate; which motion being carried, clouds of smoke obscure the deliberations of that venerable body.

7. The Juvenile American consoles himself by feasting gratuitously on bananas, oranges, and other tropical fruits.

8. And New York appreciates the change when bull-fights on Broadway become an established feature of the institutions of the city.

9. The only parties who complain are foreign nations, who vent their disgust in severe but harmless demonstrations.

FIG. 4. This 1859 image presents some of the negative effects of annexing Cuba (pictured here as a romance between "Brother Jonathan" and a demure female Cuba), including an increase in cigar smoking and unruly children. *Courtesy Library of Congress, Prints and Photographs Division.*

full development of masculine achievement. "Tell any of these distinguished men who surround me here, 'pause in your career, make no further advance up the steep hill of fame, improve and adorn what you have!' . . . Tell the seaman fresh from the decks of victory to sheathe his sword. . . . Alexander at the height of his military glory, signed for new worlds to conquer." And if Spain should, once again, "reject all reasonable terms," Mallory was clear. He would "look directly at the contingency of taking Cuba and talking about it afterwards." Representative Reuben Davis of Mississippi also repeatedly insisted in 1859 that the United States should "take" Cuba, rather than purchase it.[25]

James Dixon, a Republican senator from Connecticut, and opponent of the bill, mocked these aggressive pretentions. Slidell, according to Dixon, conducted his "negotiations" by informing Spain "that she is in the condition of a bankrupt who . . . must sell in order to save the family mansion." Even worse in his view was the address of the Whig senator Robert Toombs of Georgia, who informed Spain that "young, thriving, vigorous nations are purchasers; the weak, the feeble, the decrepit, are sellers. . . . When nations begin to decay they sell their territory, or it is taken from them by conquest."[26]

Which is exactly what happened in Central America, through the actions of William Walker, the man who was not only willing but seemingly able to capture foreign territory by force in the 1850s and who lived long enough for his actions to be debated in Congress. No discussion of Walker, or expansionism, is complete without a short digression about Franklin Pierce. Pierce has been rightfully critiqued for his failed presidency, but he had more than his share of difficulties, and Walker was one of them. No doubt when Pierce ran for president, in 1852, he thought territorial expansion would be a winning issue for him. But sadly he was proved wrong. Pierce was reviled by restrained men, who thought the Ostend Manifesto countenanced robbery and murder, but the same congressmen who had celebrated the Ostend Manifesto and the Gadsden Purchase soon learned to hate him as well. Walker was the reason.

---

[25] *Congressional Globe*, 35th Cong., 2d sess., 1859, pp. 1327, 1331–32; May, *Southern Dream*, pp. 170–71.
[26] *Congressional Globe*, 35th Cong., 2d sess., 1859, p. 1333.

## Central America

Tennessee-born William Walker, who first rose to national attention in the fall and winter of 1853 in an aborted attempt to capture land in Sonora and Baja California, seized control of Nicaragua, which was divided by a civil war, in the fall of 1855. He became commander in chief of the republic's army and, in July 1856, became president of the country.[27] At the height of his success Walker was widely lauded in all sections of the country. Alabama representative Percy Walker, who was a member of the American, or Know-Nothing, Party, and not related to William Walker, praised Walker to the House of Representatives in December 1856 as "no vulgar adventurer, but a profound observer, an earnest, scholarly man, above all mercenary considerations," but also a "young, bold, adventurous, thoughtful man, imbued with the truest spirit of Americanism" and "inspired by . . . a love of glory which has characterized the purest and noblest natures."[28] But President Pierce refused to recognize this paragon of virtue, or his regime in Nicaragua. One 1855 ditty, titled "Nicaragua Ho!" lamented, "We ain't got room enough to spread; our eagle's mighty pinions / Are clipped and fastened to his sides by Pierce and his cuss'd minions."[29] Walker would outlast Pierce's presidency and cause trouble for his successor as well.

After losing a war in May 1857 to a coalition army composed of Central American and British soldiers, William Walker returned to the United States and gathered funds for another invasion of Central America. In December 1857 he was arrested on Nicaraguan soil during a carefully planned return to the country, where he still considered himself president. He was arrested not by Nicaraguans but by an American naval officer, Commodore Hiram Paulding. Paulding justified his arrest of Walker with a critique of Walker's character, since the filibuster had not, strictly speaking, broken any laws at the time of his arrest. In his dispatch to the government Paulding explained, "I could not regard Walker and his followers in any other light than as outlaws who had escaped from the vigilance of the officers of the Government,

---

[27] May, *Manifest Destiny's Underworld*, p. 174; Greenberg, *Manifest Manhood*, pp. 32–33.
[28] *Congressional Globe*, 34th Cong., 3d sess., 1856, p. 101; on Walker's fame, see Greenberg, *Manifest Manhood*, pp. 135–69.
[29] On Pierce and Walker, see the anti-Pierce (Know-Nothing Party) newspaper, *Young Sam*, which inveighed against Pierce's Walker policy (and his manliness) for months. Quote from "Nicaragua Ho!" *Young Sam* 1 (January 1856):7.

Fig. 5. A pro–William Walker set of maps and images produced during Walker's presidency of Nicaragua suggests the potential future growth of the United States in the imaginations of expansionists. *Courtesy Library of Congress, Prints and Photographs Division.*

and left our shores for the purpose of rapine and murder." By arresting Walker, Paulding hoped to "vindicate the law, and redeem the honor of our country," he stated.[30]

Walker received extensive support in this affair, since even President Buchanan condemned Paulding for exceeding his rights in arresting Walker on foreign soil. Nonetheless, many politicians agreed with Paulding's assessment of the filibuster's character. In contrast to those, like Democratic representative George Sydney Hawkins of Florida, who praised Walker for his "uncommon personal courage, force of will, and firmness under difficulties," and compared him to Napoleon, others took a different tack.[31] President Buchanan himself claimed that Walker's expedition was little more than "an invitation to reckless and lawless men to rob, plunder, and murder the unoffending citizens of neighboring States." Democratic senator James Pearce of Maryland agreed, and very clearly laid out his critique of martial manhood in his address to the Senate. "Nothing surprises me more than the sympathy which is expressed for General Walker," he claimed. "In a few localities . . . he may be regarded as a hero; but the larger part of our countrymen view him as . . . a cold, relentless oppressor of the people whom he ruled with military rigor." Walker's martial masculinity was anachronistic. "The enterprise which he has undertaken is one that does not belong to the age, and is not in accordance with its spirit. . . . It belongs, rather to that dark period in the Christian era . . . when the Vikings and Northmen went wherever they could, disregarding the obligations of national justice, making might right, and carrying rapacity and rapine wherever they went."[32]

Paulding, by contrast, offered an admirable model of restraint. Paulding used "no language disrespectful to General Walker . . . no language . . . which could be considered disgraceful to that officer," but spoke and behaved like a gentleman. "We do not wish our officers when executing a stern duty to speak with bated breath, and accompany the act by apologetic flourishes. We want them to speak like men, like officers; to speak whatever is to be said, plainly, frankly, without apology and necessary qualification. This is

---

[30] *Congressional Globe*, 35th Cong., 1st sess., 1858, p. 360.

[31] Ibid., p. 461. Examples of condemnation of Paulding's actions on legal grounds include "Speech of W. Winslow of North Carolina" (May 31, 1858) and "Speech of Hon. Miles Taylor" (May 25, 1858), ibid., pp. 418–20, 502–3.

[32] Ibid., 35th Cong., 1st sess., 1858, p. 457; *Harper's New Monthly Magazine* 16 (March 1858):544

what Commodore Paulding has done." In contrast to Walker's martial excess, Paulding deserved praise because he refrained from undignified language and behavior and prevented violence against a weaker nation.[33]

Democratic congressman Augustus Wright of Georgia strenuously disagreed. "Commodore Paulding—what has he done?" Wright asked with wonder. "Has faction and fanaticism effaced the last vestige of justice from the mind of my countrymen? As a subaltern, he but executed the order of his superior. He did that in a most ungallant and ungracious style. . . . He insulted and brow-beat his victim. . . . Paulding faced no danger, ran no risk, accomplished nothing likely to add to his country's renown or give luster to the page of her history." How could anyone praise this man, particularly in comparison to William Walker, whom Wright called "the bravest of the brave"? Faced with the choice between an ungallant subaltern, Wright would side with the filibusters, even in the face of the "fanaticism" of his opponents. And although Cuba had nothing whatsoever to do with Walker and his arrest, in the midst of his diatribe, Wright found it necessary to inform the House of his firm belief that "Cuba ought to be subject to our jurisdiction. It is natural and just that it should be."[34]

George Sydney Hawkins of Florida went further in his condemnation of Paulding's actions, calling it "*impotence*" to pass over "the insults or outrages committed by the smaller" powers in the Western Hemisphere, instead of "displaying proper firmness" with them. "As to the territorial expansion of this country," he claimed, "it is inevitably and must be southward; faster, perhaps, than we wish." He invoked the "proud language of the Ostend manifesto," and warned that "if perchance a portion of this Union, guided by a narrow policy and false philanthropy, should oppose such an accession, from hostility to southern interests, a war of opinion may be engendered, and utterance give to it in tones loud and clear as a bugle call; and then, Mr. Chairman, hush who can its irksome echoes!"[35] In other words, those who would stop Manifest Destiny must be prepared for a war of their own. As for William Walker, he met his death in front of a Honduran firing squad in 1860, on the eve of the Civil War, which some of these partisans seemed fully anxious for.

---

[33] *Congressional Globe*, 35th Cong., 1st sess., 1858, p. 461. One has to question what sort of language Pearce considered insulting, given that Paulding called Walker an outlaw who intended rapine and murder.

[34] *Congressional Globe*, 35th Cong., 1st sess., 1858, app., pp. 459–461.

[35] Ibid., app., p. 463 (emphasis in original).

This chapter has covered a lot of territory, both in its argument and in the sheer number of countries in danger of invasion and annexation by the United States in the 1850s. This examination of congressional responses to territorial expansion has argued that attempts to gain new territories during the period of Manifest Destiny's hangover were debated, justified, and critiqued in terms of manhood, and that members of Congress clearly understood the implications of expansion. Congressmen saw that even debating whether or not to gain new territories was divisive and could potentially lead to secession and war. But they did it anyway. The lure of new lands was just too strong. Manifest Destiny did not die in 1848, but it certainly helped kill the Union at the close of the 1850s.

Spencer R. Crew

# "When the Victims of Oppression Stand Up Manfully for Themselves"

*The Fugitive Slave Law of 1850 and the Role of African Americans in Obstructing Its Enforcement*

T HE OPENING MONTHS of 1850 were a time of challenge for the nation and for the Thirty-First Congress. The successful war against Mexico and the acquisition of new lands once again raised the issue of the place of slavery in the nation. These were issues similar to those that had appeared with the Louisiana Purchase of 1803, which also dramatically increased the size of the country. Southerners wanted assurances that they could bring slaves with them as they moved onto the new lands. They perceived not having that option as a threat to both their economic well-being and the political balance in Congress. There even was talk at the time of the possibility of secession, but the Missouri Compromise of 1820 quieted those threats. Brokered by Henry Clay and others, the legislation produced an uneasy truce that began steadily unraveling and reached fever pitch by 1850.[1]

As the newly acquired Mexican territories sought recognition and eventual statehood from Congress the divide between southern slaveholding states and northern nonslaveholding states once again moved front and center. Along with issues concerning the boundaries of these new states and whether they would join the union as free or slave states, questions arose concerning the slave trade in the District of Columbia and enforcement of fugitive slave

---

The title quotation is taken from Frederick Douglass, "The Anti-slavery Movement: A Lecture by Frederick Douglass, before the Rochester Ladies' Anti-Slavery Society, Rochester, 1855," in Philip S. Foner, *The Life and Writings of Frederick Douglass*, 4 vols. (New York, 1950), 2:333–59.

[1] Holman Hamilton, *Prologue to Conflict: The Crisis and Compromise of 1850* (Lexington, 1964), pp. 11–13; John C. Waugh, *On the Brink of Civil War: The Compromise of 1850 and How It Changed the Course of American History* (Wilmington, Del., 2003), pp. 8–13.

laws. Southerners saw themselves and their way of life under attack once again. They were alarmed by the actions of nearly every northern legislature that had resulted in votes urging their congressional representatives to act to bar slavery from all territories. In addition, several others had urged the end of slavery and the slave trade in the District of Columbia.[2] Henry L. Benning, a Georgia lawyer, expressed southern concerns when he wrote, "I no more doubt that the North will abolish slavery the very first moment it feels itself able to do it without too much cost, than I doubt my existence."[3] In the face of these beliefs, momentum was growing in the South for the idea of leaving the Union to protect southern interests. As a way to seriously examine this alternative, a call was issued in June 1850 for a convention of southern states in Nashville, Tennessee, to discuss the possibilities.[4]

The South was correct that northern sentiment against the spread of slavery was growing. Abolitionists offered the loudest dissent, arguing slavery was morally corrupt and should be ended altogether. But most people in the North were not abolitionists and did not seek to end slavery in existing states. They were opposed to its spread to new states, as they believed in the importance of free labor as the backbone of American success. They saw the small independent farmer as the best future for the nation, not unpaid, enslaved labor. They recognized the acknowledgment of slavery in the Constitution and therefore were not ready to abolish it, but for them slavery was not the future of the country. The hope was that it would eventually fade away or get squeezed out of existence.[5]

As Congress assembled in December 1849, emotions continued to rise as political leaders hoped to find a solution that would placate both sides. As was the case in 1820, Henry Clay of Kentucky offered a compromise he hoped might solve the dilemma. The plan had several parts to it. Some focused specifically on California, Texas, and the land acquired from Mexico. Here the status of slavery was left to the determination of each new state as it emerged and sought admittance to the Union. Other parts of the compromise prohibited Congress from restricting the slave trade in the states. Clay's compromise continued slavery in the District of Columbia, but ended the slave trade within its borders. Finally, it closed gaps in

---

[2]Waugh, *Brink of Civil War*, p. 4.
[3]Ibid., p 4.
[4]Ibid., p. 7.
[5]Eric Foner, *Free Soil, Free Labor, Free Men: The Ideology of the Republican Party before the Civil War* (New York, 1970), pp. 38–39.

the fugitive slave law to aid slaveholders in their efforts to retrieve runaways living in the North.

Strengthening the fugitive slave law was an important part of the plan for southerners. This had been a point of contention for them for decades. They felt the Constitution absolutely made the return of fugitive slaves the law of the land. Article IV, section 2, noted that "No Person held to Service or Labour in one State, under the Laws thereof, escaping into another, shall, in Consequence of any Law or Regulation therein, be discharged from such Service or Labour, but shall be delivered up on Claim of the Party to whom such Service or Labour may be due."[6] The expectation of the creators of the Constitution was that citizens in one state would aid in the return of slaves who sought refuge within their borders. This did not happen in application, as north of the Mason-Dixon Line antislavery sentiments grew. Even as new state governments were organized after the American Revolution, many northern states either abolished slavery or passed laws mandating gradual emancipation. The new constitution of Vermont explicitly noted that as all men are born equally free and independent it would not allow slavery to exist within its borders.[7] Consequently northern states were inconsistent in their interpretation of the constitutional fugitive slave mandate or chose not to enforce it within their borders.

The most important instance of clashing views on this subject occurred beginning in 1788, in a Pennsylvania case that pitted the governor of that state against the governor of Virginia. The case involved an African American by the name of John Davis. He was a resident of Pennsylvania who had gained his freedom under its gradual abolition act of 1780. Three men from Virginia disputed this argument and forcibly took him from Pennsylvania to Virginia, claiming he was a fugitive slave. John was then sold to a planter in eastern Virginia. Friends of John who were members of the Pennsylvania Abolition Society hired an attorney to recover him but were unsuccessful. Later, with the help of Philadelphia abolitionists they were able to get the governor of Pennsylvania, Thomas Mifflin, to request the extradition of the men who had taken Davis. He also asked for the return of Davis. When he

---

[6] U.S. Constitution, art. IV, sec. 2, par. 3.

[7] Paul Finkelman, *Slavery and the Founders: Race and Liberty in the Age of Jefferson*, 2d ed. (Armonk, N.Y., 2001), p. 41; James Oliver Horton and Lois E. Horton, *In Hope of Liberty: Culture, Community, and Protest among Northern Free Blacks, 1700–1860* (New York, 1997), pp. 71–74.

contacted the governor of Virginia, Mifflin pointed out that in the eyes of Pennsylvania, Davis was a free man who had been illegally abducted, and Mifflin wanted the culprits punished.

Beverley Randolph, the governor of Virginia, refused to return Davis or extradite the three men. At loggerheads, Mifflin eventually appealed to President George Washington for a ruling on the matter. Mifflin felt the issue was a constitutional matter between two states that the federal government should resolve. Washington turned the matter over to Congress to examine and to create guidance for the future. What Congress crafted was the Fugitive Slave Law of 1793. Its goal was to clarify any confusion about interpreting the wording of the Constitution with regard to issues concerning fugitives from justice and from the service of masters.[8]

The final version of the eighteenth-century law was a victory for southern slaveholders. It favored their interests over those of alleged fugitive slaves, and over northern residents who might not agree with the accusations of slave catchers who came to their communities. With regard to fugitive slaves, several key steps were spelled out. There was no statute of limitations for runaway slaves; they were fugitives for life and subject to return. Slaveholders or their agents could seize a fugitive slave wherever they found one, take the fugitive before a judge, and get a warrant allowing them to seize the individual. Only the testimony of the slaveholder or an affidavit from their local judge was needed for extradition. Fugitives were not allowed to request trials by jury or to testify on their own behalf. And anyone who aided a fugitive or interfered with the efforts to seize a fugitive was subject to a fine of $500. Under this legislation, neither fugitive slaves nor freedmen accused of being fugitives had any rights.

If the South hoped this legislation would make an appreciable difference in northern attitudes toward the return of fugitive slaves, they were disappointed. The law served to further incense abolitionists and was opposed by numerous northern officials. These officials often exploited gaps in the legislation. It was up to the discretion of local law officials whether they would recognize the accusations of slaveholders, or whether they would play a role in the capture and jailing of an accused fugitive. It was not unusual for a local pro-abolition judge to deny the demands of a slaveholder and to set

---

[8]Finkelman, *Slavery and the Founders*, pp. 84–92.

the fugitive free. Abolitionists often sought out a sympathetic judge to issue a warrant preventing the extradition of a local African American, thereby frustrating the efforts of slave catchers.

Of key concern to northern residents was the lack of protection of the rights of free African Americans under the law. The law presumed that all African Americans were enslaved individuals and that they had to prove they were not. As a consequence, even free African Americans were subject to seizure at any moment, with little recourse to prove their status. They had no civil rights and could not even speak on their own behalf when taken before a magistrate. This made it nearly impossible for them to prevent being taken south as a fugitive. Their only hope was to have a local white resident step forward on their behalf and to come before a judge sympathetic to their predicament. Otherwise their fate was sealed.

The African Americans most vulnerable to kidnapping were individuals located close to the border of southern states. African American residents of Ohio, Indiana, Pennsylvania, Delaware, and Illinois were particularly vulnerable to sudden seizure. Richard Allen, one of the founders of Mother Bethel African Methodist Episcopal Church, in Philadelphia, was seized by a slave catcher with a warrant from a sheriff. He succeeded in winning his release. Others were not always so lucky. In the 1820s a ring of kidnappers operated in Philadelphia luring African American children onto boats along the Delaware River and then transporting them south, where they were sold into slavery.[9] Along the banks of the Ohio River near the city of Ripley, Eliza Jane Johnson in 1837 was whipped, thrown on the back of a horse, and carried to Kentucky by four horsemen. It took five months and a resolution from the Ohio House of Representatives to finally convince Kentucky officials to free her.[10]

Probably the most notable kidnapping of a freeman was the case of Solomon Northrup. A resident of Sarasota Springs, New York, Northrup in 1841 was hired to play his violin by two white men headed for Washington, D.C. While in the District of Columbia he was drugged, and when he woke up was in chains. He subsequently was sold into slavery. Despite his protesta-

---

[9]Fergus Bordewich, *Bound for Canaan: The Underground Railroad and the War for the Soul of America* (New York, 2005), p. 135; William R. Leslie, "The Pennsylvania Fugitive Slave Act of 1826," *Journal of Southern History* 18 (1952):439–40.

[10]Ann Hagedorn, *Beyond the River: The Untold Story of the Heroes of the Underground Railroad* (New York, 2002), pp. 123–27, 141–43.

tions that he was a freeman, Northrup spent the next twelve years enslaved. It was not until he got a letter to his family back in Sarasota that he eventually gained his freedom, in 1853.[11] Northrup's experience illustrated the abuses possible under the Fugitive Slave Law of 1793 and confirmed the worst fears of African Americans and white abolitionists. Both groups initiated steps, sometimes separately and sometimes together, to try to neutralize the efforts of slaveholders seeking fugitives.

As early as the turn of the nineteenth century, African Americans took an active role in helping fugitives. Some individuals, like Leonard A. Grimes, a hackman in Washington, D.C., or Polly Jackson of Ripley, Ohio, lived near the borders of southern states. Grimes used his hack to travel to Virginia to bring fugitives north.[12] Polly Jackson threw boiling water at slave catchers to keep them at bay.[13] Others, like John and Mary Jones of Chicago or Jermain W. Loguen of Syracuse, lived further north but opened their homes to fugitives passing through their cities.[14] Very often they did this as part of the local Underground Railroad network. They were a vital part of the success of this operation, as fugitives often went to the African American community first when they sought help in a strange town.

Another effort in which African Americans often took a leading role was the organization of vigilance committees. These were groups formed to provide legal aid, financial support, and other protection needed by fugitives. The largest ones operated in New York, Boston, and Philadelphia, but they also existed in smaller cities, particularly near Canada. One of their key goals was to confront slave catchers and thwart their attempts to capture fugitives. These efforts could be peaceful or violent depending on the circumstances. A particularly violent episode took place in Buffalo, New York, in 1836 when a group of fifty armed men led by William Wells Brown, himself a fugitive slave, intercepted four men attempting to return a family to enslavement. A major struggle ensued between the slave catchers, who were joined by the local sheriff, and Brown's men, with one of Brown's party losing his life. Ultimately the family gained their freedom and relocated to Canada.[15]

---

[11]Solomon Northup, *Twelve Years a Slave: Narrative of Solomon Northup, a Citizen of New-York, Kidnapped in Washington City in 1841, and Rescued in 1853* (Auburn, N.Y., 1853).
[12]Benjamin Quarles, *Black Abolitionists* (New York, 1969), p. 146.
[13]Hagedorn, *Beyond the River*, p. 89.
[14]Quarles, *Black Abolitionists*, pp. 148–49.
[15]Horton and Horton, *In Hope of Liberty*, pp. 234–35.

While the first vigilance committees in Boston, Detroit, Cleveland, and New York were predominantly African American, white abolitionists eventually actively joined in these activities as well.[16] The prototypical vigilance committee operation was in Philadelphia, guided by William Still. The original group, the Philadelphia Vigilance Committee, was founded in 1838. While its membership rolls were interracial, the most engaged members were African American. They assisted several hundred runaways passing through the city. This group disbanded after six years but was followed by a more interracial operation, the General Vigilance Committee, led day to day by William Still. With the help of the members of the committee, Still not only provided aid to fugitives but also sought ways to use Pennsylvania laws to offer freedom to enslaved people brought to Philadelphia by slaveholders.[17]

To protect abolitionists and others wishing to help fugitives, several northern states passed laws to shield state residents from what they saw as the capriciousness of the Fugitive Slave Act of 1793. The earliest measure was passed in Pennsylvania. At the urging of the Pennsylvania Society for Promoting the Abolition of Slavery and the governor, William Findlay, a bill was approved in 1820 that made kidnapping a Negro or mulatto a felony punishable with a fine and imprisonment.[18] Six years later the Pennsylvania legislature passed a second bill promoted by the society and free African Americans to counter pressure from Virginia to amend the 1820 law. Using the plight of kidnapped children from Philadelphia as leverage, they successfully lobbied for and had passed the Pennsylvania Fugitive Slave Act of 1826. This bill essentially closed any loopholes in the 1820 law and made it virtually impossible for a slaveholder to remove a fugitive slave from the state of Pennsylvania.[19]

Laws providing some protection to fugitives also were passed in Indiana (1824), Connecticut (1828), Maine (1838), New York (1840), and Vermont (1840). These laws varied, as some gave escaped enslaved individuals the right to trial by jury, some provided the right to appeal, and others granted access to an attorney. In each instance, however, the goal was to make the kidnapping of a fugitive a difficult process. The hope was that either the expense of meeting the laws or the time involved in finally gaining control

---

[16] Quarles, *Black Abolitionists*, p. 153.
[17] Ibid., pp. 153–54.
[18] Leslie, "Pennsylvania Fugitive Slave Act," p. 433.
[19] Ibid., pp. 442–45.

over the accused individual would discourage slaveholders from using the 1793 legislation.

The constitutionality of these laws was at the core of *Prigg v. Pennsylvania*. In 1837, Edward Prigg, a slave catcher, abducted Margaret Morgan, a fugitive who had lived in Pennsylvania for five years. He took her to Maryland without obtaining the proper legal documents from Pennsylvania. He was extradited, placed on trial in Pennsylvania, and found guilty of kidnapping. Prigg appealed to the U.S. Supreme Court, which reversed the lower court ruling in 1842. The justices found the 1826 Pennsylvania act unconstitutional because it contradicted the fugitive slave clause in the Constitution as well as the Fugitive Slave Act of 1793.[20]

This Supreme Court decision caused great concern within abolitionist ranks. In response to the ruling, a meeting of African Americans in Troy, New York, passed several resolutions decrying the decision and declaring, echoing Patrick Henry, that they would have liberty or they would have death.[21] Having lost one of their best weapons against slave catchers, they had to turn to other devices. One option was the organization of more vigilance committees. In Boston, African American men and women organized the New England Freedom Association. Their most celebrated, though unsuccessful, effort was the case of the fugitive slave George Latimer. He and his family escaped from Virginia to Boston. Their slaveholder pursued them and had them arrested. An initial attempt by the association to free them proved unsuccessful. An interracial coalition was then formed that denounced the Boston police, held mass protest meetings, and published news pieces decrying the kidnapping. None of these efforts worked and in the end the coalition had to raise the money to purchase Latimer's freedom. In addition they launched a huge petition campaign that attracted almost sixty-five thousand signatures that were then sent to the Massachusetts legislature. In response, it passed the Personal Liberty Act of 1843, or "Latimer Statute," which made it illegal for state officials to participate in or use state facilities in the apprehension of fugitives. This represented a major accomplishment for the Freedom Association, which three years later became part of the racially integrated Boston Vigilance Committee.[22] Vermont passed a similar law that same year.

---

[20]Joseph Nogee, "The Prigg Case and Fugitive Slavery, 1842–1850: Part I," *Journal of Negro History* 39 (1954):185–205.
[21]Quarles, *Black Abolitionists*, pp. 225–26.
[22]Horton and Horton, *In Hope of Liberty*, pp. 229–30; Quarles, *Black Abolitionists*, pp. 193–95.

In 1844, Connecticut passed a personal liberty law, as did Rhode Island in 1845 and Pennsylvania in 1848.

In the face of this rising tide of actions geared to undercut the Fugitive Slave Act of 1793, it is not surprising that southern politicians and their constituents felt that the statute needed improvement. In fact, for some it was an issue serious enough to split the Union. The legislature in Georgia had threatened secession if northern states continued to impede the rendition of fugitive slaves.[23] In January 1850, Henry Clay was very aware of these concerns and gave them high priority as he drafted his compromise legislation. Consequently, the final bill included an updated and strengthened iteration of the fugitive slave law.

Passing the final version of the overall compromise was a challenging process. While southerners sought to protect the institution of slavery, other members of Congress opposed allowing the spread of the institution and objected to having slave owners invade their towns searching for fugitives. Finding a middle ground entailed intense negotiations and skilled political maneuvering. In the end, a committee of thirteen senators was formed to hammer out a compromise bill. Extensive behind-the-scenes discussions took place, coordinated by Stephen A. Douglas of Illinois and others. The Senate, and then the House of Representatives, passed the final legislation in early September 1850. On the day of the vote for the fugitive slave bill in the House, thirty-three northern congressmen absented themselves rather than vote for it. They did not want to defeat it, but preferred not to vote in favor of it.[24] The president, Millard Fillmore, signed it into law a few days later.

There were several critical new elements to the 1850 fugitive slave bill. It placed the issue of the rendition of fugitive slaves exclusively under federal jurisdiction, overriding any local legislation. Federal marshals no longer had latitude in choosing to enforce the law. A marshal who did not arrest an illegal fugitive could be fined $1,000. If a fugitive escaped his custody for any reason he was liable for repayment of the value of the slave to the slaveholder. On the other hand, as an incentive, they received a fee for capturing fugitives. Fugitives had fewer protections under the law. Suspected fugitives could be arrested without a warrant and only the word of the accuser was

---

[23]Stanley W. Campbell, *The Slave Catchers: Enforcement of the Fugitive Slave Law* (New York, 1969), p. 5.
[24]Waugh, *Brink of Civil War*, p. 183.

necessary to initiate the arrest. The suspect could not ask for a jury trial nor testify in his or her defense. Any person aiding a runaway by providing shelter, food, or other form of assistance faced six months in jail and a $1,000 fine for each individual aided. Moreover, private citizens called upon to aid a marshal in the apprehension of a fugitive were expected to provide assistance. Finally, commissioners appointed to rule on questions of the status of an accused fugitive received $10 if they found in favor of the slaveholder but only $5 if they found in favor of the accused.

The bill addressed many of the devices and strategies used in northern states to thwart slaveholders seeking fugitives. It sought to close those loopholes to the benefit of slaveholders so as to protect their property rights with regard to slaves. Congressional supporters of the law hoped the Compromise of 1850, including the fugitive slave law, had solved many of the issues frustrating slave holders. Most significantly, to Congress and to many Americans it seemed to save the nation from the prospect of breaking apart. Daniel Webster noted to a friend after passage of the legislation, "I can now sleep nights. We have gone thro' the most important crisis, which has occurred since the foundation of the Government; & what ever party may prevail, hereafter, the Union stands firm."[25]

Early public response to the legislation seemed to show the positive support Congress desired. In the District of Columbia people took to the streets, setting bonfires and firing cannon salutes in celebration of its passage. Celebrants sought out lawmakers and serenaded them in thanks for their efforts. Dinners were given on their behalf. Joyous crowds shouted, "The Union is saved!"[26]

In Boston a one-hundred-gun salute was fired in support of the law as a "testimony of joy . . . at the adoption of the late measures of Congress." A New York City group offered a petition signed by ten thousand people approving of the legislation. In particular they declared the fugitive slave law constitutional and promised to support it.[27] At Philadelphia several thousand people gathered to hear speakers supporting the legislation. Franklin Pierce spoke to an enthusiastic crowd in Concord, New Hampshire, about

---

[25] Ibid., p. 187.
[26] Ibid., p. 187; Holman Hamilton, "'The Cave of the Winds' and the Compromise of 1850," *Journal of Southern History* 23 (1957):331–53.
[27] James Ford Rhodes, *History of the United States from The Compromise of 1850* (New York, 1896), pp. 194–95.

the legislation.[28] Similar groups of support met in Maine, Vermont, Ohio, and Connecticut offering their endorsement. In several of these meetings there were calls to create Union safety committees similar to one in New York City. There, the conservative members of the business community gathered to hear speakers denounce abolitionists, endorse the compromise, and reassure southerners of their support of the law. A large gathering in New Haven, Connecticut, took a similar position and its speaker suggested those opposed to the law should move to Canada.[29]

Southerners responded with like satisfaction. The Kentucky legislature honored Clay for his efforts on behalf of the bill. New Orleans held an enthusiastic rally. A convention in Georgia originally called to consider the issue of secession failed to endorse that idea and gave tempered support to the compromise, noting that the faithful execution of the fugitive slave bill was a critical issue for them. Other conventions previously scheduled in other southern states either had small turnouts or could not generate much enthusiasm for further discussions of secession. The meeting in Mississippi went as far as to declare that secession is "utterly unsanctioned by the Federal Constitution."[30] In North Carolina the *Weekly Raleigh Register and North Carolina Gazette* argued that the law should please both sections of the country. "It assists the South in regaining her property, and it enforces obligations which bind the North to obey the constitution."[31]

Throughout the country, the majority of people generally supported the compromise and the hope for the potential peace it offered. One newspaper, the *Daily National Intelligencer,* of Washington, D.C., noted that it could fill two pages with jubilant expressions about the law from southern and western journals alone. Buoyed by public displays of enthusiasm, in his December presidential address, Millard Fillmore said he saw the compromise as a "final settlement of the dangerous and exciting subjects [the compromises] embraced." His words reflected the optimism felt by many in the country that it had turned a corner and overcome one of its most serious challenges. The compromise, Fillmore argued, was "the best, if not the only means of restor-

---

[28] Allan Nevins, *Ordeal of the Union,* vol. 1, *Fruits of Manifest Destiny, 1847–1852* (New York, 1947), p. 348.
[29] Ibid., pp. 347–48.
[30] Rhodes, *History of the United States,* p. 198; Nevins, *Ordeal of the Union,* pp. 366, 374; *Philadelphia Christian Observer,* Dec. 21, 1850; Michael F. Holt, *The Fate of Their Country: Politicians, Slavery Extension, and the Coming of the Civil War* (New York, 2004), p. 84.
[31] *Weekly Raleigh Register and Carolina Gazette,* Aug. 28, 1850.

ing peace and quiet in the country and maintaining inviolate the integrity of the Union."[32]

While Fillmore's words had lofty aspirations, they did not account for the impact disgruntled northern antislavery groups would have in the months and years that followed. The absence of so many northern congressmen during the vote for the fugitive slave law pointed to concerns these men knew important constituents had with the legislation. The growing crescendo of voices opposed to the Fugitive Slave Act of 1793 certainly would not embrace the even tougher legislation embodied in the 1850 statute. Those opposed to slavery did not support it and very quickly they began raising objections to the law. Several points were particularly irksome in the new legislation: no trial by jury for accused fugitives; no hearing before a judge for the fugitive; a federal commissioner served that role and the commissioner received higher compensation for a guilty verdict; marshals were subject to a fine if they did not arrest an accused fugitive and they could demand aid from willing and unwilling bystanders; and aiding a fugitive could result in a heavy fine, imprisonment, and civil suits.[33] Many people found these regulations very harsh and completely in opposition to rights guaranteed in the Constitution. Accused individuals at times were established, responsible, respected residents of the community, and their seemingly arbitrary seizure angered many people.[34]

Antislavery forces offered a clear statement of their feelings about the bill while it still was under discussion in the Senate. During August 1850 the Cazenovia Slave Law Convention took place in Cazenovia, New York. More than two thousand people attended the conference, including at least thirty fugitives. Frederick Douglass served as president of the meeting. An open letter was crafted pledging to protect fugitives and encouraging the enslaved to rise up and do what they must to escape. It was one of the most militant statements on the topic to date.[35]

---

[32]Waugh, *Brink of Civil War*, pp. 188–89; Holt, *Fate of Their Country*, p. 82.
[33]Nevins, *Ordeal of the Union*, pp. 380–82.
[34]"The Agitation at the North," *National Era*, Oct. 24, 1850.
[35]Merton Dillon, *Slavery Attacked: Southern Slaves and Their Allies, 1619–1865* (Baton Rouge, 1990), pp. 215–16; Lois E. Horton, "Kidnapping and Resistance: Antislavery Direct Action in the 1850s," in *Passages to Freedom: The Underground Railroad in History and Memory*, ed. David W. Blight (Washington, D.C., 2004), p. 158; Hugh C. Humphreys, *Agitate! Agitate! Agitate!: The Great Fugitive Slave Law Convention and Its Rare Daguerreotype* (Oneida, N.Y., 1994); Mary Kay Ricks, *Escape on the Pearl: The Heroic Bid for Freedom on the Underground Railroad* (New York, 2008), pp. 220–23.

African Americans also held protest meetings all over the country shortly after Fillmore signed the law. In New York, fifteen hundred people gathered in the Zion Chapel in protest and signed two petitions condemning the law. One petition was for Congress and the other for the state legislature. Another group met in Pittsburgh in the public square, and a third in Philadelphia. Boston, Springfield (Mass.), Chicago, Zanesville (Ohio), and Columbus also had angry gatherings. These meetings and others argued for forcible resistance to the fugitive slave law.[36]

The fierce reaction by African Americans was not surprising given the impact the stronger law could have on their lives. Local laws and traditions that once had provided protection for them had lost their force. As a federal statute, the Fugitive Slave Act held sway over local legislation and officials. If accused, African Americans had no legal options to prevent their extradition south even after years of living free. This reality caused fear as well as anger among African Americans.

As the protest meetings took place, groups of African Americans decided that Canada was the only place they could live safely. They took to heart the advice of Thaddeus Stevens, who when asked about the law, commented that the safest thing to do was to "put themselves beyond its reach."[37] As a consequence they packed their belongings, armed themselves, and left as quickly as they could. The *Pittsburgh Gazette* reported that more than one hundred well-armed men had left the city by early October. They left behind families and property to greatly reduce the risk of capture and a return to slavery.[38] Many other cities witnessed similar exoduses of their African American residents. Forty left Boston within a week of the signing of the bill, and churches in Buffalo and Rochester reported the departure of most of their members. One estimate was that within ninety days of the passage of the bill as many as three thousand formerly enslaved people left for Canada.[39]

The worry was that they might suffer the same fate as James Hamlet of New York City. U.S. marshals grabbed him on the streets of the city within a week after the signing of the legislation. Hamlet had arrived in New York from Baltimore three years earlier. He was married and had two children. He argued that his mother was free, therefore he was as well, and he had

---

[36] Quarles, *Black Abolitionists*, pp. 201–2; *North Star* (Rochester, N.Y.), Oct. 24, 1850.
[37] Quarles, *Black Abolitionists*, p. 199.
[38] *Pittsburgh Gazette*, Sept. 24–25, 1850.
[39] Campbell, *Slave Catchers*, p. 64; *Independent* (Boston), Oct. 3, 1850.

been illegally enslaved in Maryland. The local commissioner refused to hear his testimony and returned him to Baltimore, where his mistress intended to sell him further south. The only thing that saved him was her willingness to sell him to someone in New York. African Americans held a meeting at Mother Zion Church with the purpose of raising the $800 needed. They raised $500 and white abolitionist friends contributed the remaining amount needed to purchase Hamlet's freedom. He returned to an emotional gathering of five thousand people wishing to celebrate their victory.[40] In the midst of the celebration, however, many attendees must have pondered Hamlet's close call and worried that the same thing might easily happen to them or a family member.

This question loomed especially large for African Americans who were high-profile participants in the antislavery movement. Since its inception in 1833, the American Anti-Slavery Society sponsored speakers who traveled the countryside offering personal testimony about their years in enslavement. Their goal was to introduce the horrors of slavery to northern audiences unaware of the day-to-day trials faced by the enslaved. An example of these efforts was the program of the New England Anti-Slavery Society to send speakers across the country in the 1843.[41] Frederick Douglass, Charles L. Redmond, Henry Highland Garnet, and other African Americans joined this effort. At other times and places, speakers like Henry "Box" Brown, Ellen and William Craft, Harriet Tubman, and Reverend Jermain Loguen also spoke about their experiences. As runaways, the fugitive slave law also put them in greater danger. In some cases it emboldened local northern ruffians as well as their former slaveholders to take steps they might not have tried earlier.

Henry "Box" Brown, who shipped himself from enslavement in Richmond, Virginia, to freedom in Philadelphia in 1849, quickly learned conditions were different. Within days of the signing of the legislation, Brown gave a speech in Providence, Rhode Island. Following his presentation, he was accosted by a group of men. When they first attacked, he was able to hold them off, but they attacked a second time and tried to push him into a carriage. Fortunately he was able to resist them again. Brown later said he

---

[40]Horton, "Kidnapping and Resistance," p. 159; Quarles, *Black Abolitionists,* pp. 197–98; *Christian Observer* (Philadelphia), Oct. 12, 1850.

[41]Bordewich, *Bound for Canaan,* p. 228; Benjamin Quarles, *Frederick Douglass* (New York, 1968), pp. 29–33.

believed this attack in broad daylight was spurred by the passage of the new law. At the advice of his antislavery friends, he left the country to lecture in England.[42]

Other antislavery participants faced similar threats and decisions. The former slaveholder of Ellen and William Craft followed their lectures and sent men to bring them back to Georgia. The men were unsuccessful, but it resulted in the Crafts also leaving for England.[43] However, other prominent figures like Rev. Jermain Loguen chose to stay despite the danger. Loguen declared to a crowd in Syracuse, "I will not live a slave, and if force is employed to reenslave me, I shall make preparations to meet the crisis as becomes a man."[44] Loguen's sentiments reflected the view of the majority of African Americans. They were not going to allow the fugitive slave law to force them to flee the country. Instead they vowed to resist the law and the individuals who came north trying to return them to slavery. Frederick Douglass captured that spirit in a speech he gave in Pittsburgh when he said that the best response or remedy to the law was a "good revolver, a steady hand, and a determination to shoot down any man attempting to kidnap."[45]

Though the strident position taken by Douglass was probably stronger than most antislavery proponents, he and African Americans were not alone in their determination to resist the new law. When African Americans in Boston requested an expression of support for their stand against the fugitive slave law, they received a rapid and positive response. Several hundred people attended a meeting called by the former mayor of the city and other white abolitionists. After several speeches two key resolutions were passed. One called for the repeal of the legislation and the other offered a promise to "not allow a fugitive slave to be taken from Massachusetts." They then established an interracial Committee of Vigilance to assist and offer advice to fugitives.[46] A meeting of Unitarian clergy in Springfield also passed a resolution condemning the law and pledging to do all they could to have it overturned. Concomitantly, a general meeting of Springfield residents

---

[42] William and Ellen Craft, *Running a Thousand Miles for Freedom: The Escape of William and Ellen Craft from Slavery* (Athens, Ga., 1999), pp. 54–58; Jeffrey Ruggles, *The Unboxing of Henry Brown: A Biography* (Richmond, 2003).

[43] Horton and Horton, *In Hope of Liberty*, pp. 253–54.

[44] Bordewich, *Bound for Canaan*, p. 325.

[45] Quarles, *Frederick Douglass*, p. 116.

[46] Ibid., pp. 202–3; *Independent* (Boston), Oct. 17, 1850.

pledged to actively resist slave catchers who came there. Similar meetings took place in Elmira and Chicago.[47]

This cooperative action illustrated an important relationship change between African Americans and abolitionists. With the establishment of the American Anti-Slavery Society, in 1833, African Americans were more welcomed among the ranks of white abolitionists. Before then, African Americans often operated separately from their white counterparts. But under the leadership of William Lloyd Garrison, who developed a close relationship with African Americans, they became important contributors to the growing antislavery movement. Just as importantly their views had an impact on abolitionist thinking. Because slavery and kidnapping was a harsh personal reality for them, African Americans had stronger sentiments about resistance. For example, in 1843 at the National Negro Convention in Buffalo, Henry Highland Garnet made a stirring speech encouraging the enslaved to rise up and take their freedom: "Strike for your lives and liberties. . . . Let your motto be resistance; no oppressed people have secured their liberty without resistance."[48] Garnet was not a solitary voice on this view. Fourteen years earlier, David Walker in his famous *Appeal in Four Articles* (1829) expressed similar thoughts. At the Buffalo convention a resolution to endorse the speech lost by one vote.[49] This sense of urgency and the need for resistance also began to infiltrate the philosophy of the overall abolitionist movement.

Until the 1850s, most of the efforts to rescue fugitives had been executed by African Americans. In Detroit in 1833, Boston in 1836, as well as Chicago and Pittsburgh in 1846, African Americans affected the escape of the accused individuals.[50] But the passage of the fugitive slave law helped to shift that dynamic. It caused more white abolitionists and antislavery sympathizers to embrace the idea of actively resisting the efforts of slave catchers. The *New York Tribune* editorialized that the law was morally wrong and while people should not use violence, the paper did support evading the law and working zealously to help slaves escape capture. Theodore Parker, the minister of the Twenty-Eighth Congregational Society in Boston, believed it

---

[47]*Independent* (Boston), Oct. 24, 1850; Nevins, *Ordeal of the Union*, p. 353; *North Star*, Oct. 24, 1850.
[48]John Hope Franklin and Alfred A. Moss, *From Slavery to Freedom: A History of African Americans* (Boston, 2000), p. 203.
[49]Horton and Horton, *In Hope of Liberty*, pp. 246–47.
[50]Quarles, *Black Abolitionists*, pp. 204–5.

was the moral duty of a good Christian to oppose the fugitive slave law: "I tear the hateful statute of kidnappers to shivers: I trample it under my feet; I do it . . . in the name of Justice and of Man, in the name of dear God."[51] He was one of the key speakers at the meeting at Faneuil Hall in Boston.

While the idea of resistance to the legislation was not the general point of view of most residents of northern states, it did gain growing acceptance among abolitionists. The most obvious manifestation of this spirit was the growing number of high-profile instances of direct resistance on the part of African American and white antislavery colleagues to efforts of slaveholders to regain control over fugitives. John Hope Franklin argues that immediately following the passage of the fugitive slave law southern slaveholders launched an extremely intense effort to capture even fugitives who had lived free for many years. Stanley Campbell also saw a major upswing in the number of fugitives arrested in 1851.[52]

The response by antislavery forces was to use whatever methods they could to prevent the return of the fugitives. These efforts took place across the North. Upstate New York had two celebrated rescues, one in Syracuse, the Jerry rescue, and the case of Charles Nalle in Troy. Both involved major confrontations. The Jerry rescue occurred first in 1851. The fugitive's real name was William Henry, a cooper, who went by the name of Jerry. Slave catchers grabbed him and took him to the courthouse. He tried to escape but was recaptured. But later that evening a group of men ran into the jail, overcame the police, and took him away. He eventually wound up in the home of a white abolitionist, where he remained in hiding for five days before going to Ontario. Twelve African Americans and fourteen whites were indicted but only one African American was found guilty. The event became a day of celebration for abolitionists in the area for the remainder of the decade.[53]

In Boston, the Shadrach case offered a vivid illustration of the steps antislavery proponents were committed to taking. Fred Wilkins, or Shadrach, a waiter, was kidnapped in February 1851 and taken to the courthouse to appear before the commissioner. When the news spread, a contingent of Afri-

---

[51]Henry Steele Commager, *Theodore Parker: Yankee Crusader* (Boston, 1982), p. 207; Nevins, *Ordeal of the Union*, p. 387.

[52]Campbell, *The Slave Catchers*, pp. 199–207; Franklin and Moss, *From Slavery to Freedom*, p. 215.

[53]Quarles, *Black Abolitionists*, pp. 209–11; Horton and Horton, *In Hope of Liberty*, p. 255; Catherine Clinton, *Harriet Tubman: The Road to Freedom* (New York, 2004), pp. 137–39.

can Americans rushed to the courtroom, grabbed Shadrach, and swept him away. He was out of the city and on his way to Canada before authorities could organize to pursue him. Two men, Lewis Hayden and Robert Morris, were arrested for the rescue but eventually were found innocent.[54] During the remainder of the year, the records of the Vigilance Committee listed helping eighty-four people get safely through the city.[55]

African Americans took an even more forceful stance several months later in Christiana, Pennsylvania. There a slaveholder, Edward Gorsuch from Maryland, came in search of four fugitives. His party of six men went to the home of William Parker, an African American and a runaway from Maryland. Parker refused Gorsuch entrance to his home to search for the fugitives, and his wife sounded the alarm, which brought two dozen African Americans there. Several white supporters arrived as well but they did not engage directly in the conflict. A battle ensued between the African Americans and Gorsuch's party. Gorsuch was killed and the fugitives along with Parker left for Canada. Thirty-five African Americans and three whites were charged by the federal government, but none were found guilty. Money for their defense was raised by abolitionists from as far away as San Francisco. The incident was judged a victory against the fugitive slave law and a warning to slaveholders of the level of danger they might face in trying to capture fugitives.[56]

But not all the efforts to protect fugitives were successful. It has been estimated that nearly 90 percent of the fugitives arrested were returned successfully. The most highly publicized case focused on Anthony Burns. An escaped slave from Virginia, Burns was seized by federal marshals as he walked home from work and was placed in jail. This set off a chain of events among Boston antislavery supporters. They first obtained a lawyer for Burns and then met to consider further actions. After a rally at Faneuil Hall, a crowd moved to the courthouse. There Lewis Hayden and other African Americans attacked the building unsuccessfully. In the process a guard was killed. At the trial Burns was judged a fugitive and turned over to federal authorities for return to Virginia. President Pierce provided federal troops and a

---

[54]Horton and Horton, *In Hope of Liberty*, p. 254; Quarles, *Black Abolitionists*, pp. 205–6.
[55]Horton, "Kidnapping and Resistance," p. 166.
[56]W. U. Hensel, *The Christiana Riot and the Treason Trials of 1851: An Historical Sketch* (New York, 1911); Roderick Nash, "William Parker and the Christiana Riot," *Journal of Negro History* 46 (1961):24–31.

federal ship to insure the sentence was carried out. Fifty thousand people gathered to watch Burns's departure, most of them frustrated and angered by the conclusion of the case.[57]

What the Burns case illustrated was a growing militancy among white antislavery supporters. While working within the law remained the first resort, more and more of them saw civil disobedience and direct action as a viable alternative. With the Joshua Glover incident in Wisconsin (1854), the Oberlin-Wellington rescue in Ohio (1858), and the Charles Nalle episode in Rochester (1860), the use of physical force came into play more often. The success of these events as well as other similar incidents and the headlines they attracted increased the skepticism of southerners about the ability of the federal government to enforce the law and protect slavery.

The inclusion of the fugitive slave law had been an essential reason many southerners reacted positively to the passage of the Compromise of 1850. They hoped that the protection of property spelled out in the Constitution finally would be enforced as the loss of fugitive slaves in particular aggravated them. Congressman David Outlaw of North Carolina gave voice to the level of frustration when he wrote to his wife that "the stealing of slaves produces more irritation, more heart-burning, among slaveholders, than all other causes combined."[58] When Georgians convened in Milledgeville in November 1850, the fifth and final resolution they passed spoke directly to the fugitive slave law, noting ominously, "upon the faithful execution of the *Fugitive Slave Bill* by the proper authorities depends the preservation of our much-loved Union."[59] Mississippi's convention that same month expressed similar thoughts. Moderates held sway in the South for the moment. They sought reconciliation but believed it depended largely on how the North enforced the elements of the compromise bill.[60] They watched carefully in the years that followed with the hope that all would work out.

The difficulty was that many southerners were frustrated by northern reactions. Despite the reality that most efforts to recover fugitives proved successful, the perception was that massive northern resistance to the recov-

---

[57] Jane H. Pease and William H. Pease, *The Fugitive Slave Law and Anthony Burns: A Problem in Law Enforcement,* ed. Harold M. Hyman (Philadelphia, 1975), pp. 25–54; Quarles, *Black Abolitionists,* p. 208.

[58] Waugh, *Brink of Civil War,* p. 183.

[59] *Journal of the State Convention, Held in Milledgeville, in December 1850* (Milledgeville, Ga., 1850), pp. 19, 29–31.

[60] Nevins, *Ordeal of the Union,* pp. 357–58, 364.

ery of fugitives was the norm. The headline-grabbing actions in Boston, Syracuse, and other northern cities fed that perception. So did the fiery speeches of William Lloyd Garrison, Jermain Loguen, Theodore Parker, Frederick Douglass, and others who counseled various forms of resistance. Douglass's words to fugitives that they should "prefer to perish in a river made red of his own blood, [to] submission to the hell hounds who were hunting and shooting him"[61] could not have been encouraging to southerners.

Also disconcerting were the actions of individuals, particularly African Americans, who traveled south to aid the enslaved to escape. Harriet Tubman topped the list with her regular sojourns into Maryland to extract family and friends. Abolitionists highlighted her efforts by featuring her as a speaker. In particular her speech in Boston after the Nalle rescue was widely reported and praised by the abolitionist newspaper *Liberator*. Slavery supporters thought it insulting for northerners to celebrate the actions of a woman who had caused the loss of over $50,000 worth of property. Southern concerns about her efforts reached such a level that Maryland slaveholders offered a reward of at least $12,000 for her capture.[62]

But Harriet was not a lone example. In Ohio near the Kentucky border, the freeman John Parker regularly rowed across the Ohio River into Mason County, Kentucky, to aid fugitives. He, like Harriet Tubman, had a bounty placed on his head. Elijah Anderson, who lived near Madison, Indiana, ventured into Kentucky as far south as Frankfort to organize escapes to Indiana and farther north. He eventually was arrested, tried, and jailed in Frankfort, where he died.[63]

Supporting the work of these individuals as they brought fugitives north were other just as well-known individuals, most of them white. Levi and Catherine Coffin were known both in Indiana and Ohio for their selfless efforts to help fugitives once they crossed onto free soil. So was John Rankin in Ripley, Ohio, who sheltered many of the people brought north by John Parker. Harriet Beecher Stowe modeled Eliza in *Uncle Tom's Cabin* after a story about a fugitive told to her by Rankin. Harriet Tubman often sought aid from Thomas Garret either going to or returning from her missions to

---

[61] Quarles, *Frederick Douglass*, p. 116.
[62] Clinton, *Harriet Tubman*, pp. 141–43.
[63] J. Blaine Hudson, *Fugitive Slaves and the Underground Railroad in the Kentucky Borderland* (Jefferson, N.C., 2002), pp. 150–53; John P. Parker, *His Promised Land: The Autobiography of John P. Parker, Former Slave and Conductor on the Underground Railroad*, ed. Stuart Seely Sprague (New York, 1996), chaps. 5–12.

Maryland. Garret at one point was sued by a slaveholder for aiding a fugitive family, found guilty, and fined $5,000, which bankrupted him. The fine slowed him but did not deter him in his support of escaping fugitives.[64]

These efforts were followed closely by slaveholders and only served to agitate them. Headlines and articles in southern newspapers indicated their growing frustration and anger. The *Mississippian and State Gazette*, under the headline, "Another Outrage upon the South," complained of resistance to the fugitive slave law and the need to begin protecting southern rights. The *Columbia (Ga.) Times* suggested that in retaliation for nonenforcement of the legislation in the North, southern state courts should refuse to address suits for the collection of debts or the redress of injuries initiated by northerners.[65] For southerners doubtful from the start about the effectiveness of the compromise bill, and particularly the fugitive slave law, the actions of northern antislavery forces served to confirm their initial concerns. Northern resistance also strengthened their argument that the federal government could not fully protect their property rights and that the South needed to consider stronger legislation or secession.

The Fugitive Slave Law of 1850 provided an issue around which antislavery forces could rally. When Congress closed loopholes in the 1793 law, its new legislation heightened concerns regarding the protection of civil liberties and the injustices inherent in the institution of slavery. The 1850 legislation also brought to the forefront discussions about civil disobedience and the use of violence as a tactic. Many groups favored using the courts, mass meetings, new legislation, and refusal to implement the law or the verbal harassment of slave catchers as the best course. They did not advocate directly intervening in the capture and return of an alleged runaway.

But not everyone embraced this point of view. Even before 1850, African Americans had included physical confrontations as a tool in their arsenal for resisting the efforts of slave catchers. Many of them were formerly enslaved or still had family held in bondage, which made protecting fugitives a very personal issue. They could find themselves in a similar situation if they did

---

[64]Clinton, *Harriet Tubman*, pp. 63–64; Hagedorn, *Beyond the River*, pp. 139, 232–37; Levi Coffin, *Reminiscences of Levi Coffin, the Reputed President of the Underground Railroad* (Cincinnati, 1876), chs. 4–11; Henrietta Buckmaster, *Let My People Go: The Story of the Underground Railroad and the Growth of the Abolition Movement* (Columbia, 1941), pp. 149–52.

[65]*Mississippian and State Gazette* (Jackson, Miss.), Feb. 28, 1851; "The Southern press is airing a new project of retaliation for the frequent obstructions to the execution of the Fugitive Slave Law at the North, and the menaced repeal of the same," *Frederick Douglass' Paper* (Rochester, N.Y.), Sept. 22, 1854.

not take steps to discourage kidnapping. Also, they were familiar with what the return to enslavement would mean for the fugitive. Thus, African Americans had less compunction about stopping slave catchers any way they could. Deception, rescues, harassment, and even gun battles were all devices used by African Americans from the very beginning. But often, at least before the 1830s, these were actions African Americans usually took on their own without the support of other antislavery proponents.

The 1850 fugitive slave law helped to shift that dynamic, as African Americans were more directly involved in the abolitionist movement. They held offices in the American Anti-Slavery Society and in regional groups. They were key operatives in interracial Vigilance committees formed to aid fugitives. As a consequence they had more influence on the discussions concerning what actions to take to disrupt the application of the law. Through the 1850s physical struggles increasingly became an alternative employed by interracial groups seeking to thwart slave catchers. Very often the people leading these actions were African Americans such as Lewis Hayden in Boston, William Parker in Christiana, and Harriet Tubman in Troy. They were willing to do whatever they must to aid fugitives. They made sure the pronouncements of Fredrick Douglass were not hyperbole but representative of the resolve of abolitionists who shared his and their level of commitment.

The implementation of the fugitive slave law had numerous impacts, some of which were intended and some of which were not. Its influence on antislavery organizations enabled African Americans to play a larger leadership role within these groups. Some white abolitionists greatly disturbed by the new law more seriously considered the idea of direct confrontation with slave catchers. They were pushed and at times pulled into these actions by a northern African American community that refused to allow the kidnapping of fugitives to occur without opposition. Denied the right to directly participate in the political process in most northern states, active opposition to implementation of the fugitive slave law in their communities was one of the most effective devices available for them to express their discontent. African Americans were at the core of what has been described as "the uprising of the people generally in 1850 and 1851, throughout northern states in opposition to the Fugitive Slave Law."[66] The reality was that these uprisings continued until the eve of the Civil War. In the process they kept attention on the issue

---

[66]Samuel J. May, *Some Reflections of Our Antislavery Conflict* (1869; reprint ed., Miami, 1969), pp. 363–64.

of fugitive slaves and the institution of slavery. These uprisings, in conjunction with other events, had an impact on the psyche of the nation that caused southerners to feel more isolated and northerners more disenchanted with the idea of slavery or its spread.

The Fugitive Slave Law of 1850 gave African Americans a protest platform that they used effectively to goad northern discussions about civic rights and direct action. Through their actions they made it clear issues concerned with slavery could not be compromised out of existence but had to be directly confronted and resolved. For African Americans and eventually for the nation the only resolution was to finally bring an end to slavery and move the nation closer to the lofty principles it espoused in the Declaration of Independence and the Constitution.

Martin J. Hershock

## "Agitation Is as Necessary as Tranquility Is Dangerous"

*Kinsley S. Bingham Becomes a Republican*

ON DECEMBER 6, 1847, in the midst of a controversial war with neighboring Mexico, the Thirtieth Congress of the United States gathered together in Washington, D.C., for the first time. Among the 230 congressmen assembled that day were 110 Democrats, 116 Whigs, two members from the new state of Wisconsin, and a handful of freshman members, among them Abraham Lincoln of Illinois, a Whig, and Kinsley Bingham, a Democrat from Michigan.

Nearly identical in age (Bingham was born on December 16, 1808, and Lincoln on February 12, 1809) and hailing from states on the old northwestern frontier, both men symbolized the West's promise of economic security, mobility, independence, and opportunity. Another parallel, though admittedly not one either man would have been proud of, is that neither Lincoln nor Bingham is much remembered for his actions during their brief stints in the House (one term, 1847–49, for Lincoln and two terms, 1847–51, for Bingham). Indeed, both men quietly returned to civilian life (Lincoln as an attorney and Bingham as a farmer) immediately following their short service in Congress and likely would have faded from the public consciousness if not for the sectional upheaval that surrounded the passage of the Kansas-Nebraska Act by Congress, in 1854, and the subsequent formation of the Republican Party, a party that provided a new political home for both men and one that ensured both men's historical legacy: Lincoln, of course, as the party's first elected president in 1860, and Bingham as one of the party's first elected governors (and later as a Republican member of the United States Senate).

In spite of the many similarities in their lives, however, the paths these two men pursued to the Republican standard were dramatically different: Bingham joined the party at its inception, in 1854, while his much more famous peer, Abraham Lincoln, remained consciously aloof from it, only cautiously embracing the new party in the spring of 1856 after it became abundantly clear that his beloved Whig Party was no longer functional. The story of Lincoln's guarded and protracted conversion to Republicanism is, thanks to historian David Donald and others, now fairly well known. Bingham's story, on the other hand, in spite of some attention from historian Eric Foner in his seminal work *Free Soil, Free Labor, Free Men*, and regardless of Bingham's arguably purer Republican pedigree, remains a relatively obscure one. This chapter seeks to partially address this gap and to shed some light on the larger issue of party restructuring during the politically contentious decade of the 1850s, by offering an overview of Kinsley Bingham's path from the Democratic Party into the Republican fold and of his motivations and his justification for undertaking this transformation.[1]

Born into a farming family of modest means near Camillus, New York, in December 1808, Kinsley Scott Bingham grew up with a profound respect for those who tilled the soil and was imbued with the fervent evangelical moralism of New York State's Yankee piety belt. Though he formally trained as a lawyer, Bingham's first love was farming, and it was this devotion that led him, in 1833, along with his new wife, Margaret, to join the thousands of other New Yorkers smitten with Michigan Fever who were streaming west to lay claim to new farmland on what was then the far western frontier. Settling just north and west of Detroit in Livingston County's Green Oak Township, Bingham rapidly established himself as a successful farmer. In 1837, after holding a number of minor elected local offices, Bingham, running as a Democrat, was chosen by voters in his home district to serve in the Michigan state legislature. Apparently Bingham's constituents approved of his actions and he was reelected to the state House of Representatives for four additional terms (two of them as Speaker of the House).[2]

---

[1] On Lincoln's tentative drift toward the Republican Party, see Reinhard H. Luthin, "Abraham Lincoln Becomes a Republican," *Political Science Quarterly* 59 (1944):420–38, and David Herbert Donald, *Lincoln* (New York, 1995), pp. 187–90. Some brief discussion of Bingham appears in Eric Foner, *Free Soil, Free Labor, Free Men: The Ideology of the Republican Party before the Civil War* (New York, 1970). A more detailed account can be found in William McDaid, "Kinsley S. Bingham and the Republican Ideology of Antislavery, 1847–1855," *Michigan Historical Review* 16 (1990):63–69.

[2] No thorough biography of Bingham exists. The sketch included in this chapter was drawn from McDaid, "Kinsley S. Bingham," pp. 40–73.

While representing his neighbors, Bingham witnessed firsthand the devastating effects of the Panic of 1837 on the new state of Michigan (the state entered the Union in January 1837) and, most especially, its impact on the state's farm families. The combination of Bingham's traditional agrarian roots, his own personal rise from obscurity to stability, and the readily apparent trauma associated with Michigan's collapsed economic order (a reminder of the all too tenuous nature of his hard-won stability) further reinforced his ties to Jackson's Democratic Party, with its ethos of autonomous self-sufficiency and hostility toward monopoly power, an ethos very much in harmony with the sentiments of a majority of Michigan's hard-pressed voters. Accordingly, Bingham railed against the state's feeble banking system, battled for "hard money," and argued for laws to protect the homesteads of Michigan's struggling farmers. Thankful for Bingham's advocacy of their interests, his farmer neighbors rewarded his service to them by nominating him as the Democratic Party candidate for Congress from the Third Congressional District in 1846. Bingham won the election going away and, in late 1847, eagerly journeyed to Washington to conduct the nation's business and to represent the people of Michigan.[3]

Tensions in Washington, however, were running high as Bingham assumed his seat among the minority Democrats, as Congress found itself immediately grappling with the question of whether slavery should be allowed to expand into the territories being added almost daily to the United States as a result of the ongoing war with Mexico. At the heart of the controversy lay the proposal put forward by a Democratic congressman from Pennsylvania, David Wilmot. In August 1846, Wilmot, hoping to put an end to the contentious debate and to maintain party unity by placing the Democrats squarely in the corner of supporting territorial expansion without slavery, appended a proviso to a wartime appropriations bill that excluded slavery from any territory obtained from Mexico as a result of the war. Though the proviso-laden bill managed to pass in the northern-dominated House, it was denounced by President James K. Polk and was repeatedly blocked in the Senate, where the number of northern and southern votes were more closely matched. The net effect of the debate, however, was the unleashing of a firestorm of sectional animosity and rancor.[4]

---

[3] Ibid., pp. 46–47.
[4] An excellent account of the Wilmot controversy is found in Michael A. Morrison, *Slavery and the American West: The Eclipse of Manifest Destiny and the Coming of the Civil War* (Chapel Hill, 1999).

Congressman Bingham, though still finding his way in Washington, wasted little time in weighing in on the Wilmot question, consistently supporting the measure at every possible turn. "Regarding slavery as a political evil," Bingham railed in an 1848 speech on the House floor, "as a hindrance to the growth and prosperity of a state; as an element of weakness wherever it exists; as wholly incompatible with that degree of intelligence which makes labor either respectable or profitable,—I insist that we should fail to discharge our duty were we to tolerate its introduction and spread over this vast extent of country which has just come into our possession free." Across the aisle, Bingham's Whig peer, Abraham Lincoln, on the other hand, avoided active participation in the Wilmot debate for much of the first session of Congress (though he did vote on at least five occasions in favor of the proposal when it was put before him). In the ensuing second session, Lincoln, a moderate by temperament and fearful of disrupting Whig Party unity before their elected presidential candidate (Zachary Taylor) could assume office, similarly kept a low profile on the issue (though again, his voting record—pro-Wilmot—left no doubt as to his personal views on the matter).[5]

Bingham's heartfelt, and very public, articulation of the intimate connection between free soil, independence, and opportunity nicely encapsulated a set of ideas that have come to be known as free-soil ideology and foreshadowed the formal positions espoused a decade later by the Republican Party as the nation veered toward civil war.[6]

Unfortunately for the young congressman, Michigan's senior statesman, Senator Lewis Cass, once also a supporter of the proviso, had concocted an alternative plan for dealing with the question of slavery in the recently acquired territories. Fearing for the nation and for the continued unity of his beloved Democratic Party, and hoping to propel himself into the White House in the upcoming presidential election, Cass, in a letter that he penned in late 1847, proposed to allow the people residing in the western territories to decide for themselves whether they wanted to have slaves or not. The doctrine, known as popular sovereignty, became the centerpiece of the Democratic Party's platform down to the Civil War and it drove a wedge between the party's small but uncompromising free-soil wing (represented by Bingham among others) and the more mainstream members of the party

---

[5] *Congressional Globe*, 30th Cong., 1st sess., 1848, app., p. 1109. Lincoln's behavior in the Wilmot debates is chronicled by Donald in *Lincoln*, pp. 136–38.

[6] The classic work on free-soil ideology is Foner, *Free Soil*.

who endorsed popular sovereignty. Hostile to any plan that held out even the slightest possibility that slavery might further tighten its grip on the nation, Bingham, in spite of his very tenuous position as a freshman congressman, refused to follow Cass's lead and toe the party line and instead steadfastly clung to his free-soil ideals and to the Wilmot Proviso. By so doing, Bingham's action threatened to hopelessly divide Michigan's Democratic Party and to paralyze the state's congressional delegation to Washington. Strict partisanship, Bingham concluded, had to give way to principle. Indeed, Bingham accepted as an article of faith that, through the Northwest Ordinance of 1787, with its prohibition against the spread of slavery into the Old Northwest, the Founders had guaranteed that "every new settler, as he crossed the border of that great territory, to establish for himself and his children a home, had the solemn assurance of the Government that free labor was never to be degraded by its contact with slavery upon that soil, and that free men could only live there." Free soil thus stood not only as a national imperative but also as the very foundation for the nation's success and as the cornerstone for American freedom. It was thus incumbent upon the present generation of leaders to ensure that that promise was extended to the current and to all future generations of Americans.[7]

By no means was Bingham alone in his beliefs. Fortunately for the congressman and other Michigan Proviso men, a new political party, the earnestly named Free-Soil Party, entered the electoral fray in 1848, committed to a platform of congressional action to prevent slavery's spread into the western territories. Michigan Free-Soilers readily appreciated the difficult position they and their new party were in. With native son Lewis Cass in the presidential field and state Democrats given their marching orders to fall into line behind popular sovereignty, the fledgling party faced the very real threat of a stillbirth. To avoid such a fate, Michigan's Free-Soilers adopted a coalition building strategy. That is, they determined to form coalitions with either proviso-supporting Whigs or Democrats in the state's three congressional districts so as to work for the election of proviso men to Congress, period. For his consistent work on behalf of the proviso, Kinsley Bingham,

---

[7] *The Rise and Fall of the Democratic Party: Speech of Hon. Kinsley S. Bingham of Michigan, Delivered in the United States Senate, May 24, 1860* (n.p., 1860), p. 2, http://www.archive.org/stream/risefallofdemocr00bing#page/n1/mode/2up. This point of view was also shared by David Wilmot, who consciously sought to craft his controversial proviso in a manner that echoed the language of the Northwest Ordinance.

already the recipient of the renomination of district Democrats, also received the Free-Soil endorsement for Congress in Michigan's Third District.[8]

Bingham did not disappoint. Throughout the campaign he railed against what he believed to be an organized national Slave Power conspiracy and its nefarious efforts to undermine the antislavery intentions of the founders and to thus force slavery upon the western settlements, thereby dooming the region and its settlers to replicate the dismal path of the backward, retrograde, southern states. Preservation of the West as free soil, as a refuge for "our own race and color," as Bingham himself stated, played well with the Michigan electorate of 1848. Still uneasy in the wake of the state's near collapse following the Panic of 1837 and the attendant devastation unleashed on the state's hapless farmers, Michigan voters took to heart Bingham's warning about the dire threat posed to opportunity and independence in the West—the nation's safety valve and the traditional place for a fresh start—and to the status of humble yeoman farmers whose hard toil, it was feared, was destined to be compared to that of southern slaves. Not surprisingly, they readily embraced Bingham's synthesis of free-soil doctrine and overt racism as it spoke to their own uncertainties and fears. Indeed, it would be this seamless amalgamation of seemingly contradictory (antislavery and concurrently racially bigoted), yet incredibly powerful and motivational themes, that would lay the foundation for the Republican Party's meteoric rise to power in the state just a few years later.[9]

When the electoral dust cleared, Lewis Cass had squeaked out a win in his home state (though with only a plurality of the state's votes) in his quest for the presidency, but the Free-Soilers' coalition strategy had also paid large dividends as Proviso candidates (William Sprague, a proviso Whig, and Kinsley Bingham) captured two of the state's three congressional seats, thus ensuring the delegation's control by Proviso men. "The defeat of Genl Cass," Bingham wrote to his wife in the election's aftermath, "has broken up a knot of slaveholding politicians who would have undertaken to trample us in the

---

[8]Martin J. Hershock, *Paradox of Progress: Economic Change, Individual Enterprise, and Political Culture in Michigan, 1837–1878* (Athens, Ohio, 2003), pp. 6–7. Lincoln did not have the opportunity to run for a second term. Ensconced in a coterie of young and ambitious Whig hopefuls, Lincoln had pledged to serve but a single term in order to solidify his nomination for Congress in 1846. The plan was designed to provide an opportunity for others to fulfill their ambition to serve in Congress as well. By 1848, though, Lincoln had come to regret his pledge. Donald, *Lincoln*, p. 124.

[9]Hershock, *Paradox of Progress*, pp. 112–13.

dust if he had succeeded." Perhaps equally as important, this same coalition-based group also controlled the balance of power in the state legislature, a fact of no small significance, given that that body would be responsible for choosing a new senator to represent the state in Washington (Cass had resigned his seat in order to run for the White House). Well aware of the impending danger and determined to regain the upper hand, Cass and his popular-sovereignty allies quickly flew into action, using their control over the state party apparatus to secure the Democratic senate nomination for Cass (though the state legislature temporarily handcuffed him with strongly worded pro-proviso voting instructions) and, later in the year, to thwart Free-Soiler efforts to capture the Democratic gubernatorial nomination for Robert McClelland, a proviso man.[10]

While Cass busied himself with reasserting his domination over the Michigan Democratic Party, back in Washington sectional animus again threatened to rip the nation apart when the newly elected president, the Whig Zachary Taylor, ignited a powder keg with his proposal to admit California, inundated with gold rush settlers and mired in chaos and disorder, directly into the union as a free state. Determined to avoid a dissolution of the union along sectional lines and hoping to avoid a repeat of the Wilmot debate, Sen. Henry Clay, the Great Compromiser from Kentucky, offered up an elaborate omnibus bill designed to present something to all sides in the debate: California's admission as a free state; a new, more stringent, federal fugitive slave law; the end of the slave trade in Washington, D.C.; popular sovereignty in the newly established New Mexico and Utah Territories; and a resolution of the Texas–New Mexico Territory boundary dispute in favor of proslavery Texas. Encouraged by the proposal's embrace of his popular sovereignty idea and its nationalist spirit, Michigan's Democratic leader, Lewis Cass, made support for the measure a litmus test of party loyalty and went so far as to threaten to resign his Senate seat if the Michigan state legislature did not rescind its 1849 instructions binding him to the Wilmot Proviso. Party stalwarts quickly moved into action in the state legislature, passing a motion to repeal the 1849 instructions and commending Cass for his ardent nationalism. In spite of the apparent shift toward moderation in Michigan, Kinsley Bingham once again refused to yield and stood fast in his opposition

---

[10]Kinsley Bingham to Mary Bingham, December 25, 1848, "August-December, 1848," Box 1, Kinsley S. Bingham Papers, 1820–1944, Bentley Historical Library, University of Michigan; Hershock, *Paradox of Progress*, pp. 7–11.

to the compromise and its proslavery provisions, asserting that, "coming as I do from the laboring classes, I should have failed to discharge my duty if I had not spoken and acted when I thought their interests in jeopardy. As a Representative of free white laboring men, I mean to defend their rights." Submitting to any compromise measure that even held out the possibility of slavery's further spread was something Bingham could not countenance.[11]

The eventual passage of the compromise measures (necessarily broken out into individual bills after the omnibus's defeat by Illinois senator, and Lincoln rival, Stephen Douglas) and Bingham's outspoken resistance to his party rendered him a political pariah among Michigan's Democratic leaders, who responded to his maverick ways by reading him out of their organization in August 1850, noting that as a result of "his efforts to promote the agitation which has for years convulsed the nation—to keep open questions the settlement of which was demanded by good judgment of our people—and by his factious opposition to measures having for their object the tranquility of the country, he has forfeited forever our respect and confidence, . . . *the democracy have done with him.*" After serving out the remainder of his congressional term, Bingham returned home in 1851 to resume his vocation as a farmer. Though retired from formal political life, Bingham did not withdraw completely from politics. On the contrary, no longer welcome within his former party, Bingham, unlike the majority of the state's Proviso Democrats who found the chords of partisan fealty too strong to easily rend asunder, openly joined the Michigan Free-Soil Party, then operating under the name of the Free Democratic Party. Here Bingham found kindred spirits in his ongoing battle against slavery's expansion. This new partisan affiliation would soon lead him into the ranks of what was to become known as the Republican Party where he would play a critical role in helping to persuade his former Democratic peers to join in the party's crusade against the slave power.[12]

---

[11]McDaid, "Kinsley S. Bingham," pp. 56–59. For his part, Abraham Lincoln had already returned home by the time the debate over the compromise reached the halls of Congress. His views on the measure are rather complex. Though a long time supporter of the compromise's originator, Henry Clay, Lincoln did not agree with the measure's embrace of popular sovereignty or of its fugitive slave provisions. At the same time, Lincoln eagerly accepted California's admission as a free state and the end of the slave trade in the nation's capital. Sadly, Lincoln did not find himself in a position to actively participate in public debate on the issue. In February 1850, his young son Edward Baker died of pulmonary tuberculosis, sending Lincoln into a bout of deep depression. Donald, *Lincoln*, pp. 153–54.

[12]*Detroit Free Press*, Aug. 25, 1850 (emphasis in original).

The relative ease with which Bingham made this transition (undeniably made simpler by his being read out of his party) stands in marked contrast to the experience of his recent congressional colleague, and the person who became the embodiment of the new party's spirit, Abraham Lincoln. One marked difference between the men was the fact that Lincoln was a son of the border, a Kentuckian by birth and a Hoosier-Illinoisan by upbringing. With his feet squarely planted in multiple worlds (North and South, upland southerner and Yankee, slave and free, commercial and traditional, urban and rural, etc.) and finding himself accustomed to having to connect with an electorate of diverse geographic and cultural origin, Lincoln was always (and prudently so) the cautious moderate and political realist.

Bingham, on the other hand, matured in an evangelical culture of moral imperatives and absolutes (both in New York's Burned-Over District and in Michigan, the Yankee West). More important still, though vastly underappreciated by historians, was Bingham's understanding of, and connection to, the ethos of his small-time farmer-producer neighbors; neighbors who were uneasily grappling with the uncertainty and disruptions associated with the fits and starts of the antebellum market revolution. It was the fear of losing one's autonomy in the face of this transformation, a fear driven home spectacularly in Michigan by the devastation associated with the Panic of 1837, that had lured Bingham and his neighbors into the Democratic Party to begin with; and it was this same fear that, as previously mentioned, informed their understanding of the meaning of free-soil doctrine. That is, it was their view that it was essential for the western territories to follow the pattern previously established in the Old Northwest so that "every new settler, as he crossed the border of that great territory, to establish for himself and his children a home, had the solemn assurance of the Government that free labor was never to be degraded by its contact with slavery upon that soil." Bingham's idealism, infused with the immediacy of the anxiety and uncertainty plaguing contemporary life on the Michigan frontier, thus facilitated Bingham's political metamorphosis and enabled his message, with its reiteration of the theme of preserving autonomous freedom in the face of encroaching power, to resonate with voters who, in the main, did not care one way or the other about the unfortunate souls enslaved in the states of the American South and but who were seeking comfort and stability in a tumultuous world of rampant social, economic, and cultural transformation.

Lincoln, of course, also sprang from the same agrarian taproot and thus certainly appreciated this point of view. In the main, however, he had largely distanced himself from that world, choosing instead to embrace the ethos of the marketplace, with its message of opportunity and mobility. Accordingly, Lincoln, whose Whig Party favored commercial expansion, banks, and soft money, and the construction of internal improvements, often found himself at philosophical odds with a great many Illinois farmers whose discomfort with the cash nexus still manifested itself in the political realm. Needing a portion of these votes to secure victory (Democrats predominated in Illinois), Lincoln picked his political battles very carefully, clinging to established political doctrines and platforms and working through existing political structures. This dogged loyalty to party also played a crucial role in shaping Lincoln's response to the crisis posed by the introduction of Stephen Douglas's Kansas-Nebraska bill, in 1854. When push came to shove and anti-Nebraska forces began to coalesce in Illinois, Lincoln, as a readily identifiable and long-term Whig, faced an uphill struggle to convince disgruntled Democrats to join him, their longtime political enemy, in a crusade against slavery's expansion. Bingham, on the other hand, as a former Democrat, faced no such disadvantage in Democratically controlled Michigan. State Democrats knew him to be reliable on the core issues that had mattered to them for so long. Moreover, his antislavery background worked to assuage the fears of Michigan Whigs, who had long embraced political antislavery as a staple of party identity and who, historian Ronald Formisano suggests, readily shed partisan restraints on moral imperatives.[13]

The contrasting political perspectives of Kinsley Bingham and Abraham Lincoln came into even sharper focus with the introduction of the controversial Kansas-Nebraska bill in January 1854. Crafted primarily as a political expedient to facilitate the construction of a transcontinental railroad with a northern terminus at Chicago, Douglas's bill, after initial southern opposition and demands for revision, explicitly repudiated the 1820 Missouri Compromise's exclusion of slavery north of 36°30' in the remainder of the

---

[13] For a detailed discussion of Michigan's antebellum political climate, see Hershock, *Paradox of Progress*. On Lincoln's Illinois and Indiana influences, see Richard Nation, *At Home in the Hoosier Hills: Agriculture, Politics, and Religion in Southern Indiana, 1810–1870* (Bloomington, Ind., 2005), and Gerald Leonard, *The Invention of Party Politics: Federalism, Popular Sovereignty, and Constitutional Development in Jacksonian Illinois* (Chapel Hill, 2000). An excellent discussion of Whigs' antiparty tendencies can be found in Ronald P. Formisano, *The Birth of Mass Political Parties: Michigan, 1827–1861* (Princeton, N.J., 1971), p. 77.

Louisiana Purchase territory, from which Kansas and Nebraska were to be created. In its stead the bill offered popular sovereignty as a vehicle for determining the status of slavery in these newly created territories, thus anointing popular sovereignty as official federal policy in the West.[14]

Both Lincoln and Bingham responded indignantly to the proposal, with the former conceding that the bill "astounded us. . . . We were thunderstruck and surprised." In spite of his shock and dismay, Lincoln remained surprisingly quiet about the measure in the early months of 1854. Undeniably, his silence had much to do with his participation in the important and time-consuming case of *Illinois Central Railroad v. McLean County*, which made its way into the Illinois supreme court in late February. But, as David Donald argues, Lincoln's silence was also a function of the fact that "as a private citizen, holding and seeking no political office, he did not feel called upon to make a public statement about the Kansas-Nebraska bill."[15]

By contrast, Kinsley Bingham felt no such reservations. On the contrary, Bingham immediately entered the fray and condemned the bill as a measure "by which traitorous ambition confederating with violators of a solemn and time-honored compact, is seeking to inflict upon the nation a deep and indelible disgrace." Mortified by the final passage of the bill, in May 1854, Bingham joined a growing chorus demanding the abandonment of traditional partisan fealties and the organization of a new political movement focused on waging war in defense of free soil. "In a republican government," Bingham affirmed, "agitation is as necessary as tranquility is dangerous. . . . To keep alive the patriotic feelings and pure motives which actuated the founders of this republic, the minds of men must be led to excitement and the necessary commotions naturally arising result in party spirit and political strife." That was not to say that the current state of political affairs, however, was to be perpetuated. Just the opposite was true, Bingham argued: "questions which at one time may have [been] leading topics the issues of which may have threatened some dire calamity to the nation, may give place to other and more essential subjects." It was this belief, as well as the necessity of organizing the diverse array of anti-Nebraska sentiment outside the contemporary party structure, that prompted Bingham, who had already been

---

[14]A succinct, yet comprehensive account of Douglas and the Kansas-Nebraska bill can be found in Robert W. Johannsen, *Stephen Douglas* (Champaign, Ill., 1997). The measure is considered more fully and in broader context in Morrison, *Slavery and the American West*.

[15]Abraham Lincoln, quoted in Donald, *Lincoln*, pp. 168, 169.

relegated an outsider by that system (which many now viewed with great suspicion), to play a lead role in the creation of Michigan's Republican Party, on July 6, 1854.[16]

Lincoln, too, heard a similar case being made in his native Illinois, yet he remained reticent about casting his political lot with anti-Nebraska forces outside his native Whig Party throughout 1854 and 1855. Indeed, there was good reason for Lincoln's hesitancy and caution. Beyond the myriad political movements seeking to give form to the assorted collection of anti-Nebraska elements in the state, including the new Republican movement that had been founded by known radicals and abolitionists, Illinois politics was also mired in chaos due to the sudden explosion of anti-immigrant nativism as a political force in 1854 and 1855. Naturally inclined toward moderation, and far too prudent a politician to ride the hobby horse of the moment, Lincoln worked to use anti-Nebraska sentiment to revive flagging support for the Whig Party, avoiding any direct involvement with the emerging Republican coalition.[17]

Bingham, meanwhile, eagerly encouraged the actions of the roughly fifteen hundred other Michiganders assembled in the city of Jackson to forge a new party on July 6, 1854. In recognition for his staunch and unwavering advocacy of free-soil principles, as well as for the trust that he engendered among Michigan's anxious population, Kinsley Bingham was rewarded with the new Republican Party's gubernatorial nomination. Following the announcement of Bingham's candidacy to those gathered under the oaks in Jackson that day, according to newspaper editor Charles DeLand, a witness to the event, "a spark of enthusiasm fired the crowd, shouts of approbation rang through the vast assemblage and if any doubt had previously existed as to who should be the man for Governor that doubt was removed."[18]

---

[16] Bingham's quote is drawn from a Free Democratic resolution that he drafted at the party's specially assembled convention. *Detroit Daily Democrat,* Feb. 20, 1854. One outcome of the convention was to nominate Bingham as the party's candidate for the governorship in that same year. "Undated and untitled essay on political parties and republican government," "Correspondence, Undated," box 1, Bingham Papers.

[17] Donald, *Lincoln,* pp., 168–71; Luthin, "Abraham Lincoln Becomes a Republican," pp. 420–28.

[18] William Stocking, *Under the Oaks: Commemorating the Fiftieth Anniversary of the Founding of the Republican Party, at Jackson, Michigan, July 6, 1854* (Detroit, 1904), p. 52. For a full description of the formation of the Republican Party in antebellum Michigan, see Hershock, *Paradox of Progress.*

That Bingham's candidacy worried Michigan Democrats cannot be denied. Large anti-Nebraska meetings had been prevalent throughout Michigan in the months leading up to the formation of the Republican Party and many Democrats had been in attendance. Moreover, a great many state residents drew a ready connection between Douglas's Kansas-Nebraska Act and Lewis Cass, the father of the popular sovereignty idea. Not surprisingly then, Cass took to the stump in Michigan to argue for popular sovereignty as the best means of preventing slavery's future spread. In addition, he and the state party machinery nominated the popular three-time former governor, John Barry, as the Democratic candidate for the governorship in the hope of minimizing Bingham's appeal among the party faithful. For their part, Republicans were also careful to include a carefully, albeit nebulously worded, plank in their party platform that also addressed state issues to help soothe the fears of state voters.[19]

Despite Cass's best efforts, however, the new party swept to a surprising victory in November 1854, capturing the governorship as well as majorities in both houses of the state legislature. Bingham worked diligently to keep the party's free-soil principles front and center throughout his first term in office, insisting at every turn that he would not allow the slave power to "nationalize slavery . . . and to sectionalize freedom." As the situation in Kansas escalated and sectionalism intensified, state residents held fast to their new party, rewarding Bingham with election to a second term in office in 1856. It was not until that year, though, with its bloodshed on the plains of Kansas and in the Senate chamber, that Abraham Lincoln finally abandoned the shell that was the Illinois Whig Party and embraced the Republican standard. Finally, the two men, who had shared a similar antislavery outlook from the time that their paths first crossed, back in 1847, found themselves in the same political camp fighting a common enemy.[20]

Two years after Lincoln's conversion to Republicanism, the party turned to him to challenge Stephen Douglas, the architect of Kansas-Nebraska and the nemesis of Republicans across the nation, for his Senate seat in Washington. Though running an able campaign and garnering much positive national

---

[19]Hershock, *Paradox of Progress*, pp. 132–35.
[20]Message of Kinsley Bingham to the Legislature of the State of Michigan, January 4, 1855, in George N. Fuller, ed., *Messages of the Governors of Michigan*, 4 vols. (Lansing, Mich., 1925–27), 2:287.

attention, Lincoln was unable to unseat Douglas. For Kinsley Bingham, however, the story line was very different. As the nation devolved further into a sectional free fall and Lincoln went down to defeat in Illinois, Bingham's party confirmed its faith in him by electing him to serve Michigan in the same body that Lincoln was denied—the U.S. Senate. In his new office, Kinsley Bingham continued to wage war against the slave power and to work diligently to restore the government to its original design. In a lengthy speech delivered on the Senate floor in late May 1860, Bingham offered a powerful, although to him unknown, epilogue on his political life, outlining his path from the Democratic to the Republican Party noting that, "step by step . . . has the Democratic Party of the North ceased to be the party of freedom, and been brought under perfect subjugation to the interests of slavery . . . and has lost the manly, independent spirit, which was the characteristic of the party in the days of General Jackson." Working through the Republican Party, Bingham affirmed,

> the people of the great Northwestern States . . . will ever hold in grateful recollection the memory of those whose statesmanlike and patriotic foresight dedicated the soil on which they live to free labor; and they are not unmindful of the duty they owe their posterity. They mean to prove to the world that the same zeal for liberty which inspired their ancestors still animates them. With Slavery in the States of this Confederacy, they claim no right to interfere. . . . But in the broad Territories of this Union they are determined that slavery shall never obtain a foothold. The auction block for fellowmen shall never be established there; the crack of the driver's whip, the clink of the fetter, or the moan of the slave mother at the loss of her offspring, shall never be heard there; but those broad plains, those fertile valleys, and those mountain gorges rich in shinning metal, shall be wrought alone by the willing hands of free men.

In concluding, Bingham assured his constituents that "a party is about to take possession of this Government, with the same name and principles of the Republican Party of 1800. An enlightened people are thoroughly aroused to the good work; and they will reverse the decisions of your Supreme Court, and the policy which has prevailed under Democratic rule; they will make freedom national and slavery sectional." Without any doubt, Bingham's conversion to Republicanism was complete.[21]

---

[21] *Rise and Fall of the Democratic Party*, pp. 15–16.

Unfortunately for Senator Bingham, he would not live to see his ultimate goal of slavery's demise and freedom's restoration achieved. The senator was able to celebrate the electoral victory he had predicted, a victory that swept into the White House his old congressional peer and relative Republican newcomer Abraham Lincoln. He also lived to see the secession of the southern states from the Union and the commencement of civil war in the United States. And while the nation's ultimate fate and the fate of the Revolutionary heritage he had so eloquently articulated in his May 1860 speech remained very much in doubt when he died of apoplexy, in October 1861, Bingham left the world knowing that he had done everything in his power to ensure that liberty, freedom, and opportunity, the values that he had worked so hard to weave into the fabric of his now beloved Republican Party, prevailed.

So what then can one learn from a study of Kinsley Bingham's political journey? Certainly one cannot help but recognize that Bingham was a man of conviction, a man of action. Indeed, in large measure, it was Bingham's deeply held conviction that precipitated and shaped the course of his political life: first as an adherent of Jacksonian Democracy, then as a proviso Democrat, and finally, as a founding member of the Free-Soil-based Republican Party. Bingham served his state and the nation at a time of tremendous tension and within a political system straining to contain sectional discord. Within this highly charged and fluid environment, political loyalties could, and sometimes (as in the case of Bingham) did, change quickly. It is important to note, however, the vital importance of local circumstances in shaping the contours of the political crisis of the era. In the end, Kinsley Bingham and his similarly minded political peers needed the support of their constituents back home to gain and, perhaps more importantly, to hold political office and promote specific policies. Given this fact, one cannot help but marvel at the political acumen of Kinsley Bingham and the skill with which he wove together the immediate concerns of his local Michigan constituents and the emerging free-soil movement. One must also note Bingham's incredible good fortune to be representing a state where a politician with strong, even controversial, opinions could reasonably expect the continuing support of his neighbors who themselves were reared in the same moralistic ethos and who thus tended to view the world in terms of moral imperatives. This environment was thus a forgiving one and it helped to smooth the way for Bingham's conversion to the Republican Party. Abraham Lincoln, Bingham's

1847 congressional mate, did not share the same good fortune and thus his path to Republicanism was more hesitant and guarded. His was a syncretic world, a world where many different peoples, ideas, and values came together, and a world where moderation and compromise were both political and social necessities and limits upon one's ability to freely follow one's conscience in the political realm. In the end, of course, Abraham Lincoln, like Bingham, would convert to Republicanism (albeit later and after much resistance). Both men would ride that movement into Washington: Bingham to the Senate and Lincoln, more famously, into the White House. While Lincoln's story is deservedly the more celebrated one, the one that all are familiar with, it is essential to note that without the efforts of Republican pioneers like Michigan's Kinsley Bingham, the party's miraculous victory in 1860, and Lincoln's subsequent fame, just might not have happened.

Jenny Wahl

## *Dred*, Panic, War

*How a Slave Case Triggered Financial Crisis and Civil Disunion*

> A single prosperous business session wipes out even the remembrance of past blunders. All is forgotten until another storm comes, and a thunderstroke shatters again the very foundations of our boasted strength and greatness. Our merchants and business men by the hundreds and thousands are now mourning over their folly.[1]

IN EERILY FAMILIAR ways, the financial panic of 1857 prefigures the current subprime mortgage crisis. Then as now, lightly regulated institutions eagerly extended credit based on exciting new financial instruments, speculators assumed that real property values would continue to climb indefinitely, and the reverberations from the inevitable collapse echoed round the world. The words of one pundit seem apt: History repeats itself because nobody listens.[2]

What follows is an account of the Panic of 1857, arguably the first truly global financial meltdown that involved multiple interlocking markets and sectors. In their landmark study of the panic, Charles Calomiris and Larry Schweikart suggest that the trigger may have been the case of *Dred Scott v. Sandford*,[3] although they acknowledge the difficulty of proving that contention. Using a heretofore untapped data source, I find empirical evidence

---

[1] *Boston Independent*, Dec. 24, 1857.
[2] Attributed to Laurence J. Peter, coauthor, with Raymond Hull, of *The Peter Principle* (New York, 1969). See for example http://www.age-of-the-sage.org/history/quotations/history_4.html. Another version of this statement—which I like even better—is "History teaches us the mistakes we are going to make."
[3] Charles Calomiris and Larry Schweikart, "The Panic of 1857: Origins, Transmission, and Containment," *Journal of Economic History* 51 (1996):807–34; 60 U.S. (19 How.) 393, 452 (1857).

that the case indeed helped set off the crisis—and set the stage for secession. By affirming the value of slave property and undercutting the value of territorial land,[4] Chief Justice Roger Taney's opinion stemmed the tide of migration westward, lowered the worth of investments in western railroads, and created havoc on Wall Street. As *Dred* led to panic, panic led to war. Because the South weathered the financial turmoil relatively better than the North, Dixie's departure from the Union became a more realistic option.

## Setting the Stage for the Impending Crisis
### Geography and Population

Between 1845 and 1853, huge changes in the geography of the United States occurred. The nation added five states in the first six years of the period, two of which—Texas and California—also increased actual acreage (see fig. 1). The disputed Oregon territory officially became part of the United States in 1846, and the Treaty of Guadalupe Hidalgo ended the Mexican-American War in 1848, granting the United States another large chunk of land. The only remaining portion of the continental United States—denoted as Mexico on the map—was the Gadsden Purchase, bought in 1853 in hopes of obtaining a southern route for a transcontinental railroad.[5]

As the nation's landmass stretched westward, so did its population. People took seriously the admonition to "Go west, young man."[6] Settlers migrated west through the 1840s and '50s, both in the North and the South (fig. 2).[7]

---

[4] Here is the relevant phrase: "It is the opinion of the court that the act of Congress which prohibited a citizen from holding and owning property of this kind in the territory of the United States north of the line therein mentioned, is not warranted by the Constitution, and is therefore void."

[5] For discussion, see Jere Roberson, "The South and the Pacific Railroad, 1845–1855," *Western Historical Quarterly* 5 (1974):163–86.

[6] The authorship of the phrase has been debated for years. Most recently, Fred Shapiro makes a strong case in the *Yale Book of Quotations* (New Haven, 2006) for Horace Greeley as opposed to John Soule, a newspaperman from Terre Haute, Indiana. For a summary, see http://www.llrx.com/features/quotedetective.htm.

[7] States and territories included in the regions indicated in figure 7.2 are as follows: NEng/MAtl = Maine, New Hampshire, Vermont, Massachusetts, Rhode Island, Connecticut, New York, New Jersey, Pennsylvania; ENC/WNC/Pac (except MO) = Ohio, Indiana, Illinois, Michigan, Wisconsin, Minnesota, Iowa, Dakota Territory, Nebraska, Kansas, Oregon Territory, California; SAtl/ESC = Delaware, Maryland, District of Columbia, Virginia, North Carolina, South Carolina, Georgia, Florida, Kentucky, Tennessee, Alabama, Mississippi; and WSC/MO/Mtn = Missouri, Arkansas, Louisiana, Texas, Colorado, New Mexico Territory, Utah Territory.

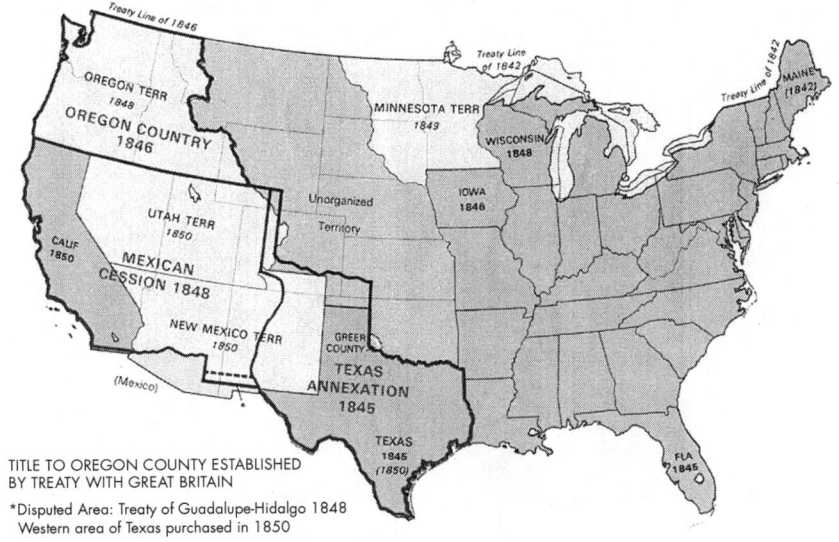

Fig. 1. Map of the United States (1850).
*Source:* http://xroads.virginia.edu/~MAP/TERRITORY/1850map.htm.

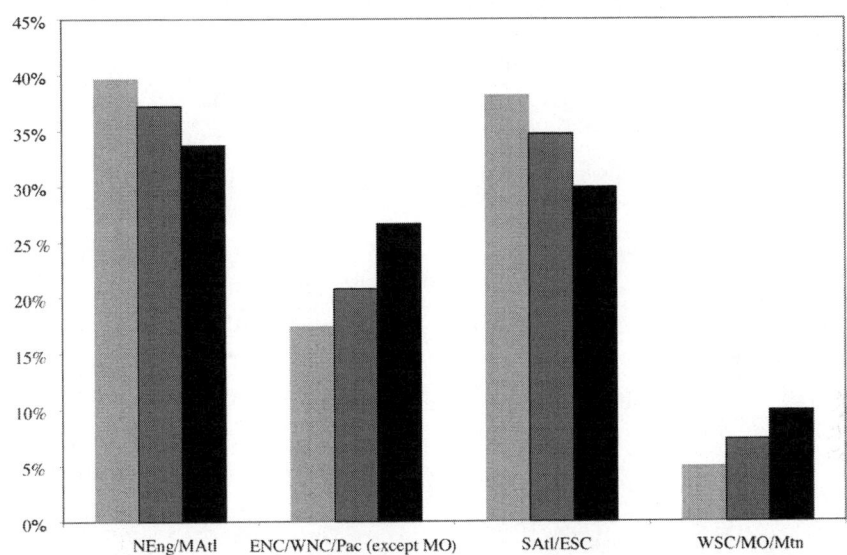

Fig. 2. Population distribution across regions, 1840, 1850, 1860.
*Source:* http://www.census.gov/population/www/documentation/twps0056.html, http://fisher.lib.virginia.edu/collections/stats/histcensus/.

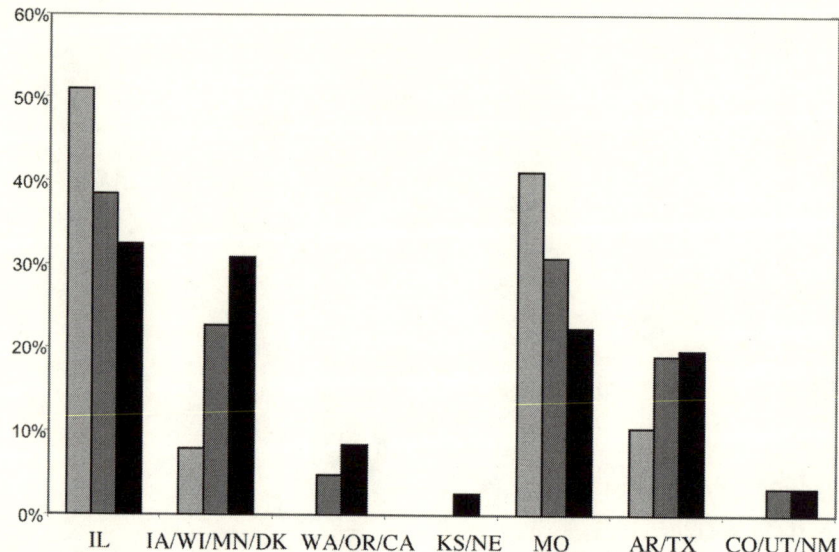

FIG. 3. Distribution of frontier population by region, 1840, 1850, 1860.
Source: http://www.census.gov/population/www/documentation/twps0056.htm, http://fisher.lib.virginia.edu/collections/stats/histcensus/.

Richard Steckel suggests that migration during this time period often took place along latitudinal lines.[8]

Take a closer look at the nation's frontier areas—Illinois, Iowa, Wisconsin, Minnesota, the Dakotas, the Pacific Northwest, Kansas, Nebraska, Missouri, Arkansas, Texas, and the mountain and southwestern states—which contained only 5 percent of the population in 1840 but 17 percent in 1860. Illinois had nearly half a million people in 1840—more than half the frontier population—growing to 1.7 million inhabitants by 1860. Missouri was next largest in 1840, with more than 40 percent of the frontier population; by 1860 it contained nearly 1.2 million people. Yet, as figure 3 indicates, frontier areas farther west grew much faster than these two, containing only 8 percent of the frontier population in 1840 but 46 percent in 1860.

U.S. land policy, particularly the Graduation Act of 1854, encouraged this western movement.[9] Figure 4 shows that people bought huge numbers

---

[8] Richard Steckel, "The Economic Foundations of East-West Migration during the Nineteenth Century," *Explorations in Economic History* 20 (1983):14–36.

[9] The act reduced the lot price to one dollar if unsold for ten years and to 12.5 cents if unsold for thirty years. Sidney Ratner, James Soltow, and Richard Sylla, *The Evolution of the American Economy*, 2d ed. (New York, 1993), p. 139. The act placed no limit on the number of acres any purchaser bought. Allan Nevins, *The Emergence of Lincoln: Douglas, Buchanan, and Party Chaos, 1857–59* (New York, 1950), p. 183.

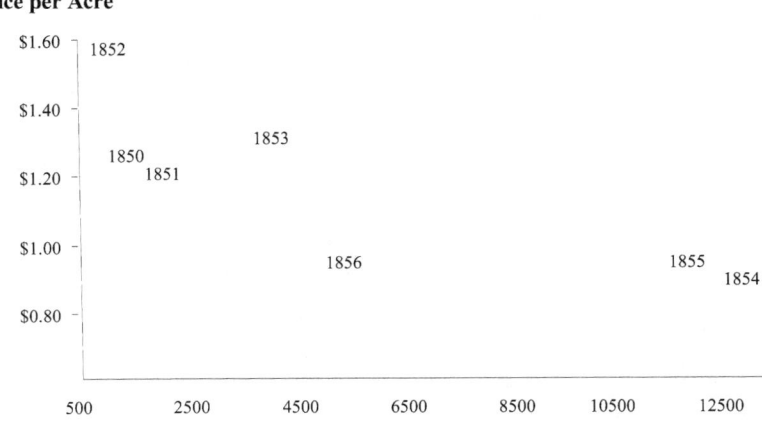

FIG. 4. Number and price of cash acres entered at public land offices, 1850–56. *Source:* Walter Smith and Arthur Cole, *Fluctuations in American Business* (Cambridge, Mass., 1935), p. 185.

of acres from public land offices in 1854 and 1855. Much of this land was located in Wisconsin, Minnesota, and Iowa.[10] Although cash acreage slacked off in 1856, the price per acre remained comparable to per-acre prices in the two previous years.[11]

The secondary market for land was where the real action took place, however. In mid-1857, lots in western cities could pass through the hands of as many as twelve people in sixty days.[12] Kenneth Stampp notes that Omaha property selling for $500 in the spring of 1856 went for $5,000 in the spring of 1857.[13] David Mitchell suggests that "everybody in the West had a share

---

[10] Walter Smith and Arthur Cole, *Fluctuations in American Business* (Cambridge, Mass., 1935), p. 55.

[11] Military warrants complicated land markets in this period. Between 1847 and 1855, Congress enacted four bounty land warrant acts granting nearly 61 million acres of unsettled public-domain lands to veterans of any war or their heirs. Jeremy Atack and Peter Passell provide a table of the significant public land laws from 1785 to 1916. Atack and Passell, *A New Economic View of American History*, 2d ed. (New York, 1994), pp. 258–59. A secondary market in these transferable warrants flourished: 60 percent of acres entered at the public land offices in 1857 and 1858 were warrant acres. Paul Gates, "The Struggle for Land and the 'Irrepressible Conflict,'" *Political Science Quarterly* 66 (1951):254. Arbitrage would tend to equalize cash and warrant prices, however, so the cash price per acre approximates annual land prices. Jenny Wahl, "Stay East, Young Man? Market Repercussions of the *Dred Scott* Decision," *Chicago-Kent Law Review* 82 (2007):361–91 contains further details.

[12] Nevins, *Emergence of Lincoln*, p. 183; Calomiris and Schweikart, "Panic of 1857," p. 810.

[13] Kenneth Stampp, *America in 1857: A Nation on the Brink* (New York, 1990), p. 218.

of God's Earth, quietly increasing at a rate of perhaps a hundred, or at least twenty per cent per annum—it was hoped."[14]

## Railroads

Although the increased size of the antebellum United States and the concurrent population movements were notable, railroads were the big story of the 1850s, because they revolutionized securities markets just as they transformed transportation. To understand the Panic of 1857, we must see how railroads fit into the picture.

### Interaction with Land Markets

Railroads interacted with land markets in the nineteenth century, because they both affected and were affected by the expected value of the land surrounding them. Owners of land could find themselves substantially richer—at least on paper—if a railroad were built nearby. They could transport both themselves and their products cheaper and faster by rail than by wagon.[15] This capitalization of reduced transportation costs into land values meant that savvy speculators did their best to ascertain where railroads were likely to be constructed so that they could buy up neighboring plots. By the same token, railroad managers were on the lookout for locations where people desired to live—a larger population meant more traffic for trains and thus greater potential profits.

Albert Fishlow offers empirical evidence to support the interwoven nature of markets. More than 60 percent of the railroad construction in Illinois up to 1853 was concentrated in one-fourth of the land area of the state: the nineteen leading wheat- and corn-growing counties. Wisconsin displayed a similar pattern. And statistics vividly show that railroad counties in Iowa had much greater population density: overall density was 9.3 persons per square mile in 1850, but typical counties with railroads could boast of twenty to thirty

---

[14] D. W. Mitchell, *Ten Years Residence in the United States* (London, 1862), p. 328.

[15] Robert Fogel, *Railroads and American Economic Growth: Essays in Econometric History* (Baltimore, 1964), pp. 82–83, provides evidence of transportation cost differentials. Scholars disagree about exactly how beneficial railroads were. In addition to Fogel, see Paul Cootner, "The Role of the Railroads in United States Economic Growth," *Journal of Economic History* 23 (1963):477–521; and Albert Fishlow, *American Railroads and the Transformation of the Ante-Bellum Economy* (Cambridge, Mass., 1965). On whether agricultural or urban land benefited more, see Michael Haines and Robert Margo, "Railroads and Local Economic Development: The United States in the 1850s," NBER Working Paper no. W12381 (July 2006).

persons per square mile. Three Iowa railroad counties had more than forty persons per square mile.[16]

## Historical Growth and Regional Patterns

Although America's great railroads trace their beginnings to the 1830s, rail transport proved fairly insignificant for the first two decades. The Baltimore and Ohio (B&O) line began in 1830 and the Erie in 1832, but only about a thousand miles of rails existed in 1835. People began to consider railroads as an alternative to canals when the Boston and Lowell Railroad started to divert traffic from the Middlesex Canal. Yet barely nine thousand miles of track had been laid by 1850, mostly in the Northeast, and many routes ran for only short distances.[17] The West contained just 12 percent of rails, all in the Old Northwest Territory and primarily in Ohio and Michigan.[18] The six years from mid-1851 to mid-1857 were frenetic ones for railroad consolidation and building (see fig. 5).[19] By 1853 people could travel by rail from New York City to Chicago; shortly thereafter, rails connected Chicago to the Mississippi River.[20]

Although figure 5 shows that total investment and mileage began to slow around 1854, the building of western roads was still gathering steam. Perhaps one of the most notable features of the rapid rail expansion of the 1850s was what happened in the northern states near the western frontier. Figure 6 shows, for example, that six states—Illinois, Indiana, Iowa, Michigan, Ohio, and Wisconsin—enjoyed fully three-quarters of new track laid in 1856 (fig. 6). Illinois acquired as much new track in 1856 as all five states of the Old Northwest Territory did in 1850.[21] Early in 1857 workers completed the Milwaukee and Mississippi Railroad, and the B&O reached St. Louis.[22]

Worth noting is where railroads were *not* located. As of 1861, the eleven Confederate states had only about one-third of the railroad lines and one-fifth of the employees in the industry.[23] This pattern is easily explained. Because

---

[16] Fishlow, *American Railroads*, pp. 173–76.
[17] For information about rail mileage, see John Stover, *American Railroads* (Chicago, 1961), pp. 28–29; Stover, *Iron Road to the West* (New York, 1978), chap. 5; and Susan B. Carter, Scott Sigmund Gartner, Michael R. Haines, Alan L. Olmstead, Richard Sutch, and Gavin Wright, eds., *Historical Statistics of the United States*, millennial edition, 5 vols. (New York, 2006).
[18] Stover, *Iron Road*, p. 13; *Historical Statistics of the U.S.*
[19] For details, see Fishlow, *American Railroads*, pp. 112–14; Stampp, *America in 1857*, pp. 214–15.
[20] Atack and Passell, *New Economic View*, p. 429.
[21] Stover, *American Railroads*, p. 39; Stover, *Iron Road*, p. 23.
[22] Stampp, *America in 1857*, p. 214.
[23] Stover *American Railroads*, pp. 54–55.

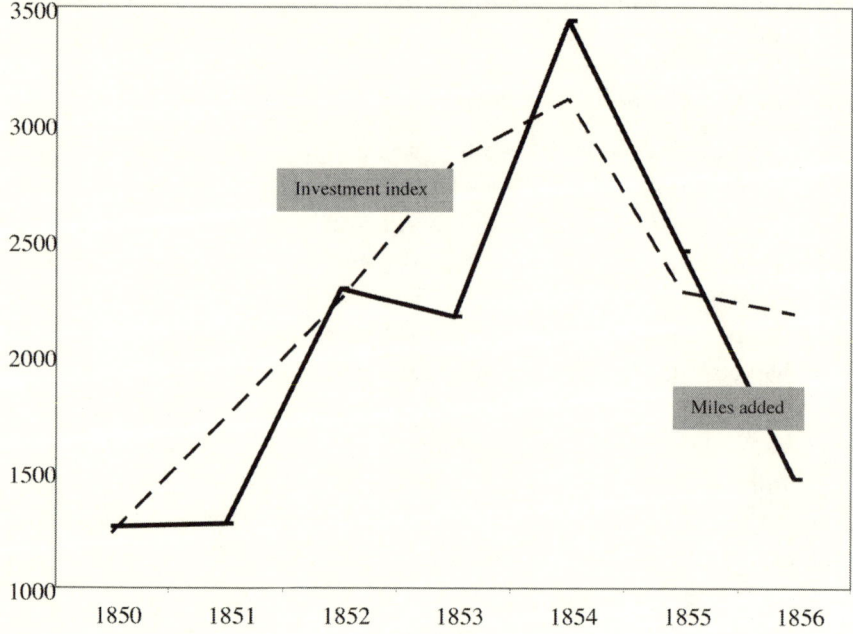

FIG. 5. Railroad investment and additional mileage, 1850–56.

*Sources:* G. Lloyd Wilson and Ellwood Spencer, "Growth of the Railroad Network in the United States," *Land Economics* 6 (1950):339; John Stover, *History of the Baltimore and Ohio Railroad* (West Lafayette, Ind., 1987), p. 317; Albert Fishlow, *American Railroads and the Transformation of the Ante-bellum Economy* (Cambridge, Mass., 1965), table 16; Susan B. Carter, Scott Sigmund Gartner, Michael R. Haines, Alan L. Olmstead, Richard Sutch, and Gavin Wright, eds., *Historical Statistics of the United States,* millennial ed., 5 vols. (New York, 2006), www.hsus.cambridge.org.

*Note:* Miles are actual miles; the investment index equals gross investment in millions of 1860 dollars multiplied by 30. Constructing the index in this way permits the two series to be graphed on the same set of axes.

the South was blessed with far more navigable inland waterways, the relative benefits of railroads were smaller there.[24] What is more, southerners had an alternative use for their capital—slaves.

## Land Grants and the Role of the Federal Government

Just as government had a hand in nineteenth-century land markets, so too did it play a part in the nineteenth-century railroad revolution. Starting with a grant to the Illinois Central in September 1850, the federal government

---

[24] Allan Nevins, *Ordeal of the Union,* vol. 2, *A House Dividing, 1852–1857* (New York, 1947), pp. 195, 208–14; Fishlow, *American Railroads,* p. 85.

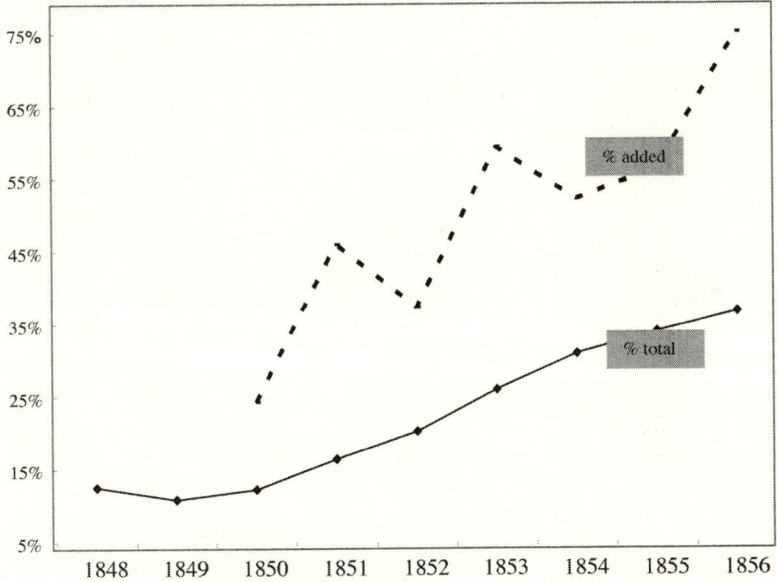

FIG. 6. Total and added rail mileage in Ohio, Indiana, Illinois, Michigan, Wisconsin, and Iowa as a percentage of U.S. amounts, 1848–56.
*Sources:* Wilson and Spencer, "Growth of the Railroad Network," p. 339; Stover, *Baltimore and Ohio Railroad*, p. 317; Fishlow, *American Railroads*, table 16; *Historical Statistics of the United States*.

gave 131 million acres of public land to railroads over the following two decades, and Texas (which did not cede its land to the national government upon statehood) donated 27 million acres.[25] Not surprisingly, the relative abundance of railroads in the North was associated with comparatively larger land grants (see table 1). The North received more total acreage; land grants as a proportion of total land area (excluding water) were also larger in the North. And acres granted per capita (using total 1850 population) were more than twice as large in the North as in the South. The only comparable North-South figures were acres granted per white person as of 1860; in all other dimensions the North benefited relatively more from federal land grants to railroads.

[25] Atack and Passell, *New Economic View*, p. 436. Albert Fishlow estimates that the land subsidy was worth about $400 million, or about 5 percent of the amount invested in railroads between 1850 and 1880. Fishlow, "Internal Transportation," in *American Economic Growth: An Economist's History of the United States*, ed. Lance Davis et al. (New York, 1972), p. 506. Also see Louis Haney, *A Congressional History of Railways*, 2 vols. (1908–10; reprint ed., New York, 1968); Stover, *Iron Road*, pp. 94–95.

**Table 1** Federal land grants for railroads, 1850–57

| Region | Acres granted | Grants/ land area (%) | Grants/ 1850 white pop. | Grants/ 1850 total pop. | Grants/ 1860 white pop. | Grants/ 1860 total pop. |
| --- | --- | --- | --- | --- | --- | --- |
| Illinois | 2,595,133 | 7.3 % | 3.07 | 3.05 | 1.52 | 1.52 |
| Iowa | 4,507,531 | 12.6 % | 23.49 | 23.45 | 6.69 | 6.68 |
| Michigan | 3,103,880 | 8.5 % | 7.86 | 7.81 | 4.22 | 4.14 |
| Wisconsin | 560,605 | 1.6 % | 1.84 | 1.84 | 0.72 | 0.72 |
| Minnesota | 7,364,269 | 14.5 % | 1,220 | 1,212 | 43.47 | 42.81 |
| NORTH | 18,131,418 | 9.4 % | 10.40 | 10.34 | 4.47 | 4.44 |
| Mississippi | 1,285,743 | 4.3 % | 4.35 | 2.12 | 3.63 | 1.62 |
| Missouri | 2,438,015 | 5.5 % | 4.12 | 3.57 | 2.29 | 2.06 |
| Alabama | 3,193,719 | 9.8 % | 7.49 | 4.14 | 6.07 | 3.31 |
| Arkansas | 3,836,595 | 11.5 % | 23.66 | 18.28 | 11.84 | 8.81 |
| Florida | 2,497,719 | 7.4 % | 52.91 | 28.56 | 32.13 | 17.79 |
| Louisiana | 699,221 | 2.5 % | 2.74 | 1.35 | 1.96 | 0.99 |
| SOUTH | 13,951,012 | 6.9 % | 7.84 | 4.85 | 5.16 | 3.30 |

*Source:* W. J. Donald, "Land Grants for Internal Improvements in the United States," *Journal of Political Economy* 19 (1911):404–10, tables 1–3, 5.

These grants generated even stronger connections among railroads, land markets, and population movements. Railroads attempted to encourage western migration by offering settlers easy credit terms and low down payments.[26] One advertisement placed by the Illinois Central Railroad offered "superior farming lands . . . not surpassed by any in the world . . . for sale on long credit [up to seven years], short credit or for cash" and promised the finest of public schools, excellent health, and the best conditions for any investment.[27]

## Securities and Financial Markets

Railroads changed the physical landscape in the United States, but they also reshaped its financial markets. Perhaps the most noteworthy feature of investors in the 1850s was their eagerness to purchase railroad securities and to trust them as collateral, despite a glaring lack of information about—or reluctance to investigate—their soundness. The *New York Herald* fruitlessly called attention to the debt burden taken on by many railroads to pay dividends, as well as the seeming ignorance of investors.[28]

Data collected by Richard Sylla, Jack Wilson, and Robert Wright (2002) offer a rare opportunity to track weekly information on securities traded in several different cities during the nineteenth century.[29] The most complete data covering the 1850s come from Baltimore, Boston, Richmond, and New Orleans.[30]

---

[26]Stampp, *America in 1857*, p. 218. Also see Paul Gates, "The Promotion of Agriculture by the Illinois Central Railroad, 1855–1870," *Agricultural History* 5 (1931):57–76.

[27]Ratner displays a copy of this advertisement. Ratner, *Evolution*, p. 140.

[28]See, for example, "Financial and Commercial Money Market," *New York Herald*, Feb. 11, 1857, p. 2; "Prices," *New York Herald*, Apr. 7, 1857, p. 5.

[29]Sylla and his collaborators have put together a large data set of prices of public securities that traded in nine U.S. markets and London between 1786 and 1862. They have made these data available via the Inter-University Consortium for Political and Social Research (ICPSR). Richard Sylla, Jack Wilson, and Robert Wright, *Price Quotations in Early United States Securities Markets, 1790–1860*, computer file ICPSR04053-v1 (New York, 2002; Ann Arbor, 2005).

[30]The exchanges mostly carried the securities of local companies, although multiple exchanges traded securities from the larger railroads. Although I would have liked to use the New York prices as well as the Boston ones for northern stock, the New York series ends well before the time of the panic. Howard Bodenhorn suggests that antebellum credit markets were reasonably well-integrated, however, and certainly more integrated than postbellum markets. Bodenhorn, "Capital Mobility and Financial Integration in Antebellum America," *Journal of Economic History* 52 (1992):585–610. An inspection of commonly reported stocks from Boston and New York exchanges shows that prices were highly, although not perfectly, correlated across the two markets between 1844 and 1853.

## The Importance of Railroad Securities

Philadelphia provided the first center for American railroad finance, followed shortly thereafter by Boston, a city that lacked a navigable inland waterway. By the time of the Civil War, New York was the financial capital of the country, although active exchanges operated in many cities, as did curbstone brokers plying their business just outside Wall Street.[31] By far the most vigorously traded securities were railroad stocks and bonds.[32]

Private investors put up about three-quarters of the more than $1 billion invested in railroads between 1828 and 1860.[33] Holding stock was not always a voluntary event: some railroads demanded that their suppliers take payment in the form of securities.[34] Companies at times also gave stock as a bonus to those who bought bonds.[35] But plenty of people also took a keen interest in playing the market. Minnesotans were said to be so eager to speculate that they had no time for politics, and Wisconsin farmers bought up railroad securities using personal notes backed by mortgages on their holdings.[36]

Railroad securities held international appeal as well. Of the total inflow of foreign capital to the United States from 1849 to 1860, half went for stocks and bonds issued by railroad companies. The secretary of the treasury estimated that foreign investors held $44 million in railroad bonds and $8 million in railroad stock out of a total of $550 million invested in U.S. railroad securities in 1853. The next most popular item in foreign portfolios was state and local bonds and, as discussed below, these often served as backing for railroad operations.[37]

---

[31] Alfred Chandler, "Patterns of American Railroad Finance, 1830–1850," *Business History Review* 28 (1954):261–62; George Garvy, "Rivals and Interlopers in the History of the New York Security Market," *Journal of Political Economy* 52 (1944):130.

[32] Garvy, "Rivals and Interlopers," p. 130; G. William Schwert, "Why Does Stock Market Volatility Change over Time?" *Journal of Finance* 44 (1989):1124; Calomiris and Schweikart, "Panic of 1857," p. 809. Allan Nevins offers a particularly vivid account of the eager response of brokers when railroad securities were called. Nevins, *Emergence of Lincoln*, pp. 180–81.

[33] Stampp, *America in 1857*, p. 215; Ratner, *Evolution*, p. 123.

[34] Harold Livesay, "The Lobdell Carwheel Company, 1830–67," *Business History Review* 42 (1968):18.

[35] Jonathan Baskin, "The Development of Corporate Financial Markets in Britain and the United States, 1600–1914: Overcoming Asymmetric Information," *Business History Review* 62 (1988):218.

[36] Stampp, *America in 1857*, p. 215. Also see James Ward, "Promotional Wizardry: Rhetoric and Railroad Origins," *Journal of the Early Republic* 11 (1991):69–88.

[37] Stover, *Iron Road*, p. 218; Fishlow, *American Railroads*, p. 117.

Figure 7 offers summary information on weekly stock prices for railroads located in various parts of the country between 1850 and 1856.[38] Among the most notable features of the figure are the early success of Atlantic roads, the general downward trend in prices of eastern railway stock throughout the period, and the downward dip in late 1854 followed by price recovery in regions outside the East, particularly for the western

---

[38]Par value for stocks varied across companies and sometimes over time within a company. To construct indices, I converted each stock price to a percentage of par value. I then combined these converted values into an index for each region. Note that the indices can only track surviving companies and thus do not capture the full effect of downturns nor the exact timing of upturns. In this regard, however, they are no different from the Dow-Jones or the Wilshire indices. Even among surviving companies, not all stock prices were quoted in all periods; this can create some potentially misleading fluctuations in the indices. I tried various methods of smoothing but decided ultimately not to use any ad hoc method.

I classified each railroad by region after inspecting various railroad maps from the 1850s. The Atlantic index includes primarily Maryland and New Jersey lines; I included New England, New York, and most Pennsylvania lines in the eastern index. The western index includes both wholly western lines (except for interior Ohio railroads) and trunk roads that led to the West. I placed two interior Ohio roads into an index separate from the other "western" lines, thinking that movement within Ohio was not truly related to westward migration. Here are the railroads included in each index: *Atlantic*—Baltimore & Hartford (until 1851), Baltimore & Susquehanna (until 1854), Camden & Amboy (1857), New Jersey (1856–59), North Central (1854–59), Northern of New Jersey (1850–59), Washington & Baltimore (brief existence), York & Cumberland (until 1854); *South*—Central (1850–56), Jackson (1853–58), Opelousas (1853–58), Pontchartrain (1852–58), Richmond (1850–59), Richmond & Danville (1852–59), Richmond & Petersburg (1850–59), Virginia Central (1855–59); *East*—Boston (1850–57), Boston & Lowell (1853–59), Boston & Maine (1850–59), Boston & New York (1854–58), Boston & Providence (1850–59), Boston & Worcester (1850–59), Cheshire (1850–89), Concord (1850–59), Concord & Montreal (1856–58), Concord & Montreal (1857–59), Connecticut River (1850–59), Eastern (1850–59), Eastern (1850–89), Fitchburg (1850–59), Grand Junction (1852–57), Harlem (1852–57), Hartford & New Hampshire (1850–59), Hudson River (1852–59), Long Island (1850–57), Manchester & Lawrence (1850–59), Nashua & Lowell (1850–59), New York & New Haven (1852–57), Norwich & Worcester (18550–7), Ogden (1850–57), Old Colony & Fall River (1854–59), Passaic (1857), Passumpsic (1850–57), Philadelphia (1850–59), Port Saco (1855–59), Providence & Worcester (1853–59), Reading (1850–59), Rutland (1855–86), Rutland & Burlington (1850–56), Stonington (1852–58), Sullivan (1850–57), Taunton (1850–53), Vermont & Canada (1852–59), Vermont Central (1850–57), Vermont & Massachusetts (1850–59), Western of Massachusetts (1850–59), Wilmington (1852–89), Worcester & Nashua (1850–59); *West*—Baltimore & Ohio (1850–59), Chicago and Rock Island (1856–59), Cleveland & Pittsburgh (1856–58), Cleveland & Toledo (1855–59), Galena & Chicago (1855–59), Illinois Central (1855–59), LaCrosse & Milwaukee (1857–58), Michigan Central (1850–59), Michigan Southern (1857–59), Milwaukee & Mississippi (1856–58), New York Central (1853–59), New York & Erie (1852–59), Wisconsin & Lake Shore (1856–57); *Ohio Interior*—Cleveland and Columbus (1856–59), Little Miami (1856–57); *Panama*—Panama.

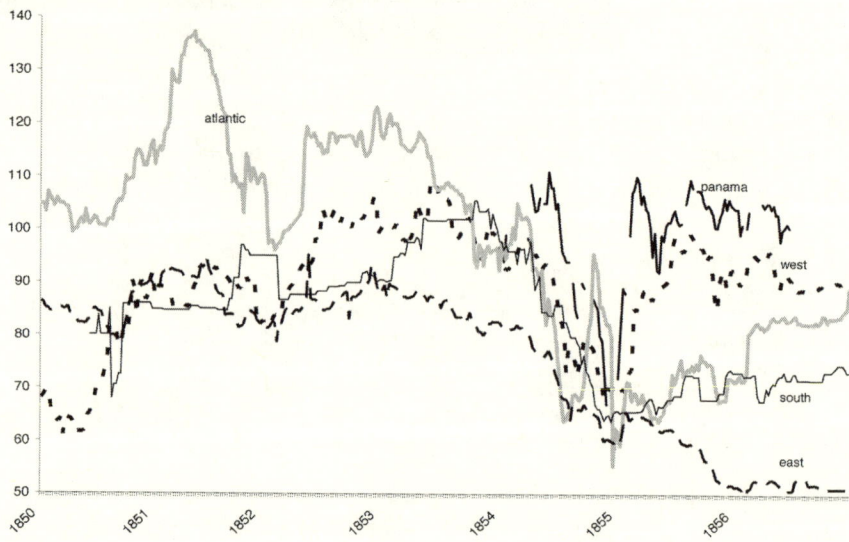

FIG. 7. Railroad stock indices, January 5, 1850–December 17, 1856.
*Sources:* Richard Sylla, Jack Wilson, and Robert Wright, *Price Quotations in Early United States Securities Markets, 1790–1860* (New York University, Stern School of Business [producer], 2002); Interuniversity Consortium for Political and Social Research, distributor (Ann Arbor, 2005), computer file ICPSR04053-vI.

and Panama railroads.[39] Prices remained fairly steady throughout 1856 in all regions.

The intense interest in railroad securities, particularly stock, was not always based on solid information about fundamentals. Generally accepted accounting principles were unheard of, and few companies offered much in the way of disclosure.[40] The New York Stock Exchange did not require annual financial reporting until 1869 and devoted no resources to enforcing

---

[39] The year 1854 was a recession year, with the downturn triggered by mismanagement in the Knickerbocker Bank and a major fraud pulled off by Robert Schuyler. Schuyler was the head of the New York & New Haven Railroad; he kept three sets of books and essentially siphoned off about $2 million for his own use, then fled to Europe. Emerson Keyes, *A History of Savings Banks in the U.S. from Their Inception in 1819 down to 1877* (New York, 1878). Morgan Kelly and Cormac O'Grada offer general information about the brief Panic of 1854, which was confined mostly to New York. Kelly and O'Grada, "Market Contagion: Evidence from the Panics of 1854 and 1857," *American Economic Review* 90 (2000):1110–24. Details about the Schuyler episode can be found in John Stover, "Southern Ambitions of the Illinois Central Railroad," *Journal of Southern History* 20 (1954):499–510, p. 500; Fishlow, *American Railroads*, p. 113; and Stover, *Iron Road*, p. 36. Schuyler at one point was president of the Illinois Central. Although he resigned from that position in 1853, his perfidy in the East affected IC investors for a time in 1854 as well until European investors stepped in to buy IC stocks and bonds.

[40] Arthur Dewing tells of the chaotic accounting of the early railroads. Dewing, "The Theory of Railroad Reorganization," *American Economic Review* 8 (1918):774–95.

that requirement.[41] As one treatise put it, "there has been no regard for the truth even in the statement of the amounts and sources of capital actually obtained by the corporation.... In many instances, shareholders are as uninformed after reading a published financial statement as if none had been rendered."[42] Top management was sometimes incompetent and occasionally venal.[43] Investors in western roads had virtually no idea how their money was being used or whether lines were even being built.[44] Contemporaneous commentators denounced the growing evil of overspeculation and the mania for playing the market.[45] The actions of state and local government—described in the next section—merely helped fuel this behavior.

Importantly, regional investment patterns varied. Most notable is the difference between North and South: southern railroads tended to have a greater proportion of local investors and to pay little in the way of dividends. The local angle meant easier monitoring of the use of funds, but it also made for shorter lines and a patchwork combination of different rail sizes in the South.[46] This hampered the South's movement of troops and supplies during the Civil War but it cushioned the impact of financial chaos resulting from speculation based on inadequate information.

*State and Local Government Involvement in Railroad Finance*

Whereas the federal government granted land to the railroads, states and municipalities offered another sort of support: they subscribed to stock and pledged their taxing powers as a guarantee on bond redemption.[47] Because investors were hit heavily by the Panic of 1837, some states began inserting constitutional provisions to limit state debt and aid to corporations in the

[41] Baskin, "Corporate Financial Markets," p. 228.
[42] Frederick Cleveland and Fred Powell, *Railroad Finance* (New York, 1912), p. 121.
[43] See Dewing, "Theory of Railroad Reorganization"; Nevins, *Ordeal of the Union*, p. 236; Stover, *Iron Road*, pp. 50–51, 152–53.
[44] Smith and Cole, *Fluctuations in American Business*, p. 113.
[45] Nevins refers particularly to an editorial denouncing the sale of $22 million of stock in one two-week period. Nevins, *Emergence of Lincoln*, p. 181.
[46] For an interesting comparison of investment patterns in Albemarle County, Virginia, and Cumberland County, Pennsylvania, see John Majewski, "Who Financed the Transportation Revolution? Regional Divergence and Internal Improvements in Antebellum Pennsylvania and Virginia," *Journal of Economic History* 56 (1996):763–88. Stover discusses dividends. Stover, *Iron Road*, pp. 62, 90.
[47] See, for instance, R. S. Cotterill, "Southern Railroads, 1850–1860," *Mississippi Valley Historical Review* 10 (1924):398, 402–3; Nevins, *Ordeal of the Union*, pp. 197–98, 202, 240; Carter Goodrich and Harvey Segal, "Baltimore's Aid to Railroads: A Study in the Municipal Planning of Internal Improvements," *Journal of Economic History* 13 (1953):2–35; Merl Reed, "Government Investment and Economic Growth: Louisiana's Antebellum Railroads," *Journal of Southern History* 28 (1962):183, 196–97, 199; John Stover, *History of the Baltimore and Ohio Railroad* (West Lafayette, Ind., 1987), p. 324; Stover, *Iron Road*, p. 217; Baskin, "Corporate Financial Markets," p. 209.

1840s.[48] Yet cities, counties, and states remained highly invested in railroad securities through the mid-1850s, particularly in the North.[49]

Southern states and cities did offer some aid. Tennessee, for example, awarded railroads $10,000 for each mile of track completed.[50] Bonds issued by New Orleans sold at a huge discount in 1854 because the city had pledged so much aid to local railroads.[51] But northern states and municipalities generally offered more support than their southern brethren.

Some public officials grew alarmed at these close relationships. After Cincinnati taxed its citizens to buy $1 million of stock in the Ohio and Mississippi Railroad, Salmon P. Chase, then governor of Ohio, begged the legislature in his January 1857 message to keep tabs on the railroads.[52] But most public figures seemed happy with, or at least complacent about, the arrangements.

Jonathan Baskin (1988) argues that the intertwining of public and private interests helped give an aura of legitimacy to railroad investments that they otherwise might not have had.[53] Not only that, the fortunes of the states were tied, at least in part, to the fortunes of the railroads. The late 1854 downturn in public-sector bond prices mirrors the pattern in privately issued security prices (see fig. 8). Note as well the climb in Illinois state bond prices from 1852 to 1856, just when the Illinois Central line commenced construction.

### NORTHERN BANKING

Banks, state governments, securities and land markets, and railroads formed an intimate network in the 1850s. In this era of free banking, banks could not print their own notes but could obtain state banknotes in exchange for

---

[48]See Reginald McGrane, *Foreign Bondholders and American State Debts* (New York, 1935); Reed, "Government Investment," p. 191; Fishlow, *American Railroads*, p. 191; D. Roderick Kiewiet and Kristin Szakaty, "Constitutional Limitations on Borrowing: An Analysis of State Bonded Indebtedness," *Journal of Law, Economics, and Organization* 12 (1996):62–97. The state bank of Illinois became so involved in state public improvement that it went bankrupt in 1842. Bray Hammond, *Banks and Politics in America: From the Revolution to the Civil War* (Princeton, N.J., 1957), p. 612.

[49]For figures on the amounts invested, see Fishlow, *American Railroads*, p. 192; Stover, *Iron Road*, p. 217. Stover reports of a restraining order obtained by private shareholders of the B&O in December 1856, who worried that the state of Maryland and the city of Baltimore had too much involvement with the railroad. The New York and Philadelphia newspapers had a field day when the Camden & Amboy wanted a twenty-year renewal of its charter plus expanded monopoly powers from the New Jersey legislature. Stover, *History of the Baltimore and Ohio Railroad*, p. 327. Nevins states that Wisconsin state officials granted land to the LaCrosse & Milwaukee after receiving bribes from the railroad's president, Byron Kilbourn. Nevins, *Ordeal of the Union*, p. 240. Stover, *Iron Road*, p. 153.

[50]Stover, *Iron Road*, p. 86. On pp. 88 and 157, Stover gives information about other southern states and counties as well.

[51]Reed, "Government Investment," p. 197.

[52]Stampp, *America in 1857*, p. 216.

[53]Ibid., p. 209.

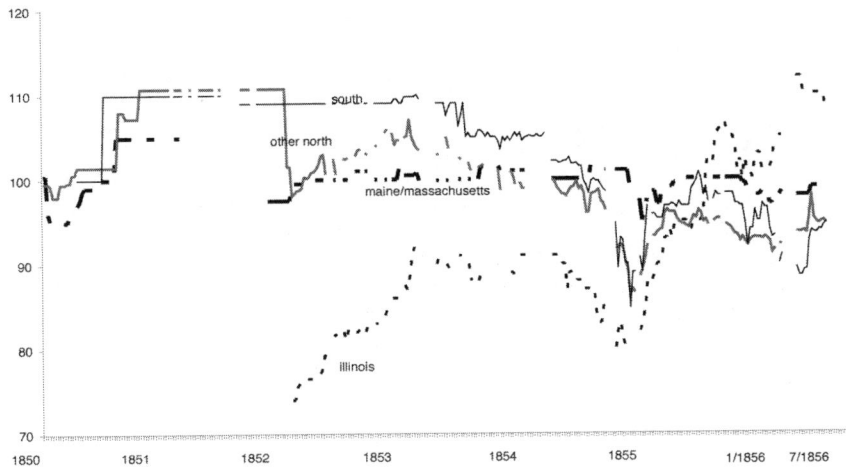

FIG. 8. Bond prices, grouped states, 1850–56.
*Source:* Sylla, Wilson, and Wright, *Price Quotations;* Inter-university Consortium for Political and Social Research, computer file ICPSR04053-v1.

state bonds which, as mentioned, sometimes backed railroad activities.[54] States in turn relied on banks to generate tax revenue and investment income.[55]

What is more, no centralized banking authority existed.[56] Instead, banks in the nation's interior used New York banks to hold their reserves. New

---

[54] In February 1857, for instance, Missouri state bonds collateralized more than two-thirds of Illinois banknotes. Andrew Economopoulos, "Illinois Free Banking Experience," *Journal of Money, Credit, and Banking* 20 (1988), p. 253.

[55] Richard Sylla, John Legler, and John Wallis, "Banks and State Public Finance in the New Republic: The United States, 1790–1860," *Journal of Economic History* 47 (1987):391–403.

[56] Although this meant an absence of a lender of last resort, some banks formed clearinghouses as an alternative. Examples include the New York clearinghouse, established in 1853, and the Suffolk Bank in New England, established three decades earlier. Hammond, *Banks and Politics,* p. 554; Gary Gorton, "Clearinghouses and the Origin of Central Banking in the United States," *Journal of Economic History* 45 (1985):277–83; Stampp, *America in 1857,* p. 216; Charles Calomiris and Charles Kahn, "The Efficiency of Self-Regulated Payments Systems: Learning from the Suffolk System," *Journal of Money, Credit, and Banking* 28 (1996):766–97; and Bruce Smith and Warren Weber, "Private Money Creation and the Suffolk Banking System," *Journal of Money, Credit, and Banking* 31 (1999):624–59. New York passed the first free-banking statute in 1838, and other states soon followed. Atack and Passell, *New Economic View,* p. 105, table 4.2. Descriptions of the free-banking era appear in Hugh Rockoff, "The Free Banking Era: A Reexamination," *Journal of Money, Credit, and Banking* 6 (1974):141–67; Arthur Rolnick and Warren Weber, "New Evidence on the Free Banking Era," *American Economic Review* 73 (1983):1080–91; Kenneth Ng, "Free Banking Law and Barriers to Entry in Banking, 1838–60," *Journal of Economic History* 48 (1988):877–89; Economopoulos, "Illinois Free Banking Experience"; Stampp, *America in 1857,* p. 217; Gary Walton and Hugh Rockoff, *History of the American Economy,* 10th ed. (Mason, Ohio, 2005), pp. 235–36. Nevins reports that 678 new banks set up shop in the ten years before 1857. Nevins, *Emergence of Lincoln,* p. 187. In his magisterial work *Banks and Politics in America,* Bray Hammond suggests that becoming a banker might have been somewhat harder than becoming a bricklayer in the free-banking era, but not much (p. 572).

York banks then lent these reserves on the call-money market, accepting stock and land mortgages as collateral.[57] This activity escalated in the second half of the decade, leaving banks with far lower specie reserves than before. The ratio of bank specie to total deposits plus notes fell from 22 percent at the beginning of 1855 to only 10.4 percent in February 1857.[58]

This complex paper edifice rested on a simple assumption: that debtors could pay. Few seem to have contemplated the possibility that everyone might call in loans at once—a classic fallacy of composition. As one contemporaneous commentator put it, using call loans with stock collateral seemed plausible as proposed by each separate bank. But "the causes which alarm one bank alarm the whole. Upon any shock to confidence, they [will] all call in at once."[59]

SOUTHERN BANKING

Southern banks engaged in fundamentally different practices than their northern counterparts. Louisiana's Forstall system, established in 1842, required one-third specie reserves held against notes and deposits, for example.[60] Banks in other southern states were not quite as conservative but nevertheless were fewer in number, more tightly knit, and more focused on solvency than northern banks.[61] Risk aversion in the South, especially af-

---

[57] Discussions of bank lending and collateralization appear in Harry Miller, "Earlier Theories of Crisis and Cycles in the United States," *Quarterly Journal of Economics* 38 (1924):294–329, p. 322; Smith and Cole, *Fluctuations in American Business*, p. 133; Nevins, *Emergence of Lincoln*, pp. 187–88; and Calomiris and Schweikart, "The Panic of 1857," p. 822. Miller and Sylla discuss the workings of the call-money market. Miller, "Crisis and Cycles," pp. 327–29; Sylla, "Origins of the New York Stock Exchange," http://icf.som.yale.edu/pdf/hist_conference/Richard_Sylla.pdf (draft 2003). Stampp notes even more tangled relationships in which railroads sold eastern bankers land mortgages they had received in exchange for stock. Stampp, *America in 1857*, p. 215. Hugh Rockoff reports that Michigan let banks use land mortgages at face value as security, regardless of their true value. Rockoff, "Free Banking Era," pp. 141–67. Likewise, Minnesota accepted railroad bonds at 95 percent of their face value, even though they were nearly worthless. Atack and Passell, *New Economic View*, p. 104.

[58] Smith and Cole, *Fluctuations in American Business*, p. 131. Edward Stevens, "Composition of Money Supply prior to Civil War," *Journal of Money, Credit, and Banking* 3 (1971):84–101, table 2, shows similar information by reporting the ratios of banknotes to bank specie, as well as bank specie to total specie.

[59] Edmund Dwight, "The Financial Revulsion and the New York Banking System," *Hunt's Merchant Magazine* 38 (1858):159, quoted in Miller, "Crisis and Cycles," p. 328.

[60] Hammond, *Banks and Politics*, p. 696; Walton and Rockoff, *American Economy*, p. 236.

[61] Hammond, *Banks and Politics*, p. 696; Rockoff, "Free Banking Era," p. 104; Larry Schweikart, "Southern Banks and Economic Growth in the Antebellum Period: A Reassessment," *Journal of Southern History* 53 (1987):28; Atack and Passell, *New Economic View*, p. 104; Calomiris and Schweikart, "Panic of 1857," p. 831.

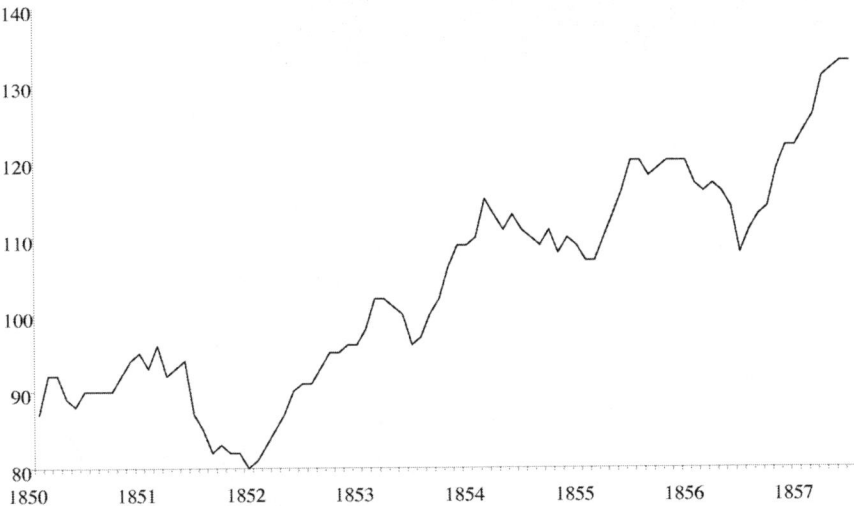

Fig. 9. Monthly commodity price index, January 1850–June 1857.
*Source:* Smith and Cole, *Fluctuations*, p. 167, table 52.

ter 1850, made borrowing difficult for small proprietors.[62] A Virginia newspaperman foreshadowed today's critics of subprime rating agencies in an editorial printed in October 1857. He decried the habits of New York banks in estimating the worth of securities "without regard to their intrinsic value."[63]

## Commodities and Slaves

Although land and railroad-security markets were beehives of activity in the 1850s, people found additional outlets for speculation, namely commodities. By midsummer 1857 commodity prices had increased 40 percent since the beginning of 1853 (see fig. 9).[64] This inflation was partly due to the infusion of gold from California.[65]

---

[62] Jeremy Atack, Fred Bateman, and Thomas Weiss, "Risk, the Rate of Return, and the Pattern of Investment in Nineteenth Century American Manufacturing, *Southern Economic Journal* 49 (1982):150–63.
[63] Nevins, *Emergence of Lincoln*, p. 186.
[64] Ibid., p. 182.
[65] Ratner, *Evolution*, p. 168.

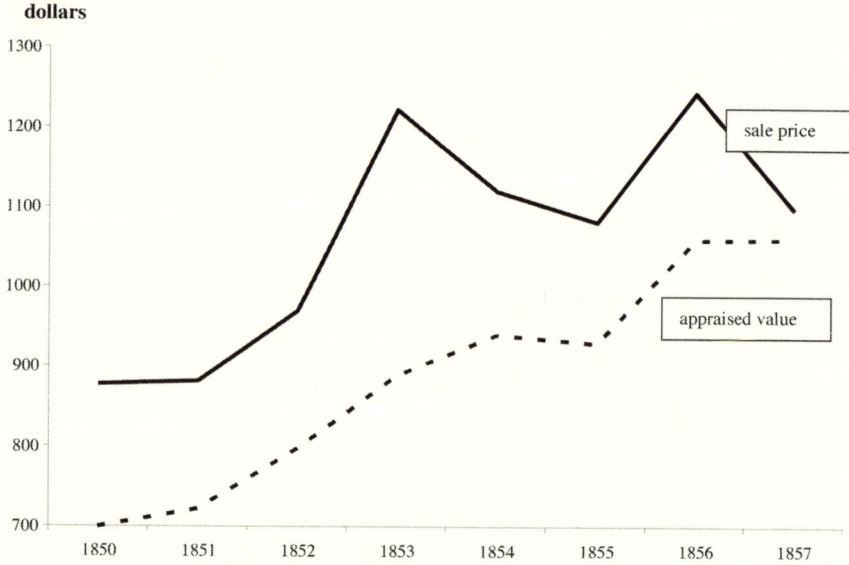

Fig. 10. Mean value of prime male slaves, 1850–57.
*Source:* Robert Fogel and Stanley Engerman, *Slave Sales and Appraisals, 1775–1865* (Rochester, N.Y., 1976); Inter-university Consortium for Political and Social Research, computer file ICPSR07421-v3.

Slave prices also escalated throughout the period (see fig. 10). The average sale price for a prime-age male went from $877 in 1850 to $1,243 in 1856. Mean appraisal values increased from $699 in 1850 to $1,058 in 1856.[66]

## The Crisis Cometh

As of late spring 1857 the nation had experienced sharply rising prices for land, railroad securities, and commodities for several consecutive months. Banks, goods traders, securities dealers, land merchants, international investors, government at all levels, and ordinary citizens shared in the largesse, anticipating continuing prosperity, particularly from western concerns. But things fell apart: the center could not hold.

[66] Data are derived from Robert Fogel and Stanley Engerman, *Slave Sales and Appraisals, 1775–1865*, computer file ICPSR07421-v3 (Rochester, N.Y.: University of Rochester [producer], 1976. Ann Arbor, Mich.: Inter-university Consortium for Political and Social Research [producer and distributor], 2006). The data are from probate records; sample sizes are much larger for appraisals than for sales, with annual numbers ranging from 437 to 710 for appraisals and 30 to 100 for sales. The larger sample size for appraisals may help explain the smoother pattern of these prices.

What happened, and why? The following sections offer a brief theoretical explanation of why the panic occurred, followed by copious empirical evidence about both short- and long-run effects.

## A Theoretical Framework

### Relevant Models of Financial Panic

Two leading theories associated with financial panics are the random-withdrawal model and the asymmetric-information model. In the first, random withdrawals from banks generate the possibility of panic in a world where depositors are served on a first-come, first-served basis.[67] A surge in the demand for funds, coupled with fractional reserves, means that the first people to arrive at a bank may retrieve their savings but later arrivals may not. I argue elsewhere that this model likely describes the Panic of 1837.[68]

A different theory centers on asymmetric information between creditors and debtors. This alternative models a financial panic starting when holders of banknotes, bank accounts, mortgages, stock certificates, or bonds revise their perception of risk when they receive bad news about the macroeconomy. Because people cannot immediately distinguish among banks or corporations, they might try to reclaim all their assets. But if at least some well-informed investors can distinguish sound from unsound operations, a panic may be just what is needed to separate the wheat from the chaff, as it tends to drive out poorly managed enterprises. According to several scholars, this model better captures the workings of the U.S. economy in the national-banking period (1863–1913).[69]

---

[67] Douglas Diamond and Philip Dybvig offer the pioneering example of this model, Diamond and Dybvig, "Bank Runs, Deposit Insurance, and Liquidity," *Journal of Political Economy* 91 (1983):401–19.

[68] Jenny Wahl, "He Broke the Bank, But Did Andrew Jackson also Father the Fed?" in *Congress and the Emergence of Sectionalism*, ed. Paul Finkelman and Donald R. Kennon, (Athens, Ohio, 2008), pp. 188–220. Spatial separation of banks could be the reason for a lack of coordination among depositors and thus the failure to overcome the first-come, first-served problem.

[69] See, for example, Gary Gorton, "Banking Panics and Business Cycles," *Oxford Economic Papers*, n.s. 40 (1988):751–81: Charles Calomiris and Gary Gorton, "The Origins of Banking Panics: Models, Fact, and Bank Regulation," in *Financial Markets and Financial Crises*, ed. Glenn Hubbard (Chicago, 1991), pp. 107–73. Fabio Canova concludes that some fundamental features of the macroeconomy could help predict panics, at least in retrospect. Canova, "Were Financial Crises Predictable?" *Journal of Money, Credit, and Banking* 26 (1994):107, referring to Jack Wilson, Richard Sylla, and Charles Jones, "Financial Market Volatility, Panics under the National Banking System before 1914, and Volatility in the Long Run, 1830–1988," in *Crises and Panics and Historical Perspective*, ed. Eugene White (Homewood, 1990). I argue that this model applied to the 1839 crisis as well. Wahl, "He Broke the Bank."

I suggest that the asymmetric-information model also applies to the panic of 1857. What existed in mid-1857 was a web of relationships among banks, securities markets, railroads, federal and state government, and investors large and small, domestic and foreign. Exuberant expectations that western land and railroad investments would continue generating breakneck price increases, coupled with spotty information about the valuation of assets and little oversight, meant large holes in the web that made it particularly vulnerable to tearing.

Then something happened that quickly sobered up investors and creditors: the decision in *Dred Scott* to open western territories to slavery. This piece of new information was enough to unleash financial panic.[70] The crisis was short-lived, however, and, financially speaking, served mainly to separate risky from stable investments and poorly run enterprises from those with good supervision. Ominously, though, the brief panic generated major political aftershocks as southerners perceived that their institutions and enterprises endured the financial upheaval better than did those in the North.

## *A Model of Antebellum Westward Migration, Land Values, and Territorial Status*

To see why *Dred Scott* precipitated a panic, consider the most salient fact known to northerners at the time of the case: land values in the South were lower and increased less rapidly than in the North.[71] As the following paragraphs discuss, the nature of regional production helps explain this pattern. One consequence of a shift in territorial status from arguably free to definitely slave was a freeze in westward migration by northerners, which in turn chilled markets for western assets.

Jeffersonian yeoman farmers epitomized the North: immobile land was their primary owned asset, and they demonstrated a preference for proprietorship—even of a small holding—over hiring themselves out.[72]

---

[70] People were aware of the case before the decision became official. Data observed for March and April 1857 may therefore underestimate the true reaction.

[71] The per-acre value of farmland in the South exceeded that in the North at the time of the American Revolution. By 1850, however, the value of farmland and buildings in the South was less than half that in the North, and the per-acre value was only one-third. Even after the cotton boom of the 1850s, the per-acre value in the South was only 43 percent of the northern value. Gavin Wright, "Capitalism and Slavery on the Islands: A Lesson from the Mainland." *Journal of Interdisciplinary History* 17 (1987):858–59.

[72] Gavin Wright, *The Political Economy of the Cotton South: Households, Markets, and Wealth in the Nineteenth Century* (New York, 1978), p. 45.

Labor was thus the scarce factor in agricultural production. Once settled, free-soil farmers put their money into land clearing, schools, towns, transportation, and other forms of local development.[73] This investment in turn affected the value of the surrounding area.[74]

The South, in contrast, held much of its wealth in mobile assets—that is, slaves.[75] Although land was also an important part of the southerner's portfolio, the very fact that property could be held in a form not affected by local development meant southerners had a different outlook on internal improvements as well as a production process that emphasized relatively abundant labor inputs. That Cyrus McCormick, with his labor-saving reaper, changed the locus of his operations from Virginia to Illinois in the mid-1840s is not surprising.[76]

Production processes were another difference between the two regions. Southerners practiced "shifting cultivation" and thus held large tracts of unimproved land, whereas northerners kept a high proportion of land in constant use. In 1860 southerners cultivated only one of every three owned acres, while northerners improved more than half their acreage.[77]

Did permitting slaves into a territory necessarily mean they would come? Stephen Douglas thought that the Kansas-Nebraska Act was all symbol and no substance: in his view, slavery itself would not be viable in the eponymous territory.[78] Yet the evidence overwhelmingly shows that slavery could

---

[73] Gavin Wright, "Slavery and American Agricultural History," *Agricultural History* 77 (2003):540.

[74] Northerners moved around, of course. The point is that their main asset was immobile. Even if people moved, they had an interest in enhancing immobile asset values because any improvements would be capitalized in the asset sale price.

[75] For dollar estimates, see Robert Fogel, *Without Consent or Contract: The Rise and Fall of American Slavery* (New York, 1989), pp. 81–89; and Roger Ransom and Richard Sutch, *One Kind of Freedom* (New York, 1977), pp. 52–53. Certainly yeoman farmers existed in the South as well, many of whom owned no slaves. See for example David Weiman, "Peopling the Land by Lottery? The Market in Public Lands and the Regional Differentiation of Territory on the Georgia Frontier," *Journal of Economic History* 51 (1991):835–60.

[76] William Hutchinson, *Cyrus Hall McCormick: Seed Time, 1809–1856* (New York, 1930), pp. 208–9, 246.

[77] John Majewski and Viken Tchakerian, "The Environmental Origins of Shifting Cultivation in the Nineteenth-Century U.S. South," (March 2006), pp. 2–3, unpublished working paper available at http://www.history.ucsb.edu/faculty/majewskiItems/EO.pdf.

[78] See Robert Johannsen, ed., *The Letters of Stephen A Douglas* (Urbana, Ill., 1961), pp. 289–90; David M. Potter, *The Impending Crisis, 1848–1861*, completed and ed. Don E. Fehrenbacher (New York, 1976), pp. 171–72. Potter and other scholars suggest that Douglas wrote the bill advocating popular sovereignty as a sop to southerners in exchange for a greater likelihood of a transcontinental railroad being built near lands that Douglas owned (pp. 152, 170).

thrive in the territories.[79] Abraham Lincoln himself displayed a map showing the climactic and soil similarities between the Kansas-Nebraska territory and various southern regions.[80] Free-Soilers therefore could reasonably believe that allowing slavery into a territory might bring slaves in, whether they arrived with their masters or were sold to new ones.[81]

Converting a territory from free-soil to slave would thus reduce the probability of migration westward for northerners due to the anticipated effect on land values. Because private and public investments would be divided among multiple assets under a slave regime rather than devoted primarily to immobile property, expected benefits for small, nonslaveholding enterprises would be less than in a free-soil environment. Add to this a large dose of racism and a panic about slave insurrections that grew palpable in the months just before *Dred Scott* was decided.[82] Even if many of the fears of freeholders were not borne out—virtually no slaves ever made it to Nevada, New Mexico, or Utah, despite the legality of slavery there[83]—expectations were what mattered.[84]

---

[79]Wright, "Slavery and American Agricultural History," pp. 527–52. Wahl offers data showing the inexorable westward movement of the slave population. Wahl, "Stay East," p. 371. David Weiman's study of the market in public lands in Georgia suggests that wealthy slave owners made up a disproportionate share of bidders at auctions, as they had the wherewithal to buy land ahead of using it. Weiman, "Peopling the Land," pp. 835–60. Opening a territory to slavery might not have brought slaves in as neighbors immediately, then, but frontier settlers could reasonably have expected them later.

[80]Doris Kearns Goodwin, *Team of Rivals: The Political Genius of Abraham Lincoln* (New York, 2005), p. 167.

[81]Jonathan Pritchett finds that about half the slaves migrated from the exporting to the importing areas of the South with their masters and half were sold. Pritchett, "Quantitative Estimates of the United States Interregional Slave Trade, 1820–1860," *Journal of Economic History* 61 (2001):467–68.

[82]Eugene Berwanger notes the prevalence of racism among northerners. Berwanger, *The Frontier against Slavery: Western Anti-Negro Prejudice and the Slavery Extension Controversy* (Champaign, Ill., 1967), pp. 1, 4. Charles Dew and Harvey Wish document the growing fears of slave insurrection in 1856 and 1857. Dew, "Black Ironworkers and the Slave Insurrection Panic of 1856," *Journal of Southern History* 41 (1975):321–38; Wish, "The Slave Insurrection Panic of 1856," *Journal of Southern History* 5 (1939):206–22. Jeffrey Adler goes so far as to claim that St. Louis declined in importance relative to Chicago because eastern capitalists became reluctant to invest in a slaveholding state. Adler, *Yankee Merchants and the Making of the Urban West: The Rise and Fall of Antebellum St. Louis* (Cambridge, 1991), pp. 175–77.

[83]U.S. Bureau of the Census, U.S. Department of Commerce, *Historical Statistics of the United States: Colonial Times to 1970* (1975), table A195–209.

[84]After *Dred Scott*, people even feared that the Supreme Court might declare that states had no say in determining whether slavery could exist within their borders. Another case—*Lemmon v. People*, 20 NY 562 (1860)—is sometimes referred to as the second *Dred Scott* case for this reason. *Lemmon* was working its way through the New York courts just before the Civil War and may have landed on the docket of the U.S. Supreme Court had not the war intervened. In *Lemmon*, slaves traveling circuitously from Virginia to the Lower South were freed by a writ of habeas corpus while in New York. The slave owner claimed that his property rights should have been protected.

Could southerners simply replace northerners? Certainly, southerners bought land in the territories and western states.[85] Yet the sheer number of potential migrants was much smaller in the South.[86] Not only that, if southern patterns of land value and growth were transplanted west, even a full replacement of population would not have yielded the same effect on land values as migration by northerners.

## A Thumbnail Sketch of Short-Run Events

Determining the status of slavery in the West occupied Americans throughout the 1850s. The Compromise of 1850 admitted California as a free state but placed no restrictions on slavery in New Mexico and Utah. The Kansas-Nebraska Act of May 30, 1854, left the matter in that territory to popular sovereignty, despite the earlier rule based on the latitude 36°36', specified by the Missouri Compromise of 1820. The ambiguous status of the Kansas-Nebraska territory led to bitter conflict both in the nation's capital and on its frontier. The Democrats lost control of the House of Representatives in the 1854–55 elections.[87] May 1856 brought the sack of Lawrence, Kansas; John Brown's murders along the Pottawatomie; and Charles Sumner's caning by Preston Brooks in the Senate chamber.[88] In February 1857 proslavery territorial legislators added to the tension by initiating a Kansas statehood movement.[89]

---

[85] Paul Gates, "Southern Investments in Northern Lands before the Civil War," *Journal of Southern History* 5 (1939):163, 173, 179.

[86] Wahl offers population figures by region. In 1860, for example, 69 percent of the white population lived in the North. Wahl, "Stay East."

[87] Don E. Fehrenbacher, *The Dred Scott Case: Its Significance in American Law and Politics*. New York, 1978), p. 188.

[88] For details, see David Donald, *Charles Sumner and the Coming of the Civil War* (New York, 1960), pp. 278–311; Potter, *Impending Crisis*, pp. 208–13; Fehrenbacher, Dred Scott *Case*, p. 193.

[89] The movement culminated in the election of proslavery delegates to a constitutional convention. Free-Soilers had refused to participate in what they considered a fraudulent process. Pro-slavers began meeting in September in Lecompton but suspended operations until after the October congressional election. Newly appointed territorial governor Robert Walker then installed a legally elected antislavery legislature that drafted its own constitution. The Kansas citizenry voted on the Lecompton constitution in December and on the antislavery constitution a few days later. In a costly move, Stephen Douglas opposed the Lecompton accord, not because it supported slavery, but because it was not the wish of the majority. In the end, Congress adopted William H. English's compromise, which proposed that Kansas be admitted under the Lecompton constitution, but only after Kansas voters approved standard federal land grants for the state. If the Kansas voters rejected the federal land grants, which they later did, then Kansas could not be considered for admission until its population had reached the federal ratio for one representative in Congress. Kansas was later admitted to the Union on January 29, 1861 (ch. 20, 12 *Stat*. 126). Fehrenbacher, Dred Scott *Case*, pp. 458–62, 465–69, 479–82.

The crowning blow to Free-Soilers was the decision in *Dred Scott*. Until Abraham Lincoln resided in the White House, nothing prevented slavery from legally entering any U.S. territory after March 6, 1857.[90] Dueling speeches delivered in late June 1857 by Stephen Douglas and Lincoln himself brought this point home to voters.[91] The outcome was a stall in westward migration, a drop in the price of western land, and faltering values of western railroad securities.

The shock to western land markets and railroads intensified when the New York newspapers revealed in August that the Michigan Southern Railroad had printed several hundred thousand dollars' worth of shares to obtain a bank loan, hoping to cover them with future profits.[92] Then followed the failure on August 24 of the New York branch of the Ohio Life Insurance and Trust Company, which had invested more than half its capital in western railroad securities and whose cashier had then embezzled a substantial portion of its assets.[93] Two days later, prominent speculative investor Jacob Little failed to meet his debts and New York banks frantically called in loans worth $4 million over the span of a single week.[94] More chaos followed: land and railroad stock prices plunged, banks suspended specie payments and refused to roll over loans, bankruptcies proliferated, and unemployed New Yorkers protested violently.[95]

In short, something concrete—the *Dred Scott* decision—occurred, which caused investors to update their evaluation of the riskiness of assets. Because markets intertwined so closely, this shock had long-reaching effects, with the brunt of the downturn borne by the North.

---

[90] A brief perusal of contemporaneous newspapers shows they were full of editorials and letters expressing fear that the *Scott* decision opened the territories—indeed, the entire nation —to slavery. Even the prospect of Oregon becoming a slave state was a serious one. See, for example, letter to the editor, (Boston) *Independent*, Mar. 19, 1857; letter to the editor, *National Era*, Mar. 26, 1857); "Oregon to Be a Slave State," *Farmers' Cabinet*, Apr. 2, 1857.

[91] Speech of Senator Douglas, Springfield, June 12, reported in *New York Daily Times*, June 23, 1857; reply to Senator Douglas by Lincoln, Indianapolis, June 26, reported in *New York Daily Times*, July 4, 1857.

[92] Nevins relates this episode. Nevins, *Emergence of Lincoln*, pp. 181–83.

[93] For a detailed account of Ohio Life's dealings, see Calomiris and Schweikart, "Panic of 1857," pp. 816–17. Also see George Van Vleck, *The Panic of 1857, an Analytical Study* (New York, 1943), p. 65; Stampp, *America in 1857*, p. 222.

[94] Nevins, *Emergence of Lincoln*, p. 190.

[95] The Tompkins Square protest occurred on November 11. Stampp, *America in 1857*, pp. 226–28.

FIG. 11. Estimated annual growth rate, Iowa population.
*Source:* Underlying population figures appear at http://iagenweb.org/census/1869-totals.htm.

## Supporting Data

Empirical evidence from several sources helps us see how various markets responded to the events of 1857. Let's take a look, both at the short-term and longer-term reactions.

### Population

Although the federal census offers only decennial reports, some states did more frequent population counts in antebellum years. The most complete data are from Iowa; figure 11 tracks the enormous decline in the annual population growth rate in 1857.

Similarities appear elsewhere. From 1850 to 1857 the average annual growth rate of population in Wisconsin was 13.3 percent; it dropped to only 2 percent from 1857 to 1860.[96] The Illinois population growth rate for the first half of the decade was 8.9 percent annually, falling to 5.7 percent in the second half.[97] After 1856, northerners got cold feet when it came to moving

---

[96] Ibid., p. 218; *Historical Statistics of the U.S.*
[97] Frederick Gerhard, *Illinois As It Is: Its History, Geography, Statistics, Constitution, Laws* (Chicago, 1857), available online at Google Books, http://books.google.com/books?id=PkYV2xFpP-UC.

farther west. We might attribute part of the decline in the growth to the fact that the land was becoming "settled up." Nevertheless, the sudden drop just after mid-decade is noteworthy.

Although data for the southern states are sketchy, the Texas almanac of 1857 suggests a 13 percent annual growth rate from 1850 to 1857, followed by a rate half that size during the last three years of the decade.[98] These figures imply that westward movement tailed off in the South as well, although slightly later and somewhat less abruptly than in the North. But why would southerners have slowed their migration west? One possibility is that the Freeport doctrine articulated by Stephen Douglas in 1858 created uncertainty for the South.[99]

*Land Prices*

Recall that public-land per-acre sale prices hovered in the 90-cent range in the 1854–56 period and western land sold in the secondary market at a feverish pace just before the crisis. The slowdown in migration coincided with fewer acres purchased and—more important—much lower prices (see fig. 12).

Finer data, quoted in biweekly editions of *Thompson's Bank Note and Commercial Reporters* reveal the drop in Iowa land prices shortly after the *Dred Scott* decision, in March 1857 (see fig. 13). The graph also shows that, at the peak of the crisis, land markets closed down completely.

Contemporaneous newspapers noted what had transpired. An editorial in the *Independent* stated, for instance, "A favorite mode of investment has been in real estate, either by mortgage or purchase of houses and lands. How many of our people last summer counted up their gains from the purchases of western lands, which had increased in value on the rise of real estate in cities, at tens and hundreds of thousands of dollars. But those lands so highly valued then are now unsaleable or of doubtful title; that city property has depreciated, and would not bring the price originally paid for it."[100]

Land prices did stabilize, albeit at a considerably lower level. By 1860–61, western land routinely sold at public land offices for about 60 cents per acre.[101]

---

[98] See http://www.texasalmanac.com/history/early/1857Population.pdf.

[99] In his debate with Abraham Lincoln on August 27, 1858, at Freeport, Illinois, Stephen Douglas stated that, despite the *Dred Scott* opinion, slavery could be excluded from a territory if the residents failed to pass laws supporting it. John Majewski thoughtfully pointed out to me the potential impact of the Freeport doctrine on southern migration patterns. E-mail from John Majewski, associate professor of history, University of California, Santa Barbara, Mar. 14, 2006.

[100] *Boston Independent,* Mar. 11, 1858.

[101] Gates, "Struggle for Land," p. 254.

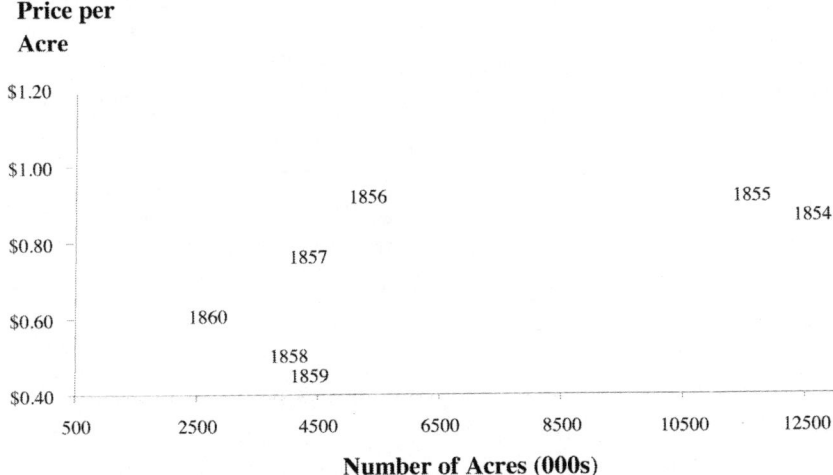

FIG. 12. Number and price of cash acres entered at public land offices, 1854–1860.
*Source:* Smith and Cole, *Fluctuations,* p. 185.

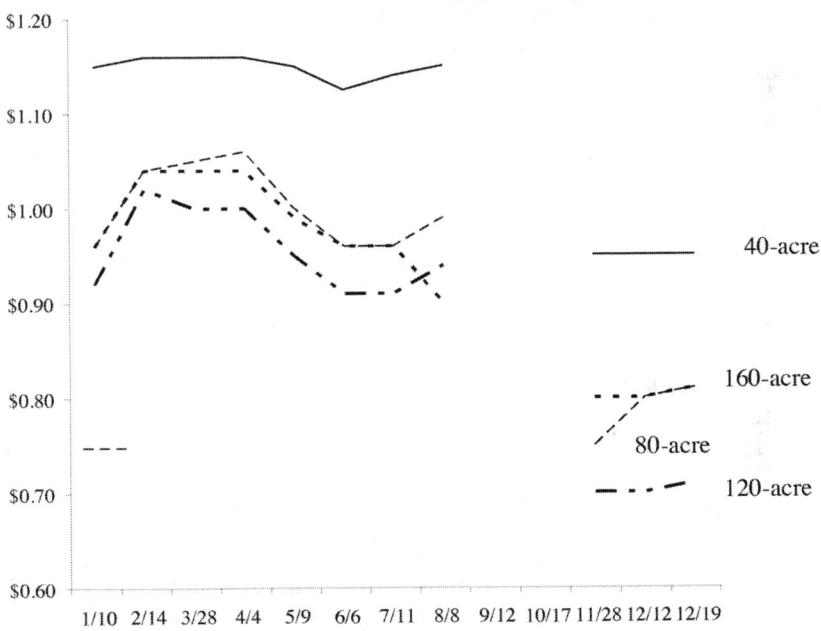

FIG. 13. Iowa land prices, 1857.
*Source: Thompson's Bank Note and Commercial Reporters* (various dates).

## Railroad Securities

Railroad securities reflected the turmoil in land markets triggered by *Dred Scott;* at the same time, western passenger traffic all but ceased.[102] Shortly after the *Scott* decision shocked investors, newly uncovered scandals took their toll on individual stock and bond values as well. Contemporaneous newspapers were filled with reports of railroad stock price declines as well as news about specific roads.[103] A prescient editorial in the *New York Herald* on April 7 commented, "No power on earth can save the railroad system of this country from a financial crisis. . . . It is . . . a matter of astonishment that public confidence has been so long sustained."[104]

### REGIONAL ANALYSIS

Figure 14 highlights regional differences in railroad construction. The percentage of railroad investment going to the South climbed from just over 25 percent in 1856 to nearly 65 percent in 1860. The percent of additional rails in the nation ending up in the Midwest plummeted from 75 percent in 1856 to below 25 percent in 1858, with a brief recovery in 1859 and another large fall in 1860. Certainly part of this decline reflects the greater buildup in the Midwest in earlier years. As I show next, however, stock price data suggest that railroad investment in the Midwest also generally became less attractive than in the South in the three years before the Civil War began.[105]

Figure 15 offers biweekly data on stock price indices for the first ten months of 1857. Note particularly the drop in prices for western (including internal Ohio) railroad stock just after the *Dred Scott* decision came out, then the ad-

---

[102] Fishlow, *American Railroads*, p. 203.

[103] The *New York Herald* reported a dive in stock prices for the New York Central, Erie, Reading, Michigan Central, Michigan Southern, Panama, Illinois Central, Cleveland & Pittsburgh, and Cleveland & Toledo on March 7, with follow-up pieces on March 9, March 21, and April 8. The *Daily National Intelligencer* reported declines on April 7; so did the *North American and U.S. Gazette* (Philadelphia) on July 11. The *Ripley (Ohio) Bee* reported reduced fares on the Erie on July 11, and the *Milwaukee Democrat* noted reduced earnings from freight on July 14 on the Michigan Central. All articles are located in America's Historical Newspapers online database, http://infoweb.newsbank.com.

[104] *New York Herald,* Apr. 7, 1857, online in America's Historical Newspapers.

[105] I performed a number of regressions on the data, casting the value (or the natural log) of stock indices and individual stock prices as functions of their own lagged values and a set of dummy variables designed to capture the possible significance of different time periods. Initial results showed a large, negative, and statistically significant coefficient on the dummy variable pertaining to the period after *Dred Scott* but before the failure of Ohio Life for the western regressions. But a unit root test indicated that the time series likely are not stationary, so these findings must be interpreted cautiously. These results are available from the author.

FIG. 14. Dollar investment and added rail mileage, regional comparison, 1856–60.
*Source:* Wilson and Spencer, "Growth of the Railroad Network," p. 339; Stover, *Baltimore and Ohio Railroad*, p. 317; Fishlow, *American Railroads*, table 16; *Historical Statistics of the United States*.

ditional fall in late summer. Stock prices for the first transcontinental line—the Panama railroad[106]—also fell sharply through August and September; Atlantic stock declined somewhat as well. Contrast these patterns with those for eastern and southern lines, where stock prices remained fairly steady throughout the period.[107]

If we take a longer view, we see that the panic had lasting effects some places but not others. In particular, stock prices for western lines remained depressed through the end of 1859 (see fig. 16). Eastern, Atlantic, and internal Ohio railroads recovered completely and in some cases enjoyed modest gains in stock prices over their early-1857 levels. Notably, stock prices of southern railroads never fell by much during 1857 and then climbed quite a

---

[106] The Panama Railroad was completed in 1855.

[107] Smith and Cole, *Fluctuations in American Business*, p. 106, and Calomiris and Schweikart, "The Panic of 1857," use other less-detailed data sources to map similar patterns, focusing primarily on the time leading up to the crisis and the crisis itself but not on subsequent periods. Lubos Pastor and Pietro Veronisi propose another potential reason for the pattern of railroad stock prices in the late 1850s: their research suggests that price bubbles occur during periods of technological revolution. In their view, the period between 1831 and 1860 was just such a time for railroads. They do not, however, address why differences across regions occurred. Pastor and Veronisi, "Technological Revolutions and Stock Prices," CRSP working paper 606 (Feb. 12, 2008), http://papers.ssrn.com/sol3/papers.cfm?abstract_id=868527.

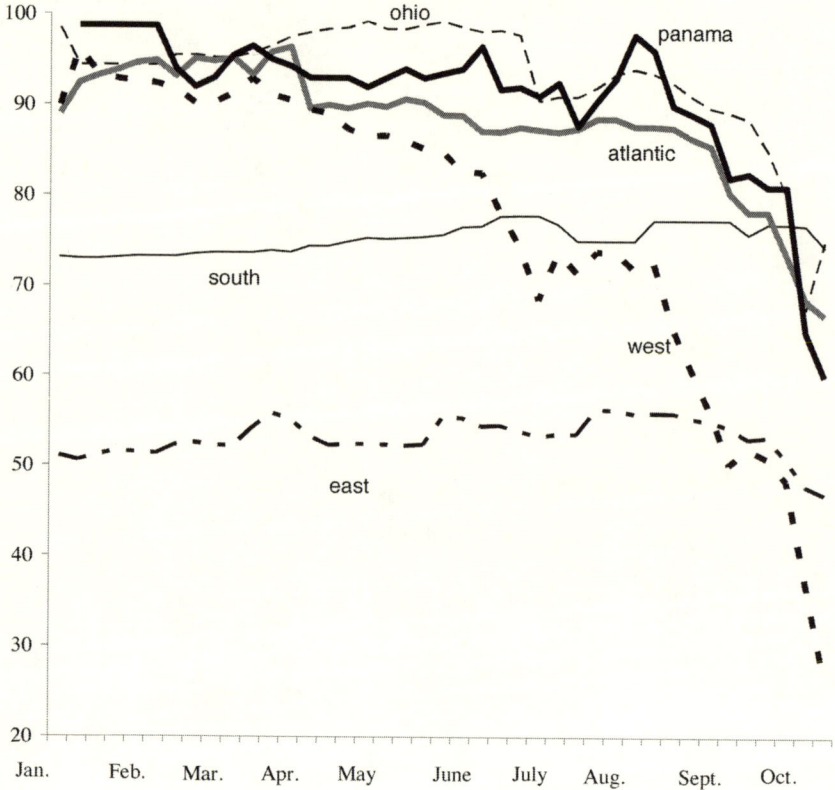

Fig. 15. Railroad stock indices, January 3–October 10, 1857.
Source: Sylla, Wilson, and Wright, *Price Quotations;* Inter-university Consortium for Political and Social Research, computer file ICPSR04053-vi.

bit through the end of 1859. Panama railroad stock also did well, perhaps because the Mountain Meadows massacre, in Utah in September 1857, made the Panama route far more attractive to California migrants than the railroad-stagecoach overland journey.[108]

INDIVIDUAL STOCKS

Figure 17 shows stock prices from 1856 to 1858 for several individual railroads, broken down into western, trunk, eastern, and southern roads. The leftmost vertical line corresponds to the date of the *Dred Scott* decision; the rightmost vertical line indicates the date of the collapse of Ohio Life.

---

[108] For an account of the massacre, see Will Bagley, *Brigham Young and the Massacre at Mountain Meadows* (Norman, Okla., 2002).

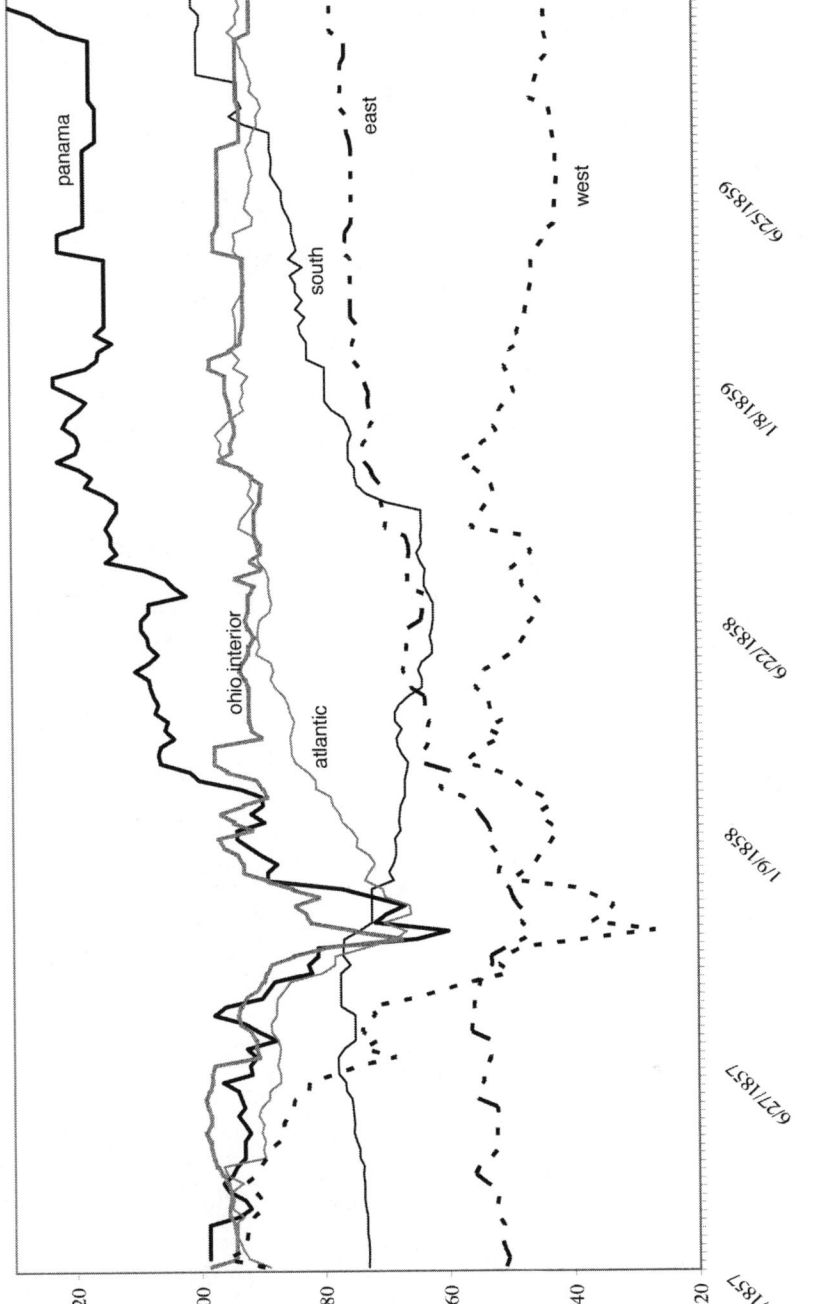

FIG. 16. Railroad stock indices, 1857–59.
Source: Sylla, Wilson, and Wright, *Price Quotations*.

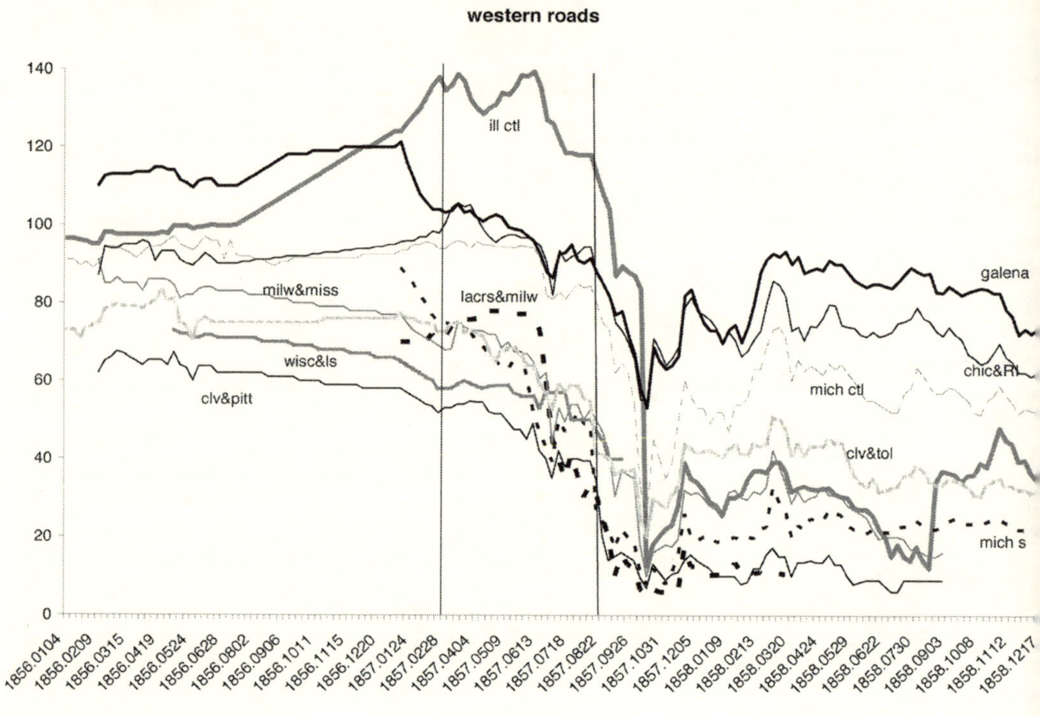

FIG. 17. Individual stock prices by region, 1856–59.

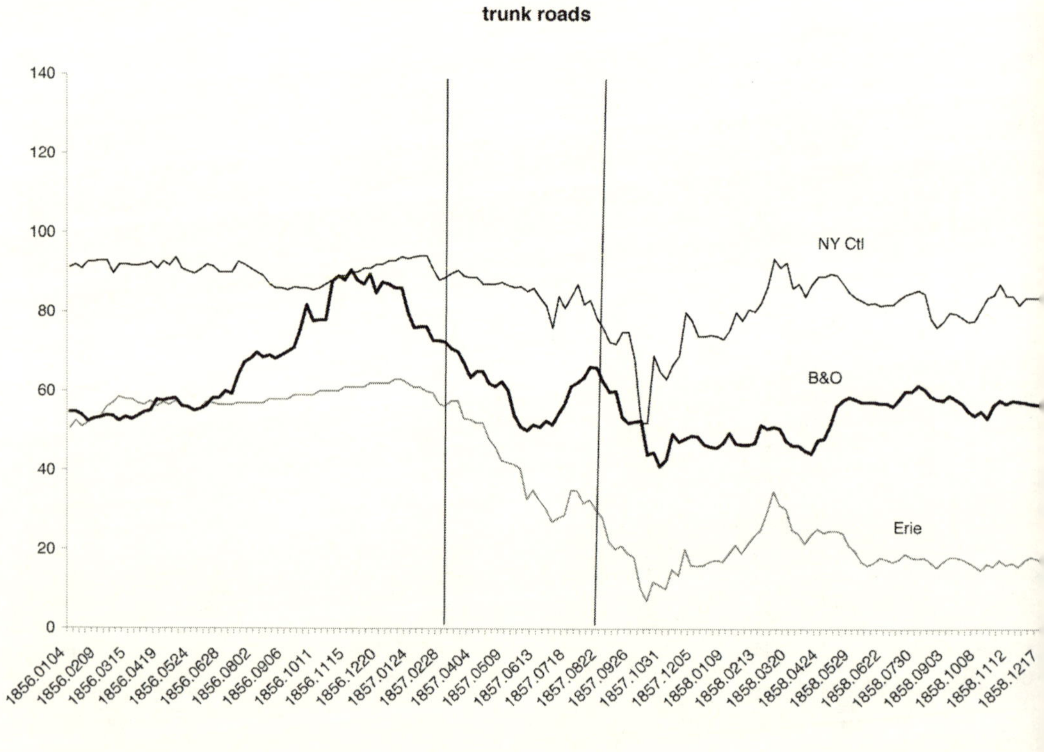

**eastern roads**

**southern roads**

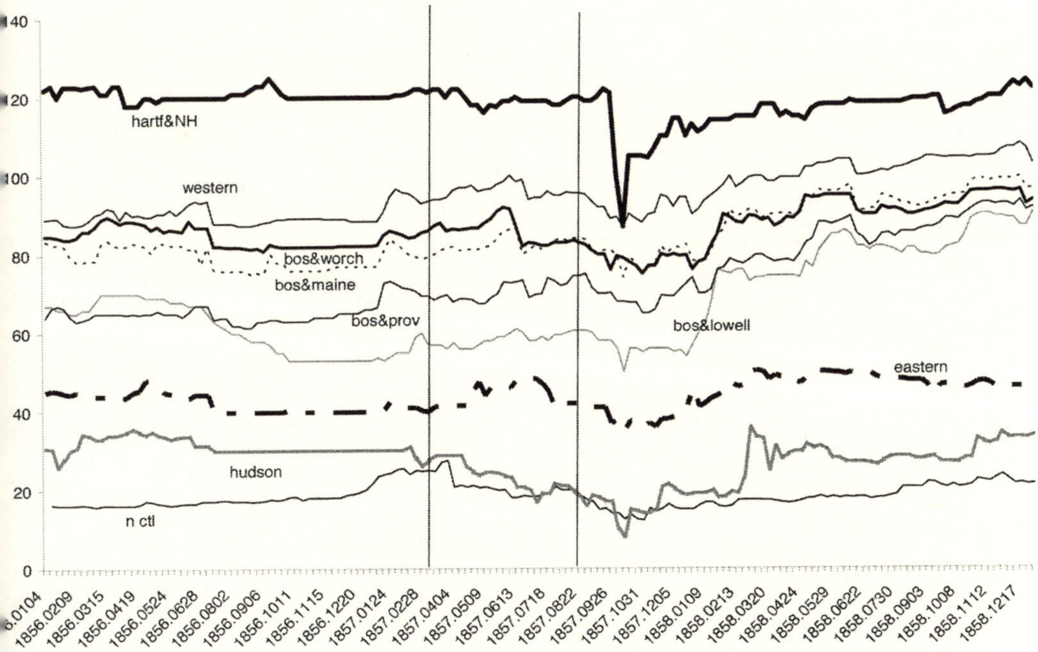

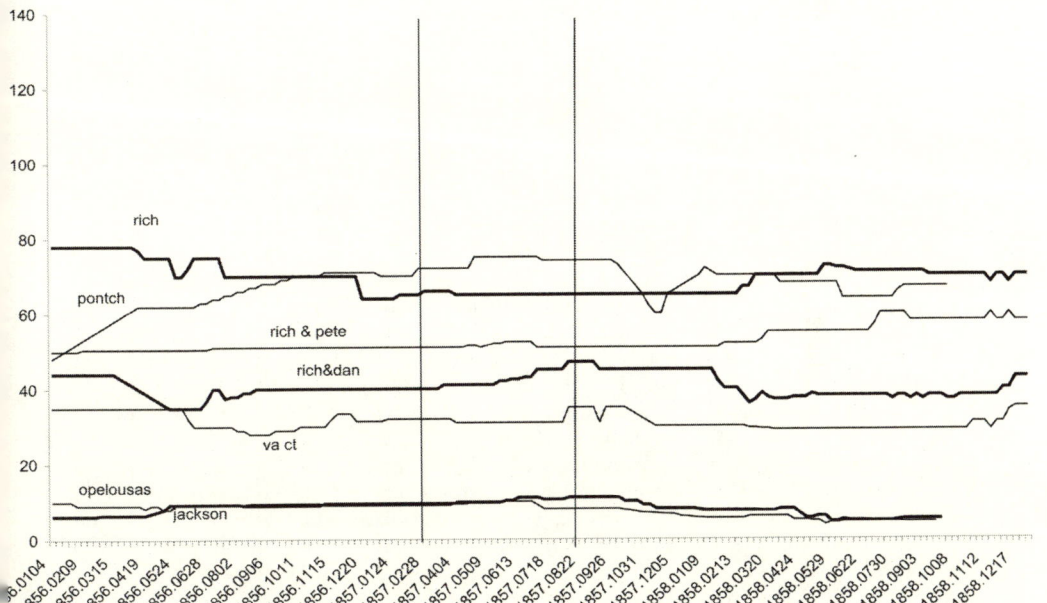

These graphs help highlight the differences in price patterns across regions. Western- and trunk-line stocks generally fell after the *Scott* decision (although B&O and New York Central stock soon recovered), then fell further after Ohio Life, with only the New York Central stock price attaining its former peak level by year's end. But security prices stayed down for many companies, particularly those revealed to have shady or incompetent management.[109] These include the infamous Michigan Southern, the Erie, and the LaCrosse and Milwaukee.[110] Illinois Central stock prices took a steep dive and remained depressed throughout 1857.[111]

By comparison, many eastern stocks appear unaffected until after the Ohio Life debacle, when they dropped slightly but recovered quickly. Southern stocks exhibit much less movement generally, with a small upward drift after *Dred Scott* but before Ohio Life.[112]

---

[109] These seem to be classic examples of Warren Buffett's "naked swimmers." As Buffett put it, "you only find out who is swimming naked when the tide goes out." Chairman's letter "To the Shareholders of Berkshire Hathaway Inc.," printed annual report 2001, available at http://www.berkshirehathaway.com/2001ar/2001letter.html.

[110] The Michigan Southern's overissue of stock is discussed earlier in the text. Daniel Drew became a member of the Erie board of directors in 1857 and used his position to manipulate the value of the stock. He later engaged in fraudulent stock transactions, along with Jay Gould and Jim Fisk, to keep the railroad out of the hands of Cornelius Vanderbilt. Byron Kilbourn, president of the LaCrosse & Milwaukee, was found guilty of bribery in obtaining a state land grant for the railroad. Stover, *Iron Road*, pp. 50–51, 153. Newspapers also commented on the frequent stock issues of the Galena & Chicago, and an overissue of $1 million in bonds by the Cleveland & Pittsburgh. "Financial and Commercial Money Market," *New York Herald*, Mar. 26, 1857; untitled article, *Pittsfield Sun*, Dec. 17, 1857.

[111] This may have had something to do with the leadership of Robert Schuyler in the early years of the Illinois Central, as I discuss in note 39.

[112] I have also conducted preliminary analysis designed to detect turning points in individual stock prices, using an analytical approach pioneered by Kristen Willard, Timothy Guinnane, and Harvey Rosen in their study of the greenback market during the Civil War. Willard, Guinnane, and Rosen, "Turning Points in the Civil War: Views from the Greenback Market," *American Economic Review* 86 (1996):1001–18. This work offers further support for the hypothesis that the *Dred Scott* decision lowered the value of investments in western railroads. Tellingly, western stocks exhibit negative turning points in their series as early as March 21, with predicted mean stock prices dropping from 1.9 percent to 17.1 percent in the period after the *Dred Scott* decision but before Ohio Life went under. Predicted average stock prices for many western lines fell even more precipitously just around the time Ohio Life failed. In contrast, southern stocks—aside from the Opelousas line, which was built but ran no cars until after the Civil War—show positive turning points in the period after *Dred Scott* but before Ohio Life, and no turning points when Ohio Life imploded. A few eastern stocks also have negative turning points in the post-*Scott*, pre–Ohio Life period that on average are smaller than those for western stocks, although many show either no turning points or positive (but typically insignificant) ones. Like southern lines, eastern lines exhibit no turning points at the time of the Ohio Life collapse. These results are available from the author.

## Banks

The close connections among land markets, securities markets, and banks—particularly via call loans—meant that many northern banks were in trouble as soon as other markets began to founder. The New York clearing house and the Suffolk Bank in New England did little to stop the hemorrhaging of funds; the poorly managed Bank of Pennsylvania closed on September 25, sixty-two of the sixty-three New York banks suspended payments by October 12, and New England and London banks soon followed.[113] The sinking of the SS *Central America* in mid-September, with its cargo of thirty thousand pounds of gold from the San Francisco mint, did not help matters. A total of 1,415 U.S. banks failed in October alone.[114] Because banks refused to roll over loans to securities brokers, several brokers went bankrupt.[115] Although New York banks began to redeem in specie by December 12, that was too late for some people.[116]

Banks were not acting unilaterally, however. Customer behavior and legal constraints mattered as well. Some commentators think that concerted effort by a few large New York banks could have stemmed the panic.[117] But banks pointed out that usury laws constrained them from raising interest rates for riskier borrowers.[118] Not only that, depositors pulled money out even faster than banks called in loans. Walter Smith and Arthur Cole (1935) show that the ratio of loans to net deposits fell from 160 in November 1854 to as low as 133, but the ratio actually climbed to 163 in August 1857 and 176 in October 1857.[119]

In contrast to banks in the Northeast, southern banks remained solvent and stable. All New Orleans banks save one continued to redeem in specie,

---

[113] The mismanagement at the Bank of Pennsylvania was well known at the time. See, for example, "The Financial Position of New York," *Independent*, Feb. 25, 1858.

[114] J. R. T. Hughes, "The Commercial Crisis of 1857," *Oxford Economic Papers*, n.s. 8, no. 2 (1956):194–222; Charles Kindleberger, *Manias, Panics, and Crashes: A History of Financial Crises* (1978; reprint ed., New York, 2000), p. 115.

[115] For a detailed account of the reaction to the crisis of banks in various states, see Calomiris and Schweikart, "Panic of 1857," p. 809. For a fascinating account of a single bank in Watertown, N.Y., during this period, see Bodenhorn, "Capital Mobility," pp. 585–610. He found, perhaps not surprisingly, that the bank was much more willing to renegotiate with customers who had enjoyed long-term relationships with it.

[116] Smith and Cole, *Fluctuations in American Business*, p. 130.

[117] Van Vleck, *Panic of 1857*. Also see "A Financial Panic," *Saturday Evening Post*, Oct. 10, 1857.

[118] A call for ending the usury laws appeared in Office of the Mercantile Agency, "Business Failures in the Panic of 1857," reprinted in *Business History Review* 37 (1963):437–43. Miller, "Crisis and Cycles," p. 321, refers to similar efforts by the New York Chamber of Commerce. See Memorial of the Chamber of Commerce of New York, *Bankers' Magazine and Statistical Register* 7 (April 1858):832–33.

[119] Smith and Cole, *Fluctuations in American Business*, p. 130, chart 45.

as did most Kentucky banks and more than half of South Carolina banks. So did the Bank of Indiana—not a southern bank, but not part of the eastern network either.[120]

## Commodities and Slaves

Like the prices of western railroad securities and land, the prices of commodities plummeted in the latter half of 1857.[121] The *New England Farmer* reported that cattle priced at more than $30 in late fall 1857 went for only $18 in January 1858, for instance.[122] Figure 18 shows the steep fall in the monthly commodity price index.

What happened in commodity markets was complicated by the reduction in tariffs during the last month of the Pierce administration. Northern ironmasters and textile manufacturers complained bitterly about the loss of protection and steep falls in the prices of their products, whereas southern cotton growers suffered relatively less from price declines.[123]

Tellingly, business failures over the life of the panic accounted for 3.24 percent of all establishments in the North but only 1.21 percent in the South. Estimated losses from the panic to the commercial community in the free states were $142 million but only about one-tenth that much in the slave states.[124]

Just as significantly, slave sales prices took only a small dip in 1857, then climbed rapidly thereafter (see fig. 19). Appraisal values remained steady or rose, even during the panic.

## Governmental and International Reverberations

Although banks had no recourse to a central bank in 1857, the country did boast an independent treasury that had some of the same powers.[125] When

---

[120]Hammond, *Banks and Politics*, p. 712; Stampp, *America in 1857*, p. 224.

[121]Smith and Cole, *Fluctuations in American Business*, p. 167.

[122]*New England Farmer* 10, no. 1 (Jan. 1858):23–24.

[123]Nevins, *Emergence of Lincoln*, pp. 195–96, 224–26.

[124]Figures were reported by the New York commercial agency Tappan and McKillop in *Bankers' Magazine*, cited in Nevins, *Emergence of Lincoln*, pp. 196–97. For commercial failures by state from January 1857 to March 1858, see Calomiris and Schweikart, "Panic of 1857," p. 814, table 2, originally reported in David Evans, *The History of the Commercial Crisis, 1857–1858, and the Stock Exchange Panic of 1859* (London, 1859).

[125]For discussions of the independent treasury, see Richard Timberlake, "The Independent Treasury and Monetary Policy before the Civil War," *Southern Economic Journal* 27 (1960):92–103; Edward Stevens, "Composition of Money Supply prior to Civil War," *Journal of Money, Credit, and Banking* 3 (1971):84–101.

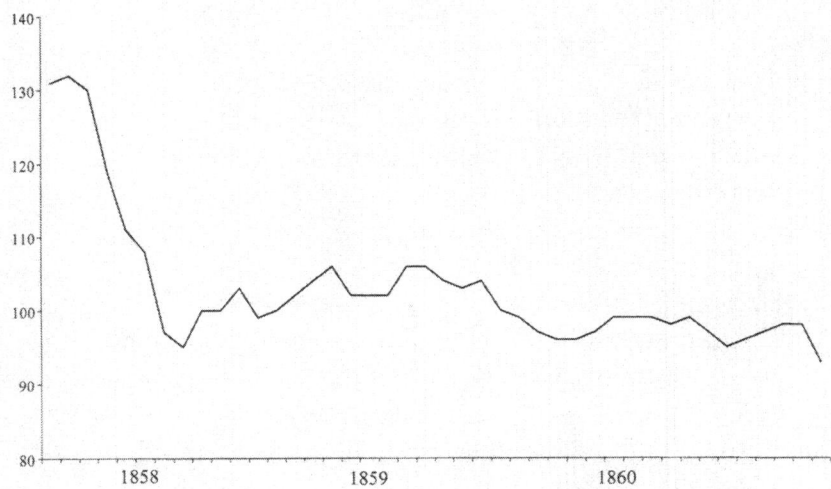

FIG. 18. Monthly commodity price index, July 1857–December 1860.
Source: Smith and Cole, Fluctuations, p. 167, table 52.

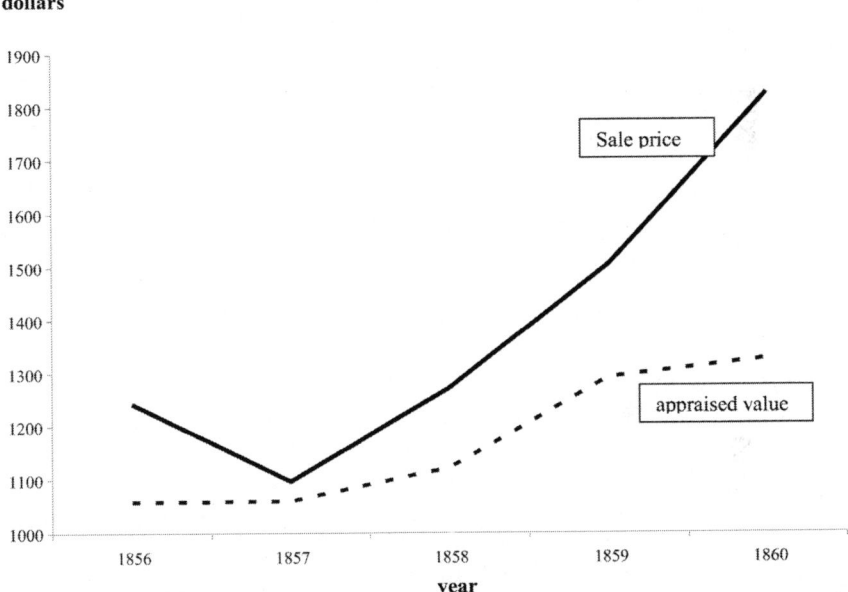

FIG. 19. Mean values for prime male slaves, 1850–57.
Source: Fogel and Engerman, Slave Sales and Appraisals; Inter-university Consortium for Political and Social Research, computer file ICPSR07421-v3.

the panic began, treasury secretary Howell Cobb took mild action, buying up private securities as well as trying to finance a growing federal deficit.[126] Some commentators think Cobb came to the rescue too early, then abandoned the nation to its fate.[127] Cobb was aware of criticism at the time, for he peevishly stated, "There are many people who seem to think it is the duty of the government to provide relief in all cases of trouble and distress."[128]

Some state governments felt the effects of the panic, in part because of their close ties to railroads. The value of Illinois state bonds dropped sharply in late autumn (see fig. 20). In contrast, other state bonds—particularly in Maine and Massachusetts—held their value fairly well, even at the height of the crisis. What the patterns suggest is that the impact on municipal bond prices generally was short lived in virtually all states except Illinois. What is more, state bond prices converged at the beginning of 1859 in nearly the same way as they had at the beginning of 1856: the most notable feature of figure 20 is not the decline in prices in the fall of 1857 but rather the huge run-up in Illinois bond values during the preceding year. Just as in land, financial, and commodity markets, the anomaly is the speculative bubble beforehand rather than its bursting afterward.

The panic spread across national borders as well, in part because of interlocking financial and securities markets.[129] British, Scottish, and French banks and individual holders of U.S. railroad stocks suffered large losses. In Europe, the panic culminated in December, when the Austrian Central Bank intervened with a loan of 10 million florins to prop up the staggering financial market.[130]

---

[126]On this episode, see Timberlake, "Independent Treasury," p. 101. The federal debt mushroomed from $29 million in 1857 to $65 million in 1860. Nevins, *Emergence of Lincoln*, p. 187.

[127]Kindleberger, *Manias, Panics, and Crashes*, p. 180; Timberlake, "Independent Treasury," p. 101.

[128]Reported in the *Congressional Globe* and quoted in Timberlake, "Independent Treasury," p. 101.

[129]Richard Sylla, Jack Wilson, and Robert Wright compile evidence about the trans-Atlantic integration of capital markets as early as 1845. Sylla, Wilson, and Wright, "Integration of Trans-Atlantic Capital Markets, 1790–1845," *Review of Finance* 10 (December 2006):1–32. Also see Bodenhorn, "Capital Mobility."

[130]Nevins, *Emergence of Lincoln*, p. 191; Hughes, "Commercial Crisis of 1857."

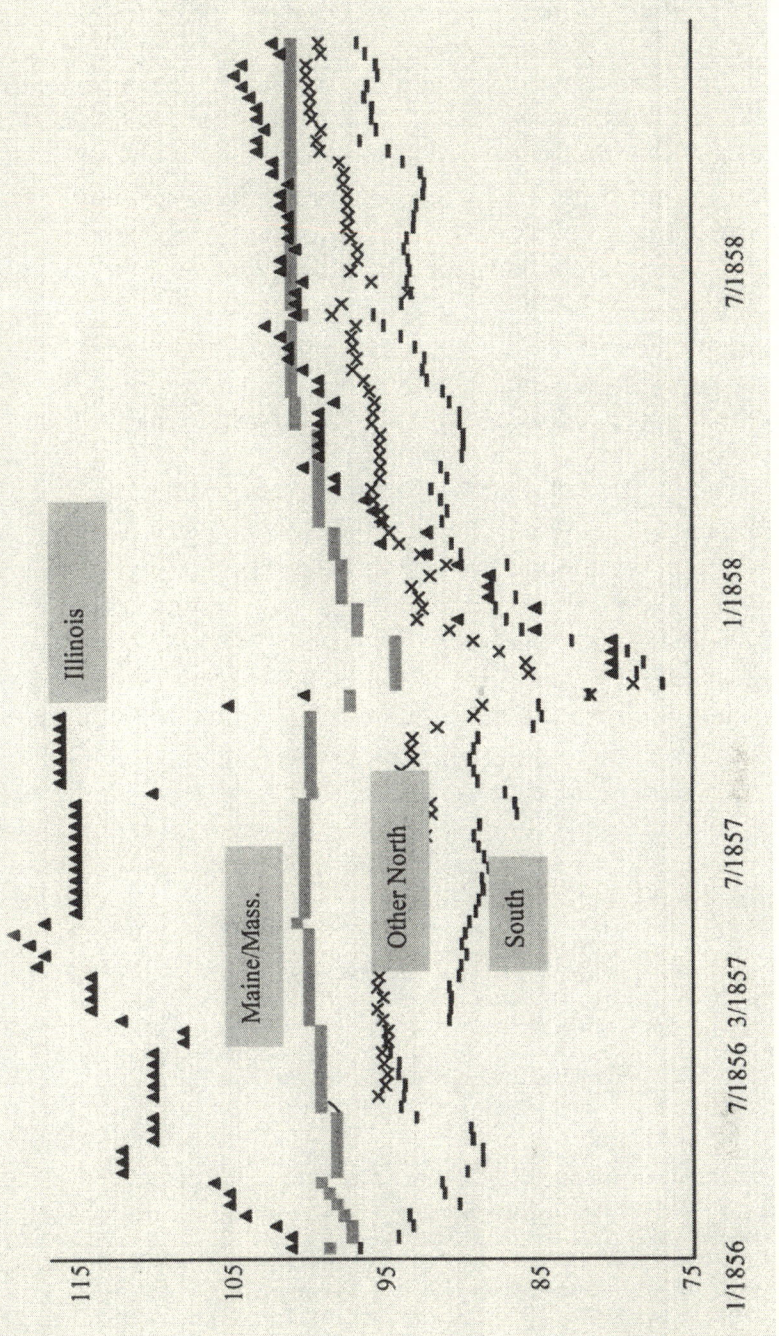

FIG. 20. Bond values, grouped states, 1856–59.
Source: Sylla, Wilson, and Wright, *Price Quotations*; Inter-university Consortium for Political and Social Research, computer file ICPSR04053-v1.

## Aftermath: *Dred* and Panic Embolden the South

Two features of the Panic of 1857 are worth noting: it did not last long in and of itself, but its uneven regional impact had long-lasting effects. The decision in *Dred Scott* helped set off the panic which, though brief, was felt particularly in the North. Northern institutions stumbled, whereas southern ones remained stable, due partly to differences in railroad financing, state involvement in transportation endeavors, banking practices, portfolio holdings, and product mix. Southerners thus felt more confident that they could succeed on their own. This is not a new thought: among others, Allan Nevins, Kenneth Stampp, and James Huston suggest a connection between the antebellum panic and secession.[131] What is new here is the abundant empirical evidence to support this contention.

Observers of today's financial crisis might be surprised at the short duration of the antebellum upheaval. Despite—or perhaps because of—the absence of strong, active public institutions, people were not helpless: private coordination among southern banks and actions of northern clearinghouses helped resolve the antebellum crisis.[132] Moreover, sound companies generally remained in business, whereas poorly run or risk-laden enterprises went bust, or at least experienced large devaluations in stock prices. Commodity prices stabilized at lower levels fairly quickly. Financial markets calmed down before Christmas and land markets soon followed.[133] Perhaps most important for future events, however, southern assets—both financial and real—experienced far smaller price shocks during the panic and exhibited more robust growth after it than northern assets.

---

[131] Nevins states that the panic was not a huge financial convulsion in and of itself, but psychologically it helped tear the nation apart. Nevins, *Emergence of Lincoln*, p. 176. Before 1857, the North seemed invincible. The panic proved otherwise. Walton and Rockoff note that the panic aggravated sectional tensions, emboldening the South to say it was better off without the North. Walton and Rockoff, *History of the American Economy*, p. 238. Also see James Huston, *The Panic of 1857 and the Coming of the Civil War* (Baton Rouge, 1987), p. 16; Stampp, *America in 1857*, pp. 229–300.

[132] On coordination in some states, see, for example, Calomiris and Schweikart, "Panic of 1857." Note that public intervention actually might prolong financial crises or make them more likely. If people—or institutions—know they will be rescued when they suffer a loss, they will take risks they would otherwise have avoided. Not only that, they have no incentive to monitor the behavior of those to whom they have entrusted their money. The end effect is to reward risky behavior and to penalize prudence—a classic example of moral hazard.

[133] Nevins, *Emergence of Lincoln*, p. 193; Kindleberger, *Manias, Panics, and Crashes*, p. 211.

So the panic cleaned house—but divided it as well. Southerners blamed the North for the crisis and for the temporary hit to their pocketbooks. Jefferson Davis blustered that the North's extravagance and speculation in railroad stocks and western land had caused the nation's problems, for example.[134] Yet Davis also noted that the South suffered less and recovered more quickly from the crisis: he reassured an audience in Jackson, Mississippi, that "[southern] prosperity was not at the mercy of such a commercial crisis. . . . Our great staple was our safety."[135]

Other prominent southerners went further, extolling the stability of the South and disparaging the volatility of the North. Alabama congressman Jabez Curry observed that northern workers "suffering from the terrible pecuniary crisis" had taken to the streets and "with hungry mouths" had cried out "Bread or Blood!" Southern slaves, in contrast, were hardly "aware of any financial pressure, because labor and capital are there harmonized, and there is no conflict between them."[136] In his famous King Cotton speech, South Carolina senator James Hammond viewed the South as the nation's savior after the panic and offered a barely veiled threat:

> When the abuse of credit had destroyed credit and annihilated confidence; when thousands of the strongest commercial houses in the world were coming down, and hundreds of millions of dollars of supposed property evaporating in thin air; . . . what brought you up? Fortunately for you it was the commencement of the cotton season, and we have poured in upon you one million six hundred thousand bales of cotton just at the crisis to save you from destruction. That cotton, but for the bursting of your speculative bubbles in the North, which produced the whole of this convulsion, would have brought us $100,000,000. We have sold it for $65,000,000 and saved you. Thirty-five million dollars we, the slaveholders of the South, have put into the charity box for your magnificent financiers, your "cotton lords," your

---

[134]Quoted in Jerry Markham, *A Financial History of the U.S.* (Armonk, N.Y., 2002), p. 202. In a somewhat ominous echo regarding today's financial turmoil, Brazilian president Luis Inacio Lula da Silva recently told British prime minister Gordon Brown, "this is a crisis caused and encouraged by the irrational behaviour of white people with blue eyes." See http://www.dailymail.co.uk/news/worldnews/article-1165089 (accessed May 17, 2011).

[135]Quoted in Marc Egnal, "Rethinking the Secession of the Lower South," *Civil War History* 50 (2004):261–90, originally from Haskell Monroe and James McIntosh, eds., *The Papers of Jefferson Davis*, 10 vols. (Baton Rouge, 1971–99), 6:157.

[136]*Congressional Globe*, 35th Cong., 1st sess., 1858, p. 819, quoted in Huston, *Panic of 1857*, p. 122.

"merchant princes." . . . The South have sustained you in great measure. You are our factors. You fetch and carry for us. . . . Suppose we were to discharge you; suppose we were to take our business out of your hands;—we should consign you to anarchy and poverty.[137]

*DeBow's Review* expressed the views of many in the South, stating that Dixie's wealth was permanent and real whereas the North's was fictitious.[138]

The decision in *Dred Scott* brought matters to a head in countless ways. But the new empirical evidence presented here strongly supports its role in triggering the subsequent financial upheaval. And, by convincing southerners of the strengths of their institutions and the weaknesses of northern ones, the Panic of 1857 helped give rise to the standoff at Fort Sumter.

---

[137]Hammond gave the speech on March 4, 1858. This excerpt appears at http://www.sewanee.edu/faculty/Willis/Civil_War/documents/HammondCotton.html.
[138]*DeBow's Review*, Dec. 1857, quoted in Nevins, *Emergence of Lincoln*, p. 196.

Brooks D. Simpson

# "Hit Him Again"

## The Caning of Charles Sumner

"WE HAVE BEFORE us a long season of excitement and ribald debate." So wrote Massachusetts senator Charles Sumner (fig. 1) in March 1856.[1] Events two months later validated his prediction. Indeed, it would be Sumner's own speech, "The Crime against Kansas," delivered in May 1856, on the eve of the escalation of political violence in Kansas, that sparked a retort that would leave its mark on American politics as well as on the senator. That retort came in the form of South Carolina congressman Preston S. Brooks's attack on Sumner on the floor of the U.S. Senate on May 22, 1856. What became known as "the caning of Charles Sumner" and the linking of "Bleeding Sumner" to Bleeding Kansas had a profound impact on American politics in 1856, and to this day it remains a vivid incident in the story of how Americans came to blows by 1861.[2]

The sensational nature of Brooks's attack on Sumner leaves us with important questions to explore. Why did it happen? What made it so sensational? How did it affect American politics in the presidential election year of 1856, the first time the antislavery Republican Party would present a candidate for the presidency? How did it affect politics in the nation's capital,

---

[1]David Donald, *Charles Sumner and the Coming of the Civil War* (New York, 1960), p. 278.
[2]On the caning, see Manisha Sinha, "The Caning of Charles Sumner: Slavery, Race, and Ideology in the Age of the Civil War," *Journal of the Early Republic* 23 (2003):233–62; William E. Gienapp, "The Crime against Sumner: The Caning of Charles Sumner and the Rise of the Republican Party," *Civil War History* 25 (1979):218–45; and Williamjames Hull Hoffer, *The Caning of Charles Sumner: Honor, Idealism, and the Origins of the Civil War* (Baltimore, 2010).

Fig. 1. A daguerreotype of Senator Charles Sumner taken between 1855 and 1860 pictures him as he appeared around the time of the caning by Congressman Preston Brooks. *Courtesy Boston Public Library.*

especially when it came to political debate and the conduct of members of Congress? What was its legacy beyond 1856? Was it truly a step toward secession and civil war?

The story is well known. In the spring of 1856, as violence continued on the plains of Kansas as proslavery and antislavery forces literally battled to control the process of constructing a territory, word circulated throughout Washington that Charles Sumner was preparing a major speech on the subject. Given Sumner's reputation as an orator and as an outspoken advocate of abolitionism, his passionately delivered words were sure to excite discussion, even controversy. On May 19, 1856, at 1 p.m., Sumner commenced a two-day philippic entitled "The Crime against Kansas." The Senate galleries were filled in anticipation of the moment, and Sumner did not disappoint.[3]

---

[3] See Michael D. Pierson, "'All Southern Society Is Assailed by the Foulest Charges': Charles Sumner's 'The Crime against Kansas' and the Escalation of Republican Anti-slavery Rhetoric," *New England Quarterly* 68 (1995):531–57.

For three hours on the nineteenth and several more hours the next day the senator described in painstaking detail, rhetorical flourishes, and classical references his understanding of how proslavery forces had invaded Kansas while Democrats in Washington defended them, all in the cause of slavery. That in itself was not exceptional: what distinguished this particular speech was Sumner's decision to attack his colleagues Stephen A. Douglas of Illinois, James M. Mason of Virginia, and Andrew P. Butler of South Carolina. As Sumner spoke, Douglas growled, "That damn fool will get himself killed by some other damn fool."[4]

For years Sumner had crossed swords with Douglas, the leader of the northern Democrats in the Senate, and Mason, the author of the Fugitive Slave Law of 1850, a favorite target of abolitionists. At times the rhetoric in these exchanges became heated and personal. But it was Sumner's references to Butler that appeared to be most objectionable. Sumner claimed that the recently widowed Butler had chosen "the Harlot, Slavery," as his mistress, which, "though ugly to others, is always lovely to him"; ridiculed Butler's slight speech impediment by asserting that the senator, "with incoherent phrases, discharged the loose expectoration of his speech" as he defended proslavery forces, adding, "He cannot open his mouth, but out there flies a blunder."[5]

No sooner had Sumner taken his seat on May 20 than several of his colleagues, including Douglas and Mason, rose to chastise him for his manner of speech. "Is it his object to provoke some of us to kick him as we would a dog in the street," wondered Douglas, "that he may get sympathy upon the just chastisement?" Clearly the senator's oration had aroused personal anger and caused some intense responses. Nor did everyone expect the confrontations to end at the close of debate that day. Several Republicans took it upon themselves to escort Sumner from the chamber, but Sumner would have none of it.[6]

That Sumner's language was exceptional is difficult to dispute, although one must add that over the years it had not been uncommon for debate to degenerate on the floor of either house of Congress. Some speakers had become masters of vituperation. Virginia's John Randolph of Roanoke gained

---

[4] Donald, *Sumner*, p. 286.
[5] For the text of Sumner's speech, see http://facweb.furman.edu/~benson/docs/sumnerksh2.htm.
[6] Donald, *Sumner*, pp. 287, 289.

quite a reputation for his bitter, sharp, and slashing attacks on fellow members during the first decades of the nineteenth century. Other members of Congress had issued retorts and offered biting personal characterizations of opponents, usually in the heat of debate. What made Sumner's characterizations all the more amazing was that they had been deliberately framed. He could not seek protection under the claim that he had spoken in the heat of the moment. After all, in previous speeches supporters had applauded his sharply etched assaults upon his foes, including Butler and Douglas, so why not repeat the process?[7]

What also rendered Sumner's insults distinctive was that they were delivered on the floor of the U.S. Senate. Rough language and more was understood to be far more typical of the give and take that characterized debates in the House chamber. The Senate was supposed to be different, a place where debate was more thoughtful, purposeful, and elevated. One might assert that this was more myth than reality, or that mutual respect had declined, especially when it came to issues that could arouse such passions, but nevertheless the perception stood. What, then, moved Sumner to speak as he did? It appears that he believed that it was time to counter attacks against his state and his cause by replying in like manner.[8] Nor did he see anything wrong in what he said. As he later observed, "I have never said anything which was not in just response ... according to parliamentary usage."[9]

The truth is that Sumner could be bitter and cutting when he spoke in public, and he appeared oblivious to the force of his own language. In turn other Senate veterans, themselves possessed of sharp tongues, found Sumner's condescension and personal commentary infuriating. Thus it was no surprise when these exchanges escalated, leaving all parties feeling aggrieved. That Sumner's insults were planned and rehearsed, however, made them a bit more difficult to stomach: that he seemed to lavish so much time and energy on them and often offered them in the context of classical allusions could only increase the irritation felt by his targets.

At first glance it seemed odd that Sumner would reserve his harshest language for Andrew P. Butler, the senator from South Carolina. As a freshman senator, Sumner found himself sitting next to Butler, who was so taken with Sumner's classical learning that he had asked his new colleague to verify

---

[7] Ibid., p. 281.
[8] Ibid.
[9] T. Lloyd Benson, *The Caning of Senator Sumner* (Belmont, Cal., 2004), p. 138.

his own classical allusions. In turn, Sumner conceded that if the South Carolinian had been a New Englander, he "would have been a scholar, or, at least, a well educated man," although one might suggest that at times the arrogant Sumner might be using the language of condescending contempt. Butler returned the favor when he rose to object to Sumner's motion to speak on behalf of his motion to repeal the fugitive slave law—the very moment Sumner had sought to deliver his inaugural oration against slavery in the Senate. Butler, joined by Douglas, carried the day.[10]

During his first four years in the Senate, Sumner had engaged in several heated exchanges with his colleagues, notably Douglas and Mason; by 1854 he had even grown upset with Butler when the two clashed yet again over the fugitive slave law.[11] Such clashes with Douglas may have been expected, but when Sumner had first entered the Senate in 1851, he found himself sitting between Butler and Mason, "with both of whom I have constant and cordial intercourse," he reported. He added, "This experience would teach me, if I needed the lesson, to shun harsh and personal criticism of those from whom I differ." Apparently the lesson did not stay with him long.[12]

Reaction to the speech was mixed. If some praised it as a strong indictment of the South, slavery, and the policies of the Pierce administration in Kansas, others were not so sure, especially some of his fellow Republicans and other politicians who disagreed with the sharp personal edge of his attacks. As one might predict, southerners and northern Democrats were outraged. As Michael D. Pierson has pointed out, not all the outrage involved Sumner's bitter characterization of his opponents: in repeatedly invoking the imagery of rape and sexual violation, the Massachusetts senator had also fashioned a philippic that bordered on the obscene in the eyes of his critics. However, that impression did not spark the anger caused by Sumner's personal attacks, and it was those attacks that brought forth a memorable response.[13]

What happened in the Senate chamber two days after Sumner concluded his remarks can be understood in part by noting that Andrew Butler was not present when Sumner delivered his two-day address. Thus the senator from South Carolina could not counter or reprimand Sumner on the spot. Rather,

---

[10] Donald, *Sumner*, pp. 209, 224–25.
[11] Ibid., pp. 258–59, 260, 263–65.
[12] Benson, *Caning*, p. 33.
[13] See Pierson, "All Southern Society."

FIG. 2. Representative Preston S. Brooks seen in an engraved portrait print made in Washington, D.C., ca. 1857. *Courtesy Library of Congress Prints and Photographs Division.*

it would be left to Butler's distant kinsman, Congressman Preston S. Brooks (fig. 2), to rise to the occasion to defend his kinsman, his state, and the South. The congressman was something of a hothead who was prone to look upon critical commentary as a matter of disputing one's honor and something that must be avenged. Colleagues had heard Brooks declare that "it was time for southern men to stop this coarse abuse used by the Abolitionists against the Southern people and States, and that he should not feel that he was representing his State properly if he permitted such things to be said; that he learned Mr. Sumner intended to do this very thing days before he made his speech; that he did it deliberately, and he thought he ought to punish him for it."[14]

Brooks planned his response with great deliberation. He would not challenge Sumner to a duel, because that would have recognized his target as

---

[14]Benson, *Caning,* p. 140.

a social equal, a gentleman, and Brooks was seeking to humiliate his foe. Rather, the congressman decided that he would have to beat his opponent with a cane, much as masters whipped slaves to keep them in line. Apparently he never considered asking Sumner to apologize to his counterpart. In the meantime reports arrived from Kansas that proslavery forces had descended upon the antislavery stronghold of Lawrence and "sacked" the town. The violence on the prairies seemed bound to continue, with bullies and bullets replacing ballots as the way to settle political differences.

The afternoon of May 22, 1856, found Charles Sumner at his desk in the Senate chamber, franking copies of his speech to distribute to admirers. The day's session had been cut short due to the death of a member of Congress, leaving him with plenty of time to address other matters. Brooks, along with fellow congressmen Laurence M. Keitt and Henry A. Edmundson, hovered about the back of the chamber, waiting for just the right moment to strike. After failing to encounter Sumner on May 21, Brooks had pondered whether it would be best to intercept him on his way to Capitol Hill or just before his entering the building itself, only to be frustrated in his design. At last he had located his target. He had entered the Senate chamber after the close of business for the day, only to learn that women remained in the galleries, and he wished to spare them the sight of what he planned to do. Brooks discussed his options with Edmundson, who then left the chamber to discuss with a senator the propriety of Brooks confronting Sumner in the upper chamber itself.

Learning that at last the chamber and gallery were clear of women, Brooks entered the chamber again. He strode toward Sumner's desk. Keitt followed, intent on gaining a good view of what was to come: he eventually made his way to the clerk's desk. Brooks approached the senator from behind: Sumner, engrossed in his busywork, did not notice the congressman.

What happened next is more difficult to describe with assurance. Brooks claimed that he came around to face Sumner, who was slow to recognize that he had a visitor (and Brooks was in any case a stranger to him). The congressman commenced by declaring (as he recalled in a letter to his brother), "Mr. Sumner, I have read your speech with care and as much impartiality as possible and I feel it my duty to tell you that you have libeled my State and slandered a relative who is aged and absent and I am come to punish you for it." Other accounts suggest that Brooks never quite got through this extended (and probably rehearsed) statement before he saw Sumner start

FIG. 3. One of many popular prints of the caning, "Southern Chivalry," depicts Brooks shattering his cane on the defenseless Sumner, shown pen in hand. *Courtesy the Harry J. Peters Collection, Smithsonian Institution, National Museum of American History.*

to rise, whereupon Brooks gave him what he later described as "a slight blow" with his cane. Sumner started to protect himself, and something snapped in Brooks, who commenced to flail away with great force on the senator's head and body. What had begun as a flogging was now a full-fledged assault, with Brooks began hitting Sumner "as hard as he could," proudly declaring, "Every lick went where I intended."[15]

Compounding the severity of the beating was the fact that Sumner struggled to get to his feet, failing to realize that since Senate desks were bolted to the floor, he had to push back on his chair and not lean forward to get to his feet. Brooks's blows soon bloodied Sumner's brow, and when the senator finally arose (having by sheer force ripped the desk from its bolted moorings), the congressman continued to strike, eventually shattering his cane (fig. 3). Even that did not stop Brooks, who used what remained of the cane to hit Sumner again and again as the senator staggered about, at one point actually grabbing his victim's lapel to steady his target in order to continue beating him senseless. "I . . . gave him about 30 first rate stripes," Brooks

---

[15]Donald, *Sumner*, p. 294.

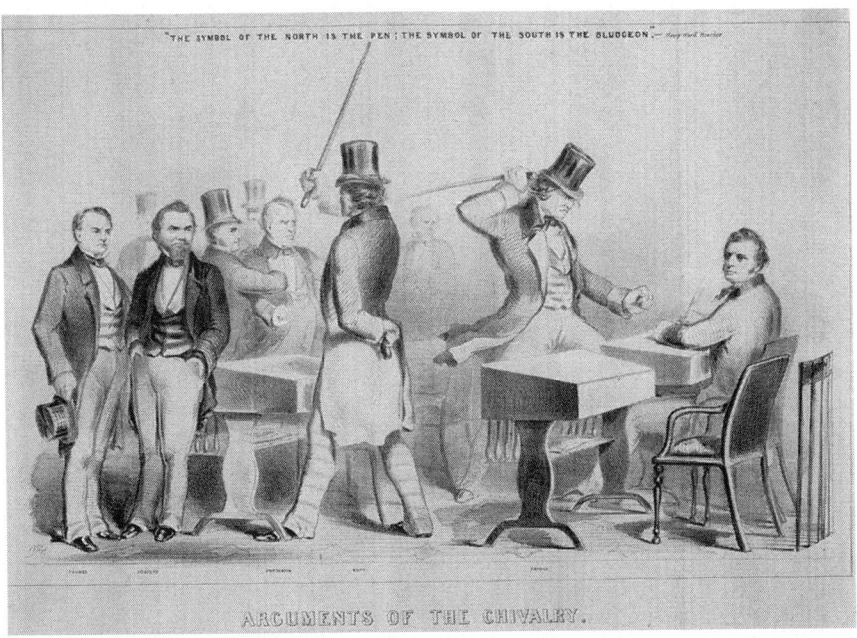

FIG. 4. Representative Lawrence M. Keitt stands guard as Brooks pummels Sumner in this contemporary lithograph. Senators Robert Toombs of Georgia (far left) and Stephen A. Douglas of Illinois (hands in pockets) make no attempt to intervene. *Courtesy Library of Congress, Prints and Photographs Division.*

boasted to his brother, adding: "Toward the last he bellowed like a calf. I wore out my cane completely but saved the head which is gold."[16]

Senators and representatives in the chamber had hurried over when Brooks began his assault. According to one witness, Keitt, who shielded Brooks, "brandished" a cane as well to prevent anyone from coming to Sumner's assistance (fig. 4), declaring, "Let them alone, God damn you."[17] Several southerners present later said they had no problem with what was happening: Douglas, who returned to the chamber when he learned of the assault, concluded that any effort to intervene might be "misconstrued." Finally, a satisfied Brooks left the chamber with Keitt and made his way back down Pennsylvania Avenue. The beating was over.[18]

It was an ugly scene, and Brooks's pride in what he had done spoke volumes for his state of mind. Aided by Senator Edwin D. Morgan of New

[16]Benson, *Caning*, pp. 131–32; Donald, *Sumner*, pp. 294–95.
[17]Benson, *Caning*, p. 139.
[18]Donald, *Sumner*, pp. 295–96.

York, Sumner managed to make his way into the Senate anteroom, where Dr. Cornelius Boyle dressed his wounds. Henry Wilson, Sumner's fellow senator from Massachusetts and a staunch antislavery Republican, then took his colleague back to his room and put him in bed; before long Dr. Boyle arrived to examine Sumner once more.[19]

Sumner never quite comprehended the force of his words or understood why they might have provoked such an extreme response. He strongly denied that he had intended to assail either Butler or South Carolina: "I have never said anything which was not in just response to his speeches according to parliamentary usage, nor anything which can be called a libel upon South Carolina or Mr. Butler."[20] Wilson and Massachusetts congressman W. S. Damrell argued that Butler had used rough language in speaking of Sumner on the Senate floor, but that argument persuaded few listeners who were not otherwise predisposed.[21]

A Senate committee dominated by southerners and not including even a single Republican concluded that it had no authority to punish a member of the lower chamber: the House failed to expel Brooks, although a majority of members (121 to 95) were in favor of that punishment when the final vote came up, on July 14. Although the representatives censured Keitt, Edmundson escaped unscathed.[22] Local law enforcement arrested Brooks, but the ensuing prosecution, such as it was, resulted in a fine of $300. Given these minimal responses, perhaps it should come as no surprise that it was not long before Brooks began issuing challenges to demand satisfaction from his critics. Henry Wilson simply dismissed the challenge, but Congressman Anson Burlingame of Massachusetts proved a cleverer opponent. He immediately accepted Brooks's challenge and proposed that the two men meet in Canada. That would compel Brooks to make his way northward through hostile crowds, and the South Carolina congressman refused the terms. Hearing of the challenge, Sumner lamented that Burlingame had "deliberately discarded the standard of Northern civilization to adopt the standard of Southern barbarism."[23] Eventually Brooks chose to resign his seat and stand for reelection, which he won easily.

---

[19]Ibid., pp. 296–97.
[20]Benson, *Caning*, p. 138.
[21]Donald, *Sumner*, p. 310 n. 2.
[22]Ibid., p. 308.
[23]Sumner to Joshua Giddings, July 22, 1856, in Beverly Palmer, ed., *The Selected Letters of Charles Sumner*, 2 vols. (Boston, 1990), 1:463.

In retrospect, one unfamiliar with the history of Congress might well express shock at a congressman caning a senator senseless. Surely it was a vicious assault. But if that had been all it was, it might not have attacked nearly the attention it did. After all, there had been acts of violence between members of Congress before. Back in 1789, representatives Matthew Lyon (Vt.) and Roger Griswold (Conn.) squared off in a battle where Griswold's cane attempted to fend off Lyon's fire tongs. There had been clashes since then, including a rather memorable one in 1838, when Representative William Graves of Kentucky killed Representative Jonathan Cilley of Maine with a rifle during a duel. Indeed, both the House and Senate had seen their share of duel challenges since the 1790s, and as recently as 1850 Mississippi's Jefferson Davis had issued a challenge. There had been other assaults over the years, several featuring the wielding of canes.[24]

As might be expected, many northern newspapers expressed outrage at the news of the caning. "For the first time has the extreme discipline of the Plantation been introduced into the Senate of the United States," observed the *Albany Evening Journal*. Apparently "the South proposes to debate with ball cartridges and bayonets." The *Boston Courier* denounced the "unmanly personal attack," launched by a "ruffian," as a sign of "barbarism." True, observed another Boston paper, there had been fights before between members of Congress, especially in the House of Representatives, "but never before has the sanctity of the Senate Chamber been violated." From now on, the paper predicted, the right to deliberate and disagree, the dignity of the Senate, and the freedom to speak and express one's position—"these will all disappear; and in their place we shall have the government of a self-constituted and revolutionary tribunal." Wasn't this already the case? "There is freedom of speech in Washington, but it is only for the champions of slavery. There is freedom of the press, but only of the press which extenuates or defends political wrongs."[25]

Yet it was almost immediately evident that something larger was at work here, and it became more evident over time. What might have been treated as an ugly incident involving a handful of individuals was often portrayed as

---

[24] See Eugene L. Wolfe, "Deliberation, Democracy and Dueling: Legislative Violence in the United States," paper presented at the Comparative Politics Workshop at the University of Chicago, May 26, 2004.
[25] *Albany Evening Journal*, May 23, 1856; *Boston Atlas*, May 23, 1856; *Boston Courier*, May 23–1856, all in Benson, *Caning*, pp. 158–62, 171–72.

something implying much more. From the beginning, for example, several northern observers chose to treat Brooks's actions as representative of how proslavery white southerners practiced politics. As the *Boston Atlas* put it on the day after the assault, "the South has taken to expedients which long use has made it familiar, and in which years of daily practice have given it a nefarious skill."[26] This sentiment—that it was the South's way of conducting politics—led a Pittsburgh paper to argue that northern congressmen should respond in kind: "These cut-throat Southrons will never learn to respect Northern men until some one of their number has a rapier thrust through his ribs, or feels a bullet in his thorax."[27] Some southern observers took note of this tendency to generalize about southern behavior from the acts of one man, adding that Brooks's critics "stigmatize the whole population of the South as 'ruffians,' 'assassins,' brutes,' 'murderers,' 'scoundrels,' 'cowards,' &c." Perhaps, the paper reasoned, it was time to separate, a sentiment expressed elsewhere in assessing northern editorial responses.[28]

The caning provided Republicans with ample ammunition to use against their Democratic opponents, even as the main target of their criticism remained southern behavior. "Now that the prejudices of the North can be appealed to in aid of a sectional controversy for the presidency, we roll up our eyes in holy horror at the offense," one observer remarked.[29] Nevertheless, it served as a perfect illustration of the slave power's determination to prevail through whatever means were necessary. Placed in context beside the gag rule controversy, the Fugitive Slave Law of 1850, the Kansas-Nebraska Act and the Border Ruffians, and the recent news about the sack of Lawrence, the caning of Sumner strengthened the case for a slave power conspiracy among people who may otherwise have dismissed it as something of a paranoid fantasy. Before long, Republicans would unite Bleeding Kansas with Bleeding Sumner, much as they would embrace "Free soil, free labor, free men, and Frémont" as the rallying cry of their party in its first presidential contest.

If context proved crucial, so did how northerners perceived the reaction of white southerners to the caning. After all, there had been acts of violence

---

[26] *Boston Atlas*, May 23, 1856, in Benson, *Caning*, p. 159.

[27] *Pittsburgh Gazette*, May 24, 1856, in Benson, *Caning*, p. 166.

[28] *Richmond Whig*, June 4, 1856, and *Charleston (S.C.) Mercury*, May 30, 1856, in Benson, *Caning*, pp. 174, 167.

[29] Joel H. Silbey, "After 'the First Northern Victory': The Republican Party Comes to Congress, 1855–56," *Journal of Interdisciplinary History* 20 (1989), 1–24 (quotation on p. 14).

between members of Congress before and none of them had produced such an uproar. But the overwhelming support shown throughout the white South for Brooks's act left an enduring impression in the minds of many northerners. What might have been dismissed as the irrational act of a lone deranged individual was now most clearly an expression of a section's sentiments. Many white southerners endorsed Brooks's actions. Just days after the assault a public meeting in Brooks's home district voted to supply their representative with a "handsome gold headed cane" to replace the one he had shattered over Sumner. Other white southerners followed suit: merchants from Charleston made sure to inscribe their gift cane with the message "Hit him again," while students at the University of Virginia presented Brooks with another gold-headed cane, which bore "a device of the human head, badly cracked and broken."[30]

Not all southern whites defended Brooks's actions: in several cases they noted that the overwhelming support for the South Carolina congressman could not but anger northerners. Several newspapers in the upper South argued that very point. The *Louisville Courier* argued that if Brooks was not held accountable for his actions, the result would "greatly strengthen the anti-slavery and anti-Southern feeling in the Northern states, and thus help the Black Republican party." The paper was particular annoyed by how South Carolinians were behaving. "The absurd and wicked resolutions which the South Carolina people are adopting will serve only to exasperate to a still greater degree the public sentiment of the North. But this is what the South Carolinians want. They rejoice in whatever seems likely to promote the dissolution of the Union." From North Carolina a Wilmington paper added that the response was "a perfect Godsend to the Abolitionists. . . . Freesoilism, languishing for an excitement has received a sudden impetus, and Sumner will be glorified into the dignity of a persecuted patriot, if not a martyr in the cause of freedom."[31]

What these critics missed, however, was that in responding to news of Sumner's caning, many white southerners had expressed the wish that other abolitionists and Republicans would receive the same treatment. It was one thing for someone to render Brooks's action understandable if not justifiable on the grounds that the senator from Massachusetts was particularly

---

[30]Donald, *Sumner*, pp. 304–5.
[31]*Louisville Courier*, May 28, 1856, and *Wilmington Herald*, May 26, 1856, in Benson, *Caning*, pp. 168–69.

obnoxious; it was another to recommend that caning become part of southern politics as an acceptable way to resolve disagreement and settle issues. Abolitionists had long been the target of mob violence and, in many cases, the mobbers were northerners. South Carolina governor James H. Adams commended Brooks's assault, recommending that the congressman continue to "break their heads"; the *Richmond Enquirer* argued that "vulgar Abolitionists in the Senate . . . must be lashed into submission," adding that Henry Wilson was "absolutely dying for a beating." In short, "Sumner and Sumner's friends must be punished and silenced." From South Carolina a newspaper hoped that Brooks's act "will prove a salutary lesson to others who may have the temerity to provoke a like act."[32] In a private letter an anonymous writer from South Carolina warned Sumner, "If you infernal abolitionists don't mind your own business at home, and let ours alone, the People at the South, will take the matter in hand themselves, and go in a mass to the Capital—tar and feather—horse-whip & expel every rascal of yours."[33]

In short, neither Sumner nor Brooks were to be treated as individuals, but as symbols of their worlds. Most southern whites praised Brooks for defending southern honor and portrayed Sumner as simply a meddlesome, self-righteous abolitionist who must be put in his place (northern Democrats were not far behind in offering this view of Sumner as archetypal troublemaker). Republicans set aside whatever reservations they might have privately expressed about the tenor and tone of Sumner's remarks and presented him as the victim of a slave power's vicious assault, best embodied in images of Brooks wielding his cane like an overseer or slaveholder wielded a whip over a beaten slave. That fit in all too well with the argument that the southern slave power sought to enslave northern whites in its efforts to prevail by whatever means worked, including trampling over the political process and resorting to violence all too easily, a choice facilitated by their experience as slaveholders who ruled through force. The fact that many white southerners supported Brooks allowed Republicans to set aside the argument that he was a lone individual and to claim that his actions were representative of how white southerners proposed to rule the nation.

Obviously Sumner's beating proved a godsend to the Republicans in the presidential campaign of 1856. Coupling Bleeding Kansas with Bleeding

---

[32]Sinha, "Caning of Charles Sumner," p. 247; *Laurensville (S.C.) Herald*, May 30, 1856, in Benson, *Caning*, p. 164.

[33]"A Friend Indeed" to Sumner, May 22, 1856, in Benson, *Caning*, pp. 189–90.

Sumner seemed an easy way to make the case against the machinations of the slave power, demonstrating the extent to which southern whites were willing to go to carry the day in defiance of democratic processes. However, it is more difficult to assess precisely what impact the beating itself had on the outcome of the election. After all, in the end the Democratic candidate still claimed victory in a field of three contestants; however, in their initial foray into presidential politics, the Republicans had come close to winning simply by building strength in the free states. Had Pennsylvania and Illinois ended in the Republican column, the party would have claimed victory. Historian William E. Gienapp believes that it was the Sumner caning that truly electrified the northern electorate, for it produced the loudest protests by people who, whatever they thought about violence in the West, found it unacceptable in the Senate chamber. Doubtless the incident bolstered Republican strength in 1856, and in Gienapp's opinion it propelled the party to political viability.[34]

Sumner's recuperation proved a lengthy process, with setbacks countering improvements in his condition. Some critics gossiped that he was shamming, but the truth seems to be that he had suffered a severe injury whose psychological effects outlasted his recovery from his wounds. Not that the senator was unaware of the political impact of his suffering: he was "much in hopes that some benefit to the antislavery cause might accrue from the affair," as an observer put it. During the fall campaign Massachusetts Republicans reminded voters of Sumner's tragic fate by arranging for a public tribute to him in Boston.[35] Early in 1857 the Massachusetts state legislature reelected him to the Senate by an overwhelming vote in the House and a unanimous vote in the Senate.[36]

Sumner returned to his seat for a short while in early 1857, in part to be sworn in for his second term in March, but he found himself unable to continue active public life. He decided to travel to Europe, spending most of his time in France and England, before returning to the United States in time

---

[34]See Gienapp, "The Crime against Sumner: The Caning of Charles Sumner and the Rise of the Republican Party," and Gienapp, *The Origins of the Republican Party, 1852–1856* (New York, 1987), pp. 299–303.

[35]Donald, *Sumner*, pp. 317–20. Donald offers an extended discussion of the injury on pp. 335–36, concluding that Sumner was suffering from posttraumatic stress syndrome; one wonders whether the work done on concussions during the last fifty years may have complicated that conclusion.

[36]Ibid., p. 322.

for the opening of the new session of Congress in December. That proved a short stay. Interpreting any health problem as related to the damages suffered during his beating, he left Washington once more to recuperate.[37] Returning to the Senate chamber on occasion, usually to cast a critical vote, he did not tarry long, to the degree that it looked as if proximity to Washington had caused him to become ill once more. In May 1858 he headed back once more to Europe in hopes that a prolonged rest might lead to an eventual recovery.[38]

One might have thought that the Brooks-Sumner affair would have given politicians pause about violence between members of Congress, but such was not the case. In February 1858 none other than South Carolina's Keitt nearly came to blows with Pennsylvania's Galusha Grow on the House floor, instigating a fracas made memorable for some when Mississippi congressman William Barksdale lost his wig.[39] Nor was such tension limited to the House, although it appeared that matters spilled over more often in the lower chamber. Missouri senator James S. Green minced no words when he called Pennsylvania's Simon Cameron "a damn liar" when Cameron had questioned Green's qualifications as a gentleman. The two offered retractions to head off talk of a duel.[40] Cameron, along with Michigan's Zachariah Chandler and Ohio's Benjamin F. Wade, actually formed an armed alliance to repel assaults, with Wade going so far as to suggest he'd be willing to duel with rifles.[41]

The long-term impact of the incident on the national political scene is more difficult to define. Certainly keeping Sumner's chair vacant was both a tribute to the senator and a mute reminder of what had happened, but what political advantage could be made of the caning had been achieved in 1856. If anything, the fact that Sumner remained in quasi seclusion for the next several years, during which debate raged over Kansas, the *Dred Scott* decision, and the fallout from the Panic of 1857, may have proved equally advantageous, for no one had to worry whether the senator would once more

---

[37] Sumner to John Jay, Mar. 2, 1857, in Palmer, *Selected Letters of Sumner*, 1:473; Donald, *Sumner*, pp. 327, 331.

[38] Donald, *Sumner*, pp. 332–33.

[39] Hans L. Trefousse, *The Radical Republicans: Lincoln's Vanguard for Racial Justice* (New York, 1968), pp. 115–16.

[40] Ibid., p. 116.

[41] Hans L. Trefousse, *Benjamin Franklin Wade: Radical Republican from Ohio* (New York, 1963), pp. 110–11, 150.

engage in rhetorical excesses in his continued denunciations of the slave power. Sumner the silent symbol may have had more value than Sumner the fiery orator.

Eventually, however, even some Republicans began to tire of Sumner's prolonged absences and his lost vote. With the help of his allies and supporters, Sumner fended off these critics, but by November 1859 it was evident that it was time for the senator to return to Washington and resume his responsibilities in the Senate. By that time, of course, he had missed the conclusion of the debate over Kansas, the introduction of a proposed federal slave code for the territories, and, most important, John Brown's raid against the federal arsenal at Harpers Ferry, Virginia. Once more Sumner remained silent, and that proved useful to Republicans, who wanted to make sure that they would make no mistakes on the eve of the 1860 presidential contest.[42]

What, then, should we make of the caning of Charles Sumner by Preston Brooks? Surely it was one of the more sensational events of the 1850s, a vivid image of the way in which the debate over slavery and its future ripped the republic apart. In the long term, however, it was but a single step on the road to disunion, soon eclipsed in importance by the *Dred Scott* decision, the debate over the Lecompton Constitution, and John Brown's attack on the federal armory at Harpers Ferry. Had it not happened, the course of events in a larger sense would probably not have been disturbed, whatever its immediate impact in 1856 may have been. The incident is best remembered, perhaps, for the way in which it encapsulated the growing rift between North and South over slavery and its expansion, and as such its symbolic imagery remains potent, a way to explain what happened in the 1850s.

For the two participants, the legacy of the beating proved challenging. Preston Brooks's sudden death, in 1857, deprived him of the mark he had hoped to make as a proslavery advocate (nearly four months later, Andrew Butler also passed away). Brooks's departure from the political scene meant that he would no longer be a target for Republican attacks, which might well have contributed to the decline of the importance of the Brooks-Sumner incident as a long-term contributing factor to the sectional crisis. For Charles Sumner, the legacy was even more problematic. Celebrated as a near martyr to the antislavery cause and a victim of the rapacious slave power, Sumner eventually returned to public life even more conscious of his greatness and

---

[42]Donald, *Sumner*, pp. 342–51.

more oblivious to how his words and actions could offend people. Even as he stood forth as one of the foremost advocates of human freedom in the Civil War era, his oratory struck some as eloquent while others saw it as bombastic egomania that could be needlessly offensive. For every person who praised his commitment to principle and his refusal to compromise, someone else would characterize him as pompous, vain, and impractical. Many people heard Sumner, but far fewer people listened to him, especially in the Senate.

The senator from Massachusetts never could quite get over the beating and the event that had sparked his remarks. Time and again he would compare current political controversies to the events of the 1850s, a practice that grew tiresome during Reconstruction, when he went so far as to invoke the Kansas crisis during the debate over the proposed annexation of the Dominican Republic. At the same time, his relentlessly sharp criticism of others offended many people, and his needlessly personal attacks finally did him in when he directed his acid tongue at Ulysses S. Grant in the 1870s. Deposed from his chairmanship of the Senate Foreign Relations Committee, in 1871, Sumner's outspokenness and demeanor led people to deplore his extreme rhetoric and question his sanity—as if Brooks's cane had left a deeper mark on Sumner's psyche and personality. Even Henry Wilson, who had stood by his colleague in 1856 and the years that followed, ultimately abandoned his friend when he accepted the Republican nomination for vice president, in 1872, as Grant's running mate, while Thomas Nast, a Grant supporter, lampooned Sumner as placing flowers at Brooks's grave, as if the Massachusetts senator had forgotten what the war was all about. By the time the senator died, in 1874, he had lost much of his political clout: although many people paid him tribute, he would remain a polarizing figure in accounts of the Civil War and Reconstruction, as many people weighed his commitment to principle against his arrogance and bitter and untoward remarks.

In the end, although Sumner's speech and Brooks's caning of Sumner were each sensational incidents in the story of the impending crisis, each gained importance because of the way politicians and editors were able to manipulate what had happened into a symbolic representation of the developing sectional rift. Brooks came to represent all proslavery white southerners at their worst, threatening to do whatever it took to prevail. Sumner, although he had enjoyed support before his speech, became the symbol of the North as victim in the eyes of many northerners, while to most white southerners he became the prototypical Yankee abolitionist bent first on insulting and then on destroying the South. Those proved powerful images during the election year of 1856, and may have done much to accelerate the growth of the Republican Party, but with each passing year other events took center stage as the nation hurtled forward toward disunion and civil war.

# Contributors

**Spencer Crew** is Clarence J. Robinson Professor of American, African American and Public History at George Mason University. His research interests are urban and Underground Railroad history. He has written numerous books and articles, including *Field to Factory: Afro-American Migration, 1915–1940* (1987) and *Black Life in Secondary Cities: A Comparative Analysis of the Black Communities of Camden and Elizabeth, N.J., 1860–1920* (1993). He coauthored *The American Presidency: A Glorious Burden* (2002) and *Unchained Memories: Readings from the Slave Narratives* (2002).

**Paul Finkelman** is President William McKinley Distinguished Professor of Law and Public Policy at Albany Law School. A specialist in American legal history, race and the law, and First Amendment issues, he is the author or editor of numerous articles and books, including *Slavery and the Founders: Race and Liberty in the Age of Jefferson* (2001), *Millard Fillmore* (2011), *A March of Liberty: A Constitutional History of the United States* (2011), and *American Legal History: Cases and Materials* (2011).

**Matthew Glassman** is an analyst on the Congress at the Congressional Research Service. He received his Ph.D. from Yale University in 2007. His primary research interests are in congressional organization, institutional design and change, and American political development.

**Amy S. Greenberg** is a professor of women's studies and history at Penn State University. She is the author of *Manifest Destiny and American Territorial Expansion: A Brief History with Documents* (2012), *Manifest Manhood and the Antebellum American Empire* (2005), and *Cause for Alarm: The Volunteer Fire Department in the Nineteenth-Century City* (1998). She is currently at work on a study of the U.S.-Mexico War of 1846.

**Martin (Marty) Hershock** is associate provost for academic affairs and associate professor of history and chair of the Department of Social Sciences at the University of Michigan–Dearborn. A specialist in nineteenth-century American history and in the history of Michigan, Hershock has written/edited four books as well as a number of academic articles and reviews. A lifelong resident of the Detroit metropolitan region, Hershock earned his Ph.D. in history from the University of Michigan–Ann Arbor. He joined the Dearborn faculty in 1999.

**Michael F. Holt** is the Langbourne M. Williams Professor of American History at the University of Virginia. A specialist in nineteenth-century political history, his many publications include *The Political Crisis of the 1850s* (1978), *Political Parties and American Political Development from the Age of Jackson to the Age of Lincoln* (1992), *The Rise and Fall of the American Whig Party: Jacksonian Politics and the Onset of the Civil War* (1999), *The Fate of Their Country: Politicians, Slavery Extension, and the Coming of the Civil War* (2004), and *Franklin Pierce* (2010).

**Brooks D. Simpson** is Foundation Professor of History at Arizona State University. He previously taught at Wofford College and was an assistant editor for the Papers of Andrew Johnson. He is the author of several books on nineteenth-century political history, including *Let Us Have Peace: Ulysses S. Grant and the Politics of Reconstruction* (1991), *The Political Education of Henry Adams* (1996), *The Reconstruction Presidents* (1998), and *Ulysses S. Grant: Triumph over Adversity, 1822–1865* (2000).

**Jenny Wahl** is a professor of economics at Carleton College. Among her recent publications are "Give Lincoln Credit: How Paying for the Civil War Transformed the U.S. Financial System" (*Albany Government Law Review*), "Blacks, Whites, and *Brown:* Effects on the Earnings of Men and Their Sons" (*Journal of African American Studies,* with Nathan Grawe), "Edith Wharton as Economist: An Economic Interpretation of *The House of Mirth* and *The Age of Innocence*" (*Edith Wharton Review*), and "The Economics of Slavery" (*Encyclopedia of Law and Economics,* Edward Elgar Press). Her current research includes an investigation of black-white labor-market inequality in the United States and an inquiry into the connections between income and wealth for American households.

# Index

abolitionists, 47, 56, 68, 107, 121–27, 130, 133–37, 139, 141, 154, 205, 208, 215–16, 221
Adams, James H., 216
Adams, John, 6
Adams, John Quincy, 46, 58
African Americans: efforts to rescue fugitive slaves, 135–38; opposition to fugitive slave laws, 120–42; and slave escapes, 139–40
African slave trade, 55
Alabama, 39, 83
*Albany Evening Journal*, 213
Alexandria, Va., 10, 53
Allen, Richard, 124
Allen, William, 25, 26
Alta California, 102
American Anti-Slavery Society, 133, 135, 141
Anderson, Elijah, 139
Andrew, John A., 17
Apaches, 103
Appalachian Mountains, 16
*Appeal in Four Articles* (Walker), 135
apportionment, 84
Arizona, 102, 104
Arkansas, 40
Atlantic slave trade, 7
Austrian Central Bank, 198

Baja California, 112, 115
balance rule: Congress and, 80–96; defined, 81, 82–84
Baltimore and Ohio Railroad, 165, 194
banking, and Panic of 1857, 174–77, 195–96
Bank of Pennsylvania, 195
Banks, Nathaniel, 3
Baptists, 58
Barksdale, William, 218
Barry, John, 155
Bartlett, John, 102, 103, 104
Bartlett-Conde agreement, 102
Baskin, Jonathan, 174
Beecher, Henry Ward, 16
Bell, Peter H., 32, 62
Bellevue, Ia., 87

Benning, Henry J., 121
Benton, Thomas Hart, 37, 41, 67
Berrien, John M., 30
Bingham, Kinsley S.: as a Democrat, 145; in Michigan state legislature, 144–45; and Republican Party, 143–58; on Wilmot Proviso, 146
Bingham, Margaret, 144
Bleeding Kansas, 13, 69, 72, 88, 203, 214, 216
Bleeding Sumner. *See* Sumner, Charles
Bocock, Thomas Stanley, 106–7
Booth, Sherman, 14
Border Ruffians, 214
Boston, Mass., 77, 127, 129, 136
Boston and Lowell Railroad, 165
*Boston Atlas*, 214
*Boston Courier*, 213
Boston Vigilance Committee, 127
Boyce, William Waters, 110–12
Boyle, Cornelius, 212
Bright, Jesse, 26
Brooks, Preston, 4, 13, 183, 203, 208–11, 212, 215, 216, 219
Brown, Albert G., 13
Brown, Henry "Box," 133–34
Brown, John, 4, 14, 16, 17, 183, 219
Brown, William Wells, 125
Buchanan, James, 2, 3, 13, 14, 15, 72, 80, 108, 112, 117
Buffalo, N.Y., 125
Burlingame, Anson, 212
Burned-Over District, 68, 151
Burns, Anthony, 14, 78, 137–38
Butler, Andrew P., 205, 206, 207, 219

Calhoun, John C., 36, 37, 41, 49, 57, 58–60
California, 102, 121, 160, 163; and Compromise of 1850 admission as free state, 8, 13, 20–21, 22, 36, 43, 48, 51, 52, 57, 60, 67; gold rush, 1, 12, 20, 45; railroads in, 40
Calomiris, Charles, 159
Cameron, Simon, 218
Camillus, N.Y., 144

225

Campbell, Stanley, 136
Canada, 14, 78, 98, 125, 132, 137
Caribbean, 98, 100
Cass, Lewis, 19, 26, 112, 146, 147, 149, 155
Cazenovia Slave Law Convention, 13
Central America, 98, 99, 101, 115–18
*Central America*, S.S., 195
Central Railroad of Georgia, 40
Chandler, Zachariah, 217
Charlotte and South Carolina Railroad, 40
Chase, Salmon P., 25, 37, 55, 60, 174
Chase, Samuel, 4
Chicago, Ill., 88
Chihuahua, 112
Christiana, Penn., 14, 77, 137
Cilley, Jonathan, 213
Civil War, 37, 89, 146
Clay, Henry: and Compromise of 1850, 2, 8, 28, 29, 36, 39, 46, 49–56, 120, 121, 128, 130, 149; in Senate, 47–49; Senate debate on Clay's compromise, 57–61
Clayton, John M., 20, 29, 32
Clemens, Jeremiah, 34
Coahuila, 102
Cobb, Howell, 34, 35, 198
Cobb, Thomas R. R., 42
Coffin, Catherine, 139
Coffin, Levi, 139
Cole, Arthur, 195
Colorado, 54, 102
*Columbia (Ga.) Times*, 140
Committee on Territories. *See* Senate Committee on Territories
commodities, speculation in, 177–78, 196
*Common Sense* (Paine), 78
Compromise of 1850, 2, 12, 15, 82, 84, 183; heroic interpretation of, 36–38; pattern of congressional votes on, 22–23; politics and patronage of, 18–35; as proslavery appeasement, 38; southern reaction to, 138
Concord, N.H., 129
Conde, Pedro García, 102–3, 104
Confederation Congress, 7
Congress, United States: and statehood process, 80–96; Thirtieth, 143, 145–58; Thirty-First, 19, 20, 25–35, 120; Thirty-Third, 3; Thirty-Fourth, 3, Thirty-Sixth, 93–94
Connecticut, 128
Constitution, United States: Article IV, section 2, 122; Article IV, section 3 (statehood), 92, 93–94

Constitutional Convention, 6, 11, 84
Continental Congress, 4
Cooper, James, 28, 34
Craft, Ellen, 133, 134
Craft, William, 133, 134
"Crime against Kansas, The" (Sumner), 203, 204–5
Crisis of the 1850s, 12–17, 43–47
Crittenden, John J., 93, 94
Cuba, 13, 14, 99, 101, 105, 107–14
Curry, Jabez, 201

*Daily National Intelligencer*, 130
Damrell, W. S., 212
Davidson, James West, 82
Davis, Jefferson, 32, 34, 42, 57, 108, 201, 213
Davis, John, 122
Davis, Reuben, 114
Dawson, William, 64
DeBow, James, 42
*DeBow's Review*, 202
Declaration of Independence, 4
DeLand, Charles, 154
Democratic Party, 3–4, 19, 58, 100, 145, 146, 147, 149, 150, 151
Denver, James W., 91
Detroit, Mich., 144
Dickinson, Daniel S., 26, 32
District of Columbia: slavery in, 1, 9–10, 45–46; slave trade in, 22, 50–53, 55, 67, 68, 73, 120, 121. *See also* Washington, D.C.
Dixon, James, 114
Dodge, Augustus C., 87
domesticity, 98
domestic slave trade, 56
Donald, David, 144, 153
Douglas, Stephen A., 26, 41, 64, 67, 68, 69, 72, 79, 87, 88, 91, 93, 94, 128, 150, 152, 155, 181, 184, 186, 205, 211
Douglass, Frederick, 15, 68, 78, 131, 133, 134, 139, 141
*Dred Scott v. Sandford*, 2, 8, 15, 38, 43, 72, 95, 96, 218, 219; and Panic of 1857, 159–202

Edmundson, Henry A., 209, 212
election of 1800, 6
election of 1860, 1
Emerson, Ralph Waldo, 16
Emory, William, 105
English Bill, 91
Erie Railroad, 194

Everett, Edward, 108
Ewing, Thomas, 27
expansionism, territorial, 97–108

Faneuil Hall, 136, 137
federal land grants. *See* land grants, federal
federal marshals. *See* marshals, federal
federal patronage, 27–28
filibustering, 76, 106, 109
filibusters, 13, 99, 101, 108. *See also* López, Narciso; Walker, William
Fillmore, Millard, 2, 3, 14, 28, 32, 33, 47, 61–69, 73, 74–78, 79, 98, 103, 108, 128, 130–31
Findley, William, 126
Fishlow, Albert, 164
Florida, 8, 39, 83
Foner, Eric, 144
Foote, Henry S., 34, 37, 99
Foreign Relations Committee. *See* Senate Foreign Relations Committee
Forstall system, 176
Founders, 84
Franklin, Benjamin, 5
Franklin, John Hope, 136
free blacks, 71–72
Free Democratic Party, 150
Freeport doctrine, 186
free soil, 73
Free-Soilers, 182, 184
*Free Soil, Free Labor, Free Men* (Foner), 144
Free Soil Party, 20, 21, 24, 147
fugitive slave clause, 7, 11
fugitive slave law, 60
Fugitive Slave Law of 1793, 123, 125, 126, 127, 128, 131
Fugitive Slave Law of 1850, 1, 4, 6, 38, 39, 43, 46, 50, 56, 67, 68, 69–72, 73–78, 205, 214; drafting and passage of, 128; provisions of, 128–29; public response to, 129–32; role of African Americans in obstructing, 120–42
fugitive slave protection laws, 126
fugitive slaves, 56, 126–27

Gadsden, James, 102
Gadsden Purchase, 100, 102–7, 109, 114, 160
Gadsden Treaty, 102, 105
Garnet, Henry Highland, 133, 135
Garnet, Thomas, 139–40
Garrison, William Lloyd, 16, 38, 135, 139
General Vigilance Committee, 126
Georgia, 39

Gerry, Elbridge, 85
Gienapp, William, 217
Gila River, 102
Glover, Joshua, 138
Gorsuch, Edward, 137
Graduation Act (1854), 162–63
Grant, Ulysses S., 220
Graves, William, 213
Great Britain, 10
Great Lakes, 74
Great Salt Lake, 20
Green, James S., 91, 218
Green Oak Township, Mich., 144
Grier, Robert, 58, 77
Grimes, Leonard, 125
Griswold, Roger, 213
Grow, Galusha, 218

habeas corpus, writ of, 71
Hale, John P., 37
Hall, Willard P., 87
Hamlet, James, 74, 132–33
Hamlin, Hannibal, 37, 60
Hammond, James, 201
Harpers Ferry, Va., 4, 16, 219
Hawaii, 98
Hawkins, George Sydney, 117, 118
Hayden, Lewis, 137, 141
Hayne, Robert Y., 49, 65
Henry, Patrick, 127
Henry, William, 136
homestead bill, 86
Houston, Sam, 37, 41, 57, 67, 96
Howard, V.E., 104
Huston, James, 200

Illinois, 39, 83, 164, 165, 185
Illinois Central Railroad, 166, 169, 174
*Illinois Central Railroad v. McLean County*, 153
Illinois Supreme Court, 6
*Impending Crisis, The* (Potter), 54
*Independent*, 186
Indiana, 39, 83, 165
Indiana Supreme Court, 6
internal improvements, 85
interstate slave trade, 50
Iowa, 12, 40, 45, 83, 87, 164, 165

Jackson, Andrew, 36, 52, 58, 65
Jackson, Mich., 154
Jackson, Miss., 201

Jackson, Polly, 125
Jefferson, Thomas, 6, 10, 58
Jerry, pseud. *See* Henry, William
Jerry rescue, 77, 136
Johnson, Eliza Jane, 124
Johnson, Hadley, 88
Johnson, Thomas, 88
Johnson, William F., 28
Jones, John, 125
Jones, Mary, 125

Kamehameha III, 98
Kansas, 4, 14, 16, 83, 89, 91–92, 95, 204, 209
Kansas-Nebraska Act of 1854, 2, 8, 15, 38, 43, 72, 80, 87, 89, 100, 105, 109, 143, 152, 155, 181, 214
Keitt, Laurence M., 209, 211, 212, 218
Kentucky, 39
Know-Nothing Party, 66

LaCrosse and Milwaukee Railroad, 194
LaGrange College, 42
land grants, federal, 166–69
land policy, United States, 162–64
land prices, 186–87
Latham, Milton Slocum, 109–10
Latimer, George, 127
Lawrence, Kans., 183, 209
Lecompton Constitution, 84, 89, 91, 92, 95, 219
*Liberator*, 139
Liberty Party, 47, 59
Lincoln, Abraham, 1, 17, 55, 93, 143, 144, 146, 151–58, 182, 184
Lincoln-Douglas campaign, 96
Livingston County, Mich., 144
Loguen, Jeremiah, 125, 133, 134, 139
López, Narciso, 76, 107, 112
Louisiana, 39, 83
Louisiana Purchase, 8, 87, 120, 153
*Louisville Courier*, 215
Lumpkin, Joseph Henry, 42
Lumpkin Law School, 42
Lynch, Thomas, 5, 6, 12
Lyon, Matthew, 213

Madison, James, 10
Maine, 83
Mallory, Stephen Russell, 98, 112, 114
manhood, concepts of: martial, 98, 100; restrained, 98–99, 100, 106
Manifest Destiny, 97–119

Mansfield, Lord Chief Justice (William Murray), 10
marshals, federal: and fugitive slave law, 70, 128–29
Maryland, 53, 55
Mason, James M., 37, 57, 205, 207
Mason, John, 108
Mason-Dixon Line, 88, 122
Massachusetts, 39
Massachusetts legislature, 127
McClelland, Robert, 149
McCorkle, Joseph, 98
McCormick, Cyrus, 181
Mesilla Valley, 105
Methodists, 58
Mexican Cession, 18, 20, 22, 29, 31, 43, 50, 54, 61, 97
Mexican War, 1, 8, 18, 43, 52, 99, 120, 160
Mexico, 99, 102
Mexico bill, 105
Michigan, 83, 145, 165
Michigan Fever, 144
Michigan Southern Railroad, 194
Michigan state legislature, 144
Middlesex Canal, 165
Mifflin, Thomas, 122–23
Miller, Jacob, 57
Milwaukee and Mississippi Railroad, 165
Minnesota, 83, 91, 95
Mississippi, 39, 52, 83
*Mississippi and State Gazette*, 140
Mississippi River, 8
Missouri, 8, 40, 83, 87
Missouri Compromise, 6, 8, 12, 15, 44, 46, 54, 64, 68, 72, 82, 84, 87, 100, 120, 152, 183
Mitchell, David, 163
Monroe Doctrine, 106
Morgan, Edwin D., 211
Morgan, Margaret, 127
Mormons, 20, 21
Morris, Gouverneur, 84
Morris, Robert, 137
Mother Bethel African Methodist Episcopal Church, 124
Mother Zion Church, 133
Mountain Meadows massacre, 190
*My Bondage and My Freedom* (Douglass), 15

Nalle, Charles, 136, 138
Nashville Convention (1850), 19, 121
Nast, Thomas, 220

National Negro Convention (Buffalo, N.Y.), 135
Nebraska Territory, 87
Nelson, Samuel, 58
Nevada, 12, 54, 102, 182
Nevins, Allan, 200
New England Anti-Slavery Society, 133
*New England Farmer*, 196
New England Freedom Association, 127
New Hampshire, 39
New Jersey, 39
New Mexico, 102; boundary of, dispute with Texas, 36, 38–39, 45, 48, 51, 53, 54, 55; slavery in, 182, 183; statehood, 21, 52, 60–67
New Mexico Territory, 4, 12, 13, 26
New Mexico Territory bill, 34
New York, 39
New York Central Railroad, 194
New York City, 129, 169
*New York Herald*, 168, 188
New York Stock Exchange, 172
*New York Tribune*, 135
Nicaragua, 101, 115
North Carolina, 39
Northrup, Solomon, 124–25
Northwest Ordinance, 5, 6, 7, 8, 52, 147
Nueces River, 44
Nuevo Mexico, 102
nullification, 37

Oberlin College, 15
Oberlin-Wellington rescue, 138
Ohio, 39, 83, 165
Ohio and Mississippi Railroad, 174
Ohio Life Insurance and Trust Company, 184, 194
Ohio River, 8
Old Northwest Territory, 165
Oregon, 80, 83, 95
Oregon Territory, 80, 81, 160
Orr, James Lawrence, 3
Ostend Manifesto, 108–14
Outlaw, David, 138

pairing, 51–52. *See also* balance rule
Panama railroad, 189
Panic of 1837, 145, 148, 151, 173
Panic of 1857, 218; and Dred Scott case, 159–202; theoretical models of, 179–83
*Paradise Lost* (Milton), 59
Parker, John, 139

Parker, Theodore, 135, 139
Parker, William, 137, 141
Paulding, Hiram, 115, 117
Pearce, James, 28, 33, 64, 117
Peckham, Russell Wheeler, 105
Pennington, William, 3
Pennsylvania, 39
Pennsylvania Abolition Society, 122
Pennsylvania Fugitive Slave Act of 1826, 126
Pennsylvania Society for Promoting the Abolition of Slavery, 126
Personal Liberty Act of 1843 (Massachusetts), 127
personal liberty laws, 127–28
Philadelphia, 129
Philadelphia Vigilance Committee, 126
Pierce, Franklin, 2, 3, 13, 14, 72, 102, 104, 105, 108, 112, 114, 115, 129, 137, 196, 207
Pierson, Michael D., 207
*Pittsburgh Gazette*, 132
Platte Territory, 87
Polk, James K., 1, 21, 47, 66, 145
population growth 1850–57, 185–86
Pottawotomie, Kans., 183
Potter, David, 41, 49, 50, 54, 55, 65, 95
Presbyterians, 58
presidential elections: (1848), 19; (1856), 216–17; (1860), 219. *See also* election of 1800; election of 1860
Prigg, Edward, 127
*Prigg v. Pennsylvania* (1842), 11, 56, 69, 72, 127
Providence, R.I., 133

Quitman, John, 108

railroads: and federal land grants, 166–68; foreign investors and, 169; and land markets, 164–65; mileage in 1850s, 39–40; and Panic of 1857, 164–68; receipts of, 40–41; securities, 168–84, 188–95; state and local government finance of, 173–74
Randolph, Beverley, 123
Randolph, John, of Roanoke, 205
Rankin, John, 139
Reconstruction, 220
Redmond, Charles L., 133
Remini, Robert, 36, 38, 39, 40, 41, 60
Republican Party, 15, 17, 38, 43, 86, 143, 148, 154–58, 203, 221
Rhett, R. Barnwell, 37
Rhode Island, 128

Richardson, William A., 87
*Richmond Enquirer*, 216
Río Bravo del Norte, 102
Rio Grande, 21, 44
Ripley, Ohio, 124, 125, 139

San Francisco, Calif., 74
Santa Fe, N.M., 21, 33, 34, 35, 62
Schermerhorn, Abraham, 68
Schweikart, Larry, 159
Scott, Winfield, 58
secession, 1, 37, 79, 200
secession crisis, 93
Senate, U.S., and Compromise of 1850, 57–61, 206
Senate Committee on Territories, 31, 87, 88, 91
Senate Foreign Relations Committee, 220
Seward, William Henry, 23, 32, 37, 60
Shadrach. *See* Wilkins, Fred
Sims, Thomas, 14
slave prices, 178
slave revolts, 7
slavery: and admission of new states, 80–96; Compromise of 1850, major issue in, 38, 50–56; churches on, 58; constitutional politics of, 4–12; and Mexican Cession, 120; spread of in 1850s, 72–77; in territories, 1, 38, 53, 97–118; in Washington, D.C., 1, 9–10, 12, 13
slave trade. *See* African slave trade; Atlantic slave trade; District of Columbia, slave trade in; domestic slave trade; interstate slave trade
Slidell, John, 112, 114
Smith, Gerrit, 106, 107
Smith, Walter, 195
*Somerset v. Stewart* (1772), 10
Sonora, 102, 112, 115
Soulé, Pierre, 108
South Carolina, 39, 93
Southwest Ordinance, 7
Spain, 14, 76, 102, 112
Sprague, William, 148
Stampp, Kenneth, 163, 200
statehood, process of, 51–52, 84–89
Steckel, Richard, 162
Stephens, Alexander, 99–100
Stevens, Robert S., 91
Stevens, Thaddeus, 132
Still, William, 126
Story, Joseph, 11, 56

Stowe, Harriet Beecher, 15, 78, 139
Sturgeon, Daniel, 26, 28, 34
Suffolk Bank, 194
Sumner, Charles, 4, 13, 183; Bleeding Sumner, 203, 214, 216–17; caning of, 203–21; Crime against Kansas speech, 203, 204–5
Supreme Court, U.S., 2, 8, 11, 38, 56, 69, 72, 127. *See also Dred Scott v. Sandford; Illinois Central Railroad v. McLean County; Prigg v. Pennsylvania*
Sylla, Richard, 169
Syracuse, N.Y., 13, 14, 77, 125, 134

Tamaulipas, 102
Taney, Roger B., 2, 15, 72, 160
Taylor, Zachary, 2, 3, 12, 19, 20, 21, 23–24, 27–28, 32, 46, 47, 48, 54, 58, 60, 61, 65, 149
Texas, 102, 121, 160, 167, 186; annexation of, 8, 47, 83; debt of, 36, 39, 45; and New Mexico boundary dispute, 1, 12, 13, 21–22, 30–31, 34, 50, 51, 53, 54, 55, 60–67; railroad mileage in, 40
*Thompson's Bank Note and Commercial Reporter*, 186
three-fifths clause, 6
Toombs, Robert, 114, 211
transcontinental railroad, 102, 105, 160
Treaty of Guadalupe Hidalgo, 18, 65, 102, 103, 160
Troy, N.Y., 127, 136
Tubman, Harriet, 133, 139, 141
Tucker, St. George, 5
Twenty-Eighth Congregational Society (Boston), 135

*Uncle Tom's Cabin* (Stowe), 15, 16, 78, 139
Underground Railroad, 125
Union safety committees, 130
Upshur, Abel, 58
Utah, 12, 26, 52, 54, 102, 182, 183, 190
Utah Territory bill, 33, 34

Van Buren, Martin, 20, 58
Vermont, 127
Victoria, Queen, 15
vigilance committees, 125–26, 134, 137, 141
Virginia, 39, 40
Virginia, University of, 215
Virginia Military Institute, 42

Wade, Benjamin F., 218
Walker, David, 135
Walker, Percy, 115

Walker, William, 101, 114, 115–18
Wall Street, 170
Washington, D.C., 85, 124–25, 129. *See also* District of Columbia
Washington, George, 10, 123
Webster, Daniel, 3, 21, 28, 33, 34, 49, 59–61, 65, 67, 68, 74, 75, 76, 79, 129
*Weekly Raleigh Register and North Carolina Gazette*, 130
Weingast, Barry, 82
Weller, John B., 104
Whig Party, 2–3, 19–20, 25, 48, 61, 64, 69, 144, 146, 155
Wilkins, Fred, 77, 136–37
Wilmot, David, 18, 43, 145
Wilmot Proviso, 12, 18, 21, 22, 43, 49, 52, 54, 59, 62, 68, 145, 147, 149
Wilson, Henry, 212, 220
Wilson, Jack, 169
Wilson, James, 5
Wisconsin, 12, 40, 45, 83, 164, 165, 185
Woman's Rights Movement, 98
Wright, Augustus, 118
Wright, Robert, 169
Wyandotte, Mo., 88
Wyoming, 54

Yulee, David Levy, 37

Zion Chapel (New York City), 132

E415.7 .C76 2012